philharmonic

autocrat

the discography of

herbert von karajan

(1908-1989)

compiled by

john hunt

(fourth edition 2016)

philharmonic autocrat
the discography of Herbert von Karajan
(1908-1989)
fourth edition 2016.

John Hunt

ISBN 978-1-901395-31-0

Travis & Emery Music Bookshop
17 Cecil Court
London
WC2N 4EZ
United Kingdom.
Tel. (+44) (0) 20 7240 2129.
newpublications@travis-and-emery.com

3

Contents

Cover drawing by courtesy of Brian Pinder

Introduction to the discography

The reputation of Herbert von Karajan (1908-1989) has remained intact in the twenty-six years since his death. Both in the history of classical music recording and in that of concert and opera presentation his name is associated with the highest possible standards, and this notwithstanding the fact that there some who, for reasons best known to themselves, found something suspect in his quest for perfection and his undeniable business acumen.

Karajan's conducting ethos can in general terms be viewed as combining the energetic precision of Arturo Toscanini with the spiritual breadth of Wilhelm Furtwängler, resulting in what Peter Csobadi has termed a "controlled ecstasy". However, I find that an even closer analogy can be made between the conducting styles of Karajan and Richard Strauss, combining beauty of sound with rhythmic integrity. Karajan's two successors in Berlin, Claudio Abbado and Simon Rattle, have gone in entirely different directions, and only Christian Thielemann, in my view, retains an affinity with the essential German musical values which Karajan himself embodied.

Herbert von Karajan's heyday coincided precisely with the golden age of recorded music, starting in the shellac era, on through the age of the long-playing record, and into that of the digital and video media. There was scarcely a major record company for which he did not at some stage work, although his main loyalties remained clearly with EMI and Deutsche Grammophon. Both these major legacies continue to be marketed for the enjoyment of new generations of listeners and students.

introduction/continued

Alongside the body of official recordings, rivalled but never quite eclipsed by the likes of Leonard Bernstein, Georg Solti and Bernard Haitink, there is also a vast cornucopia of radio broadcasts and in-house tapes. Despite the caveat that most of these are unauthorised, there are many items of importance which highlight significant moments in Karajan's career. For this reason I have interspersed these in a listing alongside the official studio recording sessions, resulting in an impressive chronology of uninterrupted activity from 1938 (the very first session with Mozart's *Zauberflöte* overture) until 1989 (final sessions and concerts in Vienna). All the repertoire commercially recorded by Herbert von Karajan can be found in these pages, both complete works and excerpted pieces such as overtures or arias. However, issues of excerpts from recordings which exist complete are not covered.

The recordings are grouped into sessions, each allocated a session number between 001 and 889; numbers with an added suffix "a" or "b" merely denote items added to the discography at a late stage in the preparation. The session heading gives the known details about recording venue, orchestra, soloists and recording producer. In the case of much video material Karajan himself is named as producer (the company executives who may have played important assisting roles are not named).

The chronological discography is followed by a listing by composer, which can be cross-referenced to the chronological one by means of the session numbers. This composer listing will be specially helpful in showing at a glance how many versions are accessible for every single piece in Karajan's vast repertoire, be they officially sanctioned editions or off-air tapings.

introduction/continued

As far as studio recording sessions are concerned, I have attempted to list the main issues in the various formats: 78rpm shellac discs (original matrix numbers are included for the first time), LP catalogue numbers for most major territories, the same for CDs and, finally, the various video formats (in Karajan's case these include both studio-made films and televised concerts). It should be noted that many of his earler video performances (Unitel) are available for "streaming" on the Berlin Philharmonic Orchestra's Digital Concert Hall.

Also new to this edition of the discography are numbers for EMI's Reel-to-reel tapes which were published for selected titles during the 1950s and 1960s: although never commercially profitable, these tape records are now keenly sought on the internet and seem to fetch similar prices to those for audiophile LPs from the same period.

Many interesting comparisons can be made between the various multiple versions of the same piece, be it symphony, tone poem or opera, particularly when the sound quality of an unofficial version is acceptable (when that is not the case, I have sometimes added a warning comment to this effect). Personally, I find particular value in complete orchestral concerts published in their entirety and therefore highlighting the conductor's brand of programme building. He was one of the first to break away from the traditional pattern of overture/concerto/symphony, preferring for example to couple a major symphony or tone poem with a baroque, classical or even near-contemporary piece in the first half of the concert.

introduction/continued

And mention of the near-contemporary reminds us that
although Karajan's repertory of twentieth-century works
may not have been extensive, he preferred to concentrate
on honing selected ones like Stravinsky *Sacre* and *Apollon,*
Shostakovich 10, Prokofiev 5 and some Mahler (4. 5, 6,
9 and *Lied von der Erde*), let alone Sibelius, Debussy,
Ravel and the Second Viennese School, until they emerged
in performance in as fluent a manner as any standard
Classical repertoire.

During the 1990s I assisted archivist Anneliese Eggebrecht
(based in Hannover) in cataloguing the conductor's
professional activity, information which was intended
to reach the Herbert-von-Karajan-Zentrum which had been
set up in Vienna. This included details of radio transmissions
which I then included in my 1999 discography as "unpublished
radio broadcasts". Careful comparison with the previous
discographies will reveal that some of these "broadcasts"
are no longer mentioned in this new listing, nor are they
known to the Eliette-und-Herbert-von-Karajan-Institut
(currently based in Salzburg). This suggests that mention of
certain elusive items may merely have been the result of
wishful thinking on the part of over-enthusiastic collectors.
Also omitted from the new discography are items previously
appearing on certain Italian pirate LP and CD labels (Natise,
Artemis and Urania, for example), which transpired to be
blatant copies of Columbia and DG originals.

introduction/concluded

Important live concert material can now also be found on Japanese labels like NHK (there is, for example, an impressive set of CDs and DVDs issued in 2008 for the Karajan centenary) and Universal (the conductor's last three Tokyo concerts in May 1988); and on the European market the website *rarebroadcasts.wordpress* lists high quality radio transmissions (these are denoted in the discography as "Private Edition Vienna").

Deserving of special mention must be the re-issue by Warner Classics of Herbert von Karajan's entire orchestral and choral output made between 1946 and 1984 for Columbia and then EMI/Electrola: sadly EMI's previous CD versions of the material did little justice to the mellowness and sonic depth of the original LPs, but this has been amply rectified by Warner's technicians, with transfers that should prove a revelation to younger listeners in particular. Furthermore, the music is presented in thirteen convenient multi-disc sets (arranged by category) in contrast to the daunting CD boxes of DG Recordings currently on offer from Universal, each one containing around 80 discs.

Finally I would like to acknowledge the colleagues who have assisted with research, advice or suggestions (and in some cases supplied me with copies of rare recorded material) in the period since I published the previous Karajan discography: Yasushi Aisa, John Baker, Pia Bernauer, Lyn Clemo, Peter Csobadi, Michael Gray, John Hancock, John Hooper, Roderick Krüsemann, David Lampon, Ernst Lumpe, Luis Luna, Aman Pedersen, Matthias Röder, Neville Sumpter and Ates Tanin.

John Hunt 2016

Herrn
John Hunt

37 Chester Way /Flat 6
LONDON   SE11 4UR   Salzburg, 1987-11-24

England

Sehr geehrter Herr Hunt,

Herr von Karajan hat die Zusendung Ihres Buches er-
halten und läßt Ihnen, ebenso wie Frau Hemedinger,
auf das herzlichste dafür danken.

Mit besten Empfehlungen und freundlichen Grüßen

(Lore Salzburger)

HERBERT VON KARAJAN: THE CHRONOLOGICAL DISCOGRAPHY

001/9 december 1938/grammophon session in berlin alte-jakob-strasse

staatskapelle berlin

mozart die zauberflöte overture

825ge 67465/decca LY 6145

826ge

cd: deutsche grammophon 423 5312/423 5252/457 6892/ 477 6237/unlimited classics HDNC 0017

002/february 1939/grammophon sessions in berlin alte-jakob-strasse

staatskapelle berlin

verdi la forza del destino overture

5gz 67466

6gz

wagner die meistersinger von nürnberg overture

1020 ½ gs 67532

1021 ½ gs

cd issues of both items: deutsche grammophon 423 5262/ 423 5252/477 6237/unlimited classics HDNC 0017

003/april-may 1939/grammophon sessions in berlin alte-jakob-strasse

staatskapelle berlin

wagner die meistersinger von nürnberg: act three prelude

1115 ½ gs 67527

1116 ½ gs

cherubini anacreon overture

1117 ½ gs 67514

1119 ½ gs

cd issues of both items: deutsche grammophon 423 5312/ 423 5252/477 7237/unlimited classics HDNC 0017

004/23 june 1939/grammophon sessions in berlin

alte-jakob-strasse

philharmonisches orchester berlin

tchaikovsky symphony no 6 in b minor op 74 "pathetique"

1189gs IX	67499
1190gs IX	
1191gs IX	67500
1192gs IX	
1193gs IX	67501
1194gs IX	
1195gs IX	67502
1196gs IX	
1197gs IX	67503
1198gs IX	
1199gs IX	67504
1200gs IX	

lp: top classic TC 9055

cd: deutsche grammophon 423 5302/423 5252/477 6237/
unlimited classics HDNC 0017

some issues were incorrectly dated 15 april 1939

005/6-22 june 1940/grammophon sessions in berlin
alte-jakob strasse

philharmonisches orchester berlin

smetana the moldau

1482 ¾ ge IX	67583
883ge IX	
884ge IX	67584
885ge IX	

lp: deutsche grammophon LPEM 19 078

cd: deutsche grammophon 423 5302/423 5252/477 6237/
unlimited classics HDNC 0017

side one of the recording (1482 ¾ ge IX) was re-made on
9 june 1941

Johann strauss künstlerleben waltz

886gs IX	67585
887gs IX	

cd: deutsche grammophon 423 5302/423 5252/477 6237/
unlimited classics HDNC 0017/pristine audio PACO 070

this item was incorrectly dated february 1940

dvorak symphony no 9 in e minor op 95 "from the new world"

890gs IX	67519/cetra OR 5019
891gs IX	
892gs IX	67520/cetra OR 5020
893gs IX	
894gs IX	67521/cetra OR 5021
895gs IX	
900gs IX	67522/cetra OR 5022
901gs IX	
902gs IX	67523/cetra OR 5023
903gs IX	
904gs IX	67524/cetra OR 5024
905gs IX	

cd: deutsche grammophon 423 5282/423 5252/477 6237/
unlimited classics HDNC 0017

this item was incorrectly dated march 1940

006/24 may 1941/french newsreel film of a concert
encore in the paris opera during guest visit by the
berlin staatsoper

staatskapelle berlin

wagner die meistersinger von nürnberg overture, concluding bars
laserdisc: japan TES 132/LSZS 009191
dvd video: deutsche grammophon 073 4392/immortal IMM 950001

007/9 june 1941/grammophon session in berlin
alte-jakob-strasse

philharmonisches orchester berlin

johann strauss kaiserwalzer

1483 5/8 ge IX	67649
1484 5/8 ge IX	

cd: deutsche grammophon 423 5282/423 5252/477 6237/
unlimited classics HDNC 0017/pristine audio PACO 070

008/june 1941/grammophon sessions in berlin
alte-jakob strasse

staatskapelle berlin

beethoven symphony no 7 in a op 92

1492 5/8 ge	67643
1493 ¾ ge	
1494 ¾ ge	67644
1495 ¾ ge	
1485 ¾ ge	67645
1486 ¾ ge	
1487 5/8 ge	67646
1490 ¾ ge	
1491	67647
1488 ½ ge	
1489 ½ ge	67648

cd: deutsche grammophon 423 5262/423 5252/477 6237/
unlimited classics HDNC 0017

009/april 1942/test recordings in berlin

alte-jakob-strasse

dresdner philharmonie

rossini semiramide overture

conductor paul van kempen also participated in these
experimental tests, which appear not to have survived

010/october 1942/grammophon-fonit sessions
in turin

eiar orchestra torino

mozart symphony no 35 in d K385 "haffner"

1941 ½ gs	67986/cetra RR 8035
1942 4/4 gs	
1943 4/4 gs	67987/cetra RR 8036
1944 4/4 gs	
1945 4/4 gs	67988/cetra RR 8037

lp: decca (usa) DL 9513

cd: deutsche grammophon 423 5292/423 5252/477 6237/
unlimited classics HDNC 0017

78rpm discs were also published in automatic coupling
with the numbers 69104-69106

mozart symphony no 40 in g minor K550

1946 4/4 gs	67983
1947 4/4 gs	
1948 ½ gs	67984
1949 ½ gs	
1950 ½ gs	67985
1951 4/4 gs	

cd: deutsche grammophon 423 5292/423 5252/477 6237/
unlimited classics HDNC 0017

78rpm discs were also published in automatic coupling
with the numbers 69171-69173

010/october 1942/grammophon-fonit sessions in turin/concluded

mozart symphony no 41 in c K551 "jupiter"

1952 4/4 gs	67993
1953 ½ gs	
1954 ½ gs	67994
1955 4/4 gs	
1956 4/4 gs	67995
1957 ½ gs	
1958gs	67996

cd: deutsche grammophon 423 5292/423 5252/477 6237/ unlimited classics HDNC 0017
78rpm discs were also published in automatic coupling with the numbers 69363-69366

rossini semiramide overture

1959 ½ gs	68154
1960 ½ gs	
1961 ½ gs	68155
1962 ½ gs	

cd: deutsche grammophon 423 5312/423 5252/477 6237/ unlimited classics HDNC 0017

verdi la traviata: preludes to acts one and three

| 1963 ½ gs | 68156 |
| 1964 ½ gs | |

cd: deutsche grammophon 423 5312/423 5252/477 6237/ unlimited classics HDNC 0017

011/21 october 1942/grammophon session in berlin
alte-jakob-strasse

philharmonisches orchester berlin

johann strauss der zigeunerbaron overture

1975gs IX	67997
1976gs IX	

cd: deutsche grammophon 423 5312/423 5252/459 0012/
459 0652/477 6237/unlimited classics HDNC 0017/
pristine audio PACO 070

johann strauss die fledermaus overture

1977gs IX	68043
1978gs IX	

cd: deutsche grammophon 423 5282/423 5252/477 6237/
unlimited classics HDNC 0017/pristine audio PACO 070

this item was incorrectly dated december 1943

012/6-17 september 1943/grammophon sessions in
amsterdam concertgebouw

concertgebouworkest

brahms symphony no 1 in c minor op 68

2477 ½ ge	68175
2478 ½ ge	
2479 ½ ge	68176
2480 ½ ge	
2486 ½ ge	68177
2487 ½ ge	
2488 ½ ge	68178
2481 ½ ge	
2482 ½ ge	68179
2483 ½ ge	
2484 ½ ge	68180
2485 ½ ge	

cd: deutsche grammophon 423 5272/423 5252/477 6237/
unlimited classics HDNC 0017/audiophile classics
APL 100 555/naxos 8.111298

automatic coupling numbers 69176-69181

012/6-17 september 1943/grammophon sessions in
amsterdam concertgebouw/concluded

weber der freischütz overture

2489 ½ ge	68354
2490 ½ ge	
2491 ½ ge	68355

cd: deutsche grammophon 423 5312/423 5252/477 6237/
unlimited classics HDNC 0017

strauss salome: dance of the seven veils

| 2492 ½ ge | 68126 |
| 2493ge | |

cd: deutsche grammophon 423 5272/423 5252/477 6237/
unlimited classics HDNC 0017/audiophile classics APL 101 555/
naxos 8.111298

beethoven leonore no 3 overture

2494 ½ ge	68181
2495 ½ ge	
2496 ½ ge	68182
2497 ½ ge	

cd: deutsche grammophon 423 5262/423 5252/477 6237/
unlimited classics HDNC 0017/naxos 8.111298
78rpm discs were also published in automatic coupling
with the numbers 69182-69183

strauss don juan

2498 ¾ ge	68127
2499 ¾ ge	
2500 ¾ ge	68128
2501 ¾ ge	
2502 ½ ge	68129

lp: decca (usa) DL 9529
cd: deutsche grammophon 423 5272/423 5252/477 6237/
unlimited classics HDNC 0017/audiophile classics APL 101 555

013/26-28 june 1944/reichsrundfunk recording of a
magnetophon concert in berlin haus des rundfunks
staatskapelle berlin
bruckner symphony no 8 in c minor: second and third movements
cd: koch 3-1448-2/membran 232 779

014/19 september 1944/experimental twin-channel
recording by reichsrundfunk in berlin haus des rundfunks
staatskapelle berlin
bruckner symphony no 8 in c minor: fourth movement
lp: discocorp RR 391/RR 508
cd: arkadia CD 705/Koch 3-1448-2/unlimited classics HDNC 0017/
membran 232 779

015/14 december 1944/reichsrundfunk recording in
salzburg grosser saal des mozarteums
linz-bruckner-reichsorchester
bach die kunst der fuge BWV 1080
*information about this recording, which may not have survived,
came from ernst lumpe*

016/december 1944/reichsrundfunk recording of a
magnetophon concert in berlin haus des rundfunks
staatskapelle berlin
beethoven symphony no 3 in e flat op 55 "eroica"
lp: arfon (russia) 91 00049
cd: disques refrain 92 0040/unlimited classics HDNC 0017/
koch 31-5092
most issues of this recording were incorrectly dated may 1944

017/13-20 october 1946/columbia sessions in vienna musikvereinssaal

wiener philharmoniker/*producer walter legge*

beethoven symphony no 8 in f op 93

CHAX 200	LX 988/LFX 824/LVX 48
CHAX 201	
CHAX 202	LX 989/LFX 825/LVX 49
CHAX 203	
CHAX 204	LX 990/LFX 826/LVX 50
CHAX 205	

45: columbia (usa) EL 51

lp: toshiba EAC 30102/emi RLS 7714/1C137 54370-54373M

cd: emi 566 3912/763 3262/566 4832/512 0382/
warner 2564 633618

78rpm discs were also published in automatic coupling with the numbers LX 8557-8559

schubert symphony no 9 in c D944 "great"

CHAX 206	LX 1138/LFX 818/GQX 11130
CHAX 207	
CHAX 208	LX 1139/LFX 819/GQX 11131
CHAX 214	
CHAX 215	LX 1140/LFX 820/GQX 11132
CHAX 216	
CHAX 217	LX 1141/LFX 821/GQX 11133
CHAX 209	
CHAX 210	LX 1142/LFX 822/GQX 11134
CHAX 211	
CHAX 212	LX 1143/LFX 823/GQX 11135
CHAX 213	

lp: columbia (usa) ML 4631/toshiba EAC 30104/
emi 2C153 03200-205M

cd: emi 566 3892/566 4832/512 0382/warner 2564 633618

78rpm discs were also published in automatic coupling with the numbers LX 8644-8649 and GQX 11271-11276

018/18-19 october 1946/columbia sessions in
vienna brahmssaal des musikvereins
wiener philharmoniker/*producer walter legge*
mozart symphony no 33 in b flat K319

CHAX 220	LX 1006/LFX 781/LVX 84/M 778
CHAX 221	
CHAX 218	LX 1007/LFX 782/LVX 85/M 778
CHAX 219	
CHAX 222	LX 1008/LFX 783/LVX 86/M 778

lp: FCX 145/QCX 145/C 90633/columbia (usa) ML 4370/
toshiba EAC 30107
cd: emi 476 8972/763 3262/566 4832/556 3892/512 0382/
deutsche grammophon 476 8762/warner 2564 633618
*78rpm discs were also published in automatic coupling
with the numbers LX 8568-8570*

019/21-23 october 1946/columbia sessions in
vienna brahmssaal des musikvereins
wiener philharmoniker/**elisabeth schwarzkopf/
producer walter legge*
mozart le nozze di figaro overture
CHAX 223   LX 1008/LFX 783/LVX 86/GQX 11169/M 778
lp: toshiba EAC 30107/emi RLS 7714/1C153 54370-54373M/
2C153 03200-03205M
cd: emi 566 3682/566 4832/512 0382/warner 2654 633618

mozart deutsche tänze K600 no 5 and K605 no 3
CHAX 224   unpublished
cd: emi 763 3262/566 4832/566 3882/512 0382/
warner 2564 633618

019/21-23 october 1946/columbia sessions in vienna
brahmssaal des musikvereins/concluded

mozart serenade no 13 in g K525 "eine kleine nachtmusik"

CHAX 225	LX 1293/LCX 134/LFX 832/GQX 11157/LZX 215
CHAX 227	
CHAX 228	LX 1294/LCX 135/LFX 833/GQX 11158/LZX 216
CHAX 226	

lp: columbia (usa) ML 4370/toshiba EAC 30108/
emi 2C153 03200-205M
cd: emi 476 8762/566 3882/566 4832/512 0382/deutsche
grammophon 476 8762/warner 2564 633618

mozart divertimento no 17 in d K334: adagio

| CHAX 229 | unpublished |
| CHAX 388 | |

cd: emi 763 3262/566 3912/566 4832/512 0382/
warner 2564 633618
side 2 (CHAX 388) was recorded on 13 december 1947

*mozart die entführung aus dem serial: martern aller arten

| CHAX 230 | unpublished |
| CHAX 231 | |

lp: emi RLS 763/RLS 7714/154 6133/1C151 43160-43163M/
1C137 54370-54373M
cd: emi 763 7082/566 3942/566 4832/511 9732/
preiser 93444/warner 2564 633618

020/28-31 october 1946/columbia sessions in vienna musikvereinssaal

wiener philharmoniker/*hans hotter/*producer walter legge*

tchaikovsky romeo and juliet fantasy overture

CHAX 235	LX 1033/LCX 105/LFX 720/GQX 11184
CHAX 236	
CHAX 237	LX 1034/LCX 106/LFX 721/GQX 11185
CHAX 238	
CHAX 239	LX 1035/LCX 107/LFX 722/GQX 11186
CHAX 240	

lp: toshiba EAC 30112

cd: emi 764 8552/763 3262/566 3922/566 4832/512 0382/ warner 2564 633618

78rpm discs were also published in auomatic coupling with the numbers LX 8583-8585

johann strauss der zigeunerbaron overture

CHAX 241	LX 1009/LFX 773/LVX 4/GQX 11139
CHAX 242	

lp: toshiba EAC 30110

cd: emi 764 2992/764 2942/566 3952/566 4832/512 0382/ warner 2564 633618

johann strauss kaiserwalzer

CHAX 243	LX 1021/LCX 108/LVX 2/GQX 11148
CHAX 244	

lp: columbia (usa) AL 28/toshiba EAC 30111

cd: emi 763 3262/566 3952/566 4832/512 0382/ warner 2564 633618

johann strauss künstlerleben waltz

CHAX 245	LX 1012/LZX 218/LVX 3/GQX 11173
CHAX 246	

45: SEL 1503/C 50142/SELW 503/SEBQ 101/ERBF 109

lp: columbia (usa) AL 28/toshiba EAC 30111

cd: emi 566 3952/566 4832/512 0382/warner 2564 633618

020/28-31 october 1946/columbia sessions in vienna
musikvereinssaal/concluded

johann strauss an der schönen blauen donau
CHAX 247   LX 1118/LCX 123/LFX 840/LZX 217
CHAX 248
45: SCD 2144
lp: toshiba EAC 30110
cd: emi 476 8792/566 3952/566 4832/512 0382/
warner 2564 633618

johann strauss leichtes blut polka; josef and johann strauss
pizzicato polka
CHA 957   unpublished
CHA 958
cd: emi 476 8792/566 3962/566 4832/512 0382/
warner 2564 633618

*wagner die meistersinger von nürnberg: wahnmonolog;
fliedermonolog
CHAX 249   unpublished
CHAX 250
CHAX 251   unpublished
CHAX 252
recordings probably incomplete

021/20 october-3 november 1947/columbia sessions
in vienna musikvereinssaal

wiener philharmoniker/*wiener singverein/*elisabeth
schwarzkopf/*hans hotter/*producer walter legge*

* brahms ein deutsches requiem

CHAX 290	LX 1055/LVX 68/GQX 11239/SL 157/M755
CHAX 291	
CHAX 292	LX 1056/LVX 69/GQX 11240/SL 157/M755
CHAX 293	
CHAX 294	LX 1057/LVX 70/GQX 11241/SL 157/M755
CHAX 295	
CHAX 296	LX 1058/LVX 71/GQX 11242/SL 157/M755
CHAX 297	
CHAX 298	LX 1059/LVX 72/GQX 11243/SL 157/M755
CHAX 299	
CHAX 300	LX 1060/LVX 73/GQX 11244/SL 157/M755
CHAX 301	
CHAX 302	LX 1061/LVX 74/GQX 11245/SL 157/M755
CHAX 303	
CHAX 304	LX 1062/LVX 75/GQX 11246/SL 157/M755
CHAX 305	
CHAX 306	LX 1063/LVX 76/GQX 11247/SL 157/M755
CHAX 307	
CHAX 308	LX 1064/LVX 76/GQX 11248/SL 157/M755
CHAX 309	

lp: toshiba EAC 30103/emi RLS 7714/1C137 54370-53473M/
2C153 03200-03205M

cd: emi 761 0102/479 9312/512 0382/naxos 8.111038/
warner 2564 633618

78rpm discs were also published in automatic coupling with the
numbers LX 8595-8604

021/20 october-3 november 1947/columbia sessions
in vienna musikvereinssaal/concluded

strauss metamorphosen

CHAX 310	LX 1082/LVX 64
CHAX 311	
CHAX 312	LX 1083/LVX 65
CHAX 313	
CHAX 314	LX 1084/LVX 66
CHAX 315	
CHAX 316	LX 1085/LVX 67

lp: toshiba EAC 30109/emi RLS 7714/1C137 54370-53473M/
2C153 03200-03205M
cd: emi 476 8772/763 3262/566 3902/566 4832/512 0382/
warner 2564 633618

78rpm discs were also published in automatic coupling
with the numbers LX 8606-8609

022/3-6 november and 10-14 december 1947/
columbia sessions in vienna musikvereinssaal
wiener philharmoniker/wiener singverein/
elisabeth schwarzkopf/elisabeth höngen/julius
patzak/hans hotter/*producer walter legge*
beethoven symphony no 9 in d minor op 125 "choral"

CHAX 321	LX 1097/LFX 846/LVX 32/GQX 11250
CHAX 322	
CHAX 323	LX 1098/LFX 847/LVX 33/GQX 11251
CHAX 324	
CHAX 325	LX 1099/LFX 848/LVX 34/GQX 11252
CHAX 326	
CHAX 327	LX 1100/LFX 849/LVX 35/GQX 11253
CHAX 328	
CHAX 329	LX 1101/LFX 850/LVX 36/GQX 11254
CHAX 330	
CHAX 331	LX 1102/LFX 851/LVX 37/GQX 11255
CHAX 332	
CHAX 333	LX 1103/LFX 852/LVX 38/GQX 11256
CHAX 334	
CHAX 335	LX 1104/LFX 853/LVX 39/GQX 11257
CHAX 336	
CHAX 383	LX 1105/LFX 854/LVX 40/GQX 11258
CHAX 384	

45: columbia (usa) EL 51
lp: toshiba EAC 30101/emi RLS 7714/1C137 54370-54373M/
2C153 03200-03205M
cd: emi 761 0762/476 8782/479 9312/512 0382/
warner 2564 633618
78rpm discs were also published in automatic coupling
with the numbers LX 8612-8620

023/3 december 1947/columbia session in vienna
brahmssaal des musikvereins
wiener philharmoniker/*producer walter legge*
mozart adagio and fugue in c minor K546
CHAX 367   LX 1076
CHAX 368
lp: columbia (usa) ML 4370/toshiba EAC 30108/emi RLS 7714/
1C137 54370-54373M/2C153 03200-03205M
cd: emi 566 3912/566 4832/512 0382/warner 2564 633618

024/8 december 1947/columbia session in vienna
musikvereinssaal
wiener philharmoniker/*producer walter legge*
reznicek donna diana overture
CHAX 375   LX 1402/LWX 403/LCX 145/LFX 1013/GQX 11437
45: columbia SCB 112/SCD 2075/SCBQ 3017/SCBW 107
lp: columbia (usa) ML 5141/toshiba EAC 30111/emi RLS 7714/
1C137 54370-54373M
cd: emi 764 2942/764 2992/566 3962/566 4832/512 0382/
warner 2563 633618

025/9 december 1947/columbia session in vienna
brahmssaal des musikvereins
wiener philharmoniker/erich kunz/elisabeth
schwarzkopf/irmgard seefried/*producer walter legge*
mozart le nozze di figaro: non piu andrai (kunz)
CHAX 376　　　　　　LX 1123
45: SEL 1574
lp: C 70407/VS 811/emi RLS 764/1C137 43187-43188M/
1C147 03580-581M
cd: emi 566 3932/566 4832/511 9732/preiser 90345/
testament SBT 1059/warner 2564 633618

mozart don giovanni: la ci darem la mano (kunz/seefried)
CHA 988　　　　　　unpublished
lp: emi RLS 764/1C137 43187-43188M/EX 29 12363
cd: emi 566 3932/566 4832/511 9732/warner 2564 633618

mozart die zauberflöte: bei mannern welche liebe fühlen
(kunz/schwarzkopf)
CHA 989　　　　　　unpublished
cd: emi 566 3942/566 4832/511 9732/warner 2564 633618

026/9 december 1947/columbia session in vienna
musikvereinssaal
wiener philharmoniker/elisabeth schwarzkopf/
irmgard seefried/*producer walter legge*
strauss der rosenkavalier: mir ist die ehre widerfahren
CHAX 377　　　　　　LX 1225
CHAX 378
CHAX 379　　　　　　LX 1226
lp: columbia (usa) ML 2126/world records SH 286/
emi RLS 763/RLS 7714/154 6133/1C151 43160-43163M/
1C137 54370-54373M
cd: emi 769 7952/566 3942/566 4832/567 6342/511 9732/
regis RRC 1167/istituto discografico italiano IDIS 6447-6448/
warner 2564 633618

027/11 december 1947/columbia session in vienna
brahmssaal des musikvereins

wiener philharmoniker/irmgard seefried/*producer*
walter legge

mozart le nozze di figaro: deh vieni non tardar
CHAX 380　　　　　　LX 1145
lp: emi RLS 764/1C137 43187-43189M/EX 29 12363
cd: emi 566 3932/566 4832/511 9372/preiser 90345/
warner 2564 633618/orfeo C577 154I
mozart le nozze di figaro: voi che sapete; don giovanni: batti batti
CHA 990　　　　　　　LB 76/LO 82
CHA 991
lp: emi RLS 764/1C137 43187-43189M/EX 29 12363
cd: emi 566 3932/566 4832/511 9372/orfeo C577 154I
(voi che sapete)/warner 2564 633618

028/12 december 1947/columbia session in vienna
musikvereinssaal

wiener philharmoniker/*producer walter legge*

puccini manon lescaut intermezzo
CHAX 385　　　　　　unpublished
this recording was re-made on 30 november 1948 (session 038)

029/13 december 1947/columbia session in vienna
brahmssaal des musikvereins

wiener philharmoniker/*producer walter legge*

mozart maurerische trauermusik K477
CHAX 386　　　　　　LX 1155/LFX 950/columbia (usa) 72846D
CHAX 387
lp: toshiba EAC 30108/emi 2C153 03200-03205M
cd: emi 476 8772/763 3262/566 3902/566 4832/512 0382/
warner 2564 633618
session also included completion of the adagio from
divertimento K334 (see session 0019)

030/15-16 december 1947/columbia sessions in vienna musikvereinssaal

wiener philharmoniker/*hilde konetzni/*producer walter legge*

*strauss der rosenkavalier: da geht er hin (monologue part 1)
CHAX 391   LX 1135/LVX 45
cd: emi 566 3942/566 4832/511 9372/preiser 90078/90345/
rca-bmg 74321 694272/74321 694282/dutton CDLX 7034/
warner 2564 633618

*smetana the bartered bride: sweet dream of love/
sung in german
CHAX 392   LX 1074/LVX 54
CHAX 393
lp: emi RLS 764/1C137 43187-43189M
cd: emi 566 3942/566 4832/511 9372/preiser 90078/
warner 2564 633618

*strauss der rosenkavalier: quinquin er soll jetzt geh'n
(monologue part 2)
CHAX 394   LX 1135/LVX 45
cd: emi 566 3942/566 4832/511 9372/preiser 90078/
dutton CDLX 7034/warner 2564 633618

chabrier espana
CHAX 395   unpublished
CHAX 396
cd: emi 566 3932/566 4832/512 0382/warner 2564 633618

030a/16 december 1947/hmv session in vienna musikvereinssaal

wiener philharmoniker/maria cebotari/*producer walter legge*

mozart don giovanni: crudele? non mir dir

2VH 7065   DB 7638
2VH 7066

mozart don giovanni: or sai chi l'onore

2VH 7067   unpublished

45: 7ER 5126 (crudele non mi dir)

lp: E 60050/WDLP 563/preiser PR 9860/emi RLS 764/
1C137 43187-9M/1C147 29118-9M

cd: preiser 90034/90345 (or sai chi l'onore)/emi 566 3932/
566 4832/511 9732/warner 2564 633618

original and some lp issues of these recordings incorrectly named conductor as felix prohaska

031/8-10 april 1948/columbia sessions in london abbey road studios

philharmonia orchestra/dinu lipatti/*producer walter legge*

schumann piano concerto in a minor op 54

CAX 10206	LX 1110/LCX 8012/GQX 11207
CAX 10207	
CAX 10208	LX 1111/LCX 8013/GQX 11208
CAX 10209	
CAX 10210	LX 1112/LCX 8014/GQX 11209
CAX 10211	
CAX 10212	LX 1113/LCX 8015/GQX 11210
CAX 10213	

lp: 33C 1001/FCX 322/FCX 491/FCX 30096/FC 1016/FC 25078/
WC 1001/C 70082/VC 803/QC 1016/QCX 322/columbia (usa)
ML 2195/ML 4525/3216 0141/toshiba EAC 37001-37019/
emi XLP 30072/HLM 7046/1C061 00770M/1C047 00770M/
1C197 53780-53786M/2C051 03173

cd: emi 767 1632/769 7922/512 0382/warner 2564 633625/
207 3182/opus kura OPK 2072/dutton CDBP 9719

78rpm discs were also published in automatic coupling LX 8624-8627

032/14 may 1948/concert recordings in turin
sala del conservatorio
orchestra sinfonica di torino della rai
mozart symphony no 41 "jupiter"; ravel rapsodie espagnole;
beethoven symphony no 5 in c minor
these recordings remain unpublished

032a/28 july 1948/short newsreel footage of rehearsal
in salzburg felsenreitschule
wiener philharmoniker/ballet der wiener staatsoper
gluck orfeo ed euridice: dance of the furies

033/4-10 november 1948 and 21 january 1949/columbia
sessions in vienna musikvereinssaal
wiener philharmoniker/*producer walter legge*
tchaikovsky symphony no 6 in b minor op 74 "pathetique"

CHAX 409	LX 1234/LVX 87/columbia (usa) M 15147
CHAX 403	
CHAX 404	LX 1235/LVX 88/columbia (usa) M 15148
CHAX 405	
CHAX 408	LX 1236/LVX 89/columbia (usa) M 15149
CHAX 397	
CHAX 398	LX 1237/LVX 90/columbia (usa) M 15150
CHAX 399	
CHAX 400	LX 1238/LVX 91/columbia (usa) M 15151
CHAX 407	
CHAX 410	LX 1239/LVX 92/columbia (usa) M 15152
CHAX 406	

lp: 33CX 1026/FCX 105/WCX 1026/C 90302/columbia (usa) ML 4299/
toshiba EAC 30105/emi 2C153 03200-03205M
cd: emi 566 3922/566 4832/512 0382/preiser 90445/
warner 2564 633618
78rpm discs were published in automatic coupling with the
numbers LX 8699-8704

033a/6-10 november 1948/columbia sessions in
vienna brahmssaal des musikvereins
wiener philharmoniker/elisabeth schwarzkopf/
ljuba welitsch/erich kunz/*producer walter legge*
puccini la boheme: si mi chiamano mimi (schwarzkopf)
CHAX 401   unpublished
lp: emi ALP 143 5501/154 6133
cd: emi 763 5572/566 3932/566 4832/511 9732
warner 2564 633618

puccini la boheme: donde lieta usci (schwarzkopf)
CHAX 402   unpublished

puccini gianni schicchi: o mio babbino caro (schwarzkopf)
CHA 1002   LB 85/LV 7/LM 4/GQ 7240
45: SEL 1575
lp: toshiba EAC 30112/emi RLS 763/154 6133/1C151 43160-3M
cd: emi 566 3932/566 4832/511 9732/warner 2564 633618

mozart le nozze di figaro: se vuol ballare (kunz)
CHA 1003   unpublished

puccini turandot: tu che di gel sei cinta (schwarzkopf)
CHA 1004   unpublished

puccini la boheme: quando m'en vo (welitsch)
CHA 1005   LB 82
lp: emi HLM 7002/1C047 01267M/world records SH 289/
angel seraphim 60202
cd: polyhymnia 01212/melodram MELCD 1204 004/emi
761 0072/566 3932/566 4832/511 9732/warner 2564 633618
melodram edition incorrectly dated 1952

mozart don giovanni: or sai che l'onore (welitsch)
CHAX 411   unpublished

034/11-17 november 1948/columbia sessions in vienna musikvereinssaal

wiener philharmoniker/_producer walter legge_

beethoven symphony no 5 in c minor op 67

CHAX 412	LX 1330/LCX 140/LVX 79
CHAX 413	
CHAX 414	LX 1331/LCX 141/LVX 80
CHAX 415	
CHAX 416	LX 1332/LCX 142/LVX 81
CHAX 417	
CHAX 418	LX 1333/LCX 143/LVX 82
CHAX 419	

lp: 33CX 1004/FCX 107/QCX 107/VCX 506/
columbia (usa) RL 3068/toshiba EAC 30111
cd: emi 566 3912/566 4832/512 0382/warner 2564 633618
78rpm discs were also published in automatic coupling with the numbers LX 8752-8755

035/16 november 1948/hmv session in vienna brahmssaal des musikvereins

wiener philharmoniker/maria cebotari/_producer walter legge_

strauss ariadne auf naxos: es gibt ein reich

2VH 7105	DB 6914
2VH 7106	

45: 7ER 5141
lp: world records SH 286/preiser PR 9860/emi RLS 764/
1C137 43187-43189M/1C147 29118-29119M
cd: emi 569 7432/566 3942/566 4832/511 9732/
preiser 90034/warner 2564 633618

johann strauss der zigeunerbaron: o habet acht!

2VH 7107	DB 6947

lp: columbia (usa) RL 3068/preiser PR 9860/emi RLS 764/
1C137 43187-43189M/1C147 29118-29119M/
1C147 30226-30227M
cd: emi 566 3942/566 4832/511 9732/preiser 90034/
warner 2564 633618

036/19 november 1948/columbia session in
vienna musikvereinssaal

wiener philharmoniker/chor der wiener staatsoper/
*gertrud schüster/*producer walter legge*
*wagner der fliegende holländer: summ und brumm
CHAX 420 LX 1440
lp: toshiba EAC 30109
cd: emi 566 3942/566 4832/511 9732/warner 2564 633618

wagner lohengrin: treulich geführt
CHAX 422 unpublished

037/22-24 november 1948/columbia sessions in
vienna musikvereinssaal

wiener philharmoniker/ljuba welitsch/*gertrud
schüster/*josef witt/*producer walter legge*
*strauss salome: du wolltest mich nicht deinen mund
küssen lassen (with orchestral introduction)
CHAX 423 unpublished
CHAX 424
CHAX 425 unpublished
CHAX 428
CHAX 429 unpublished
CHAX 430
lp: world records SH 286
cd: emi 566 3942/566 4832/511 9732/warner 2564 633618
*all issues omit the section "öffne deine augen....geheimnisvolle
musik" as the matrix CHAX 424 was irreparably damaged in
transit from vienna to london*

johann strauss g'schichten aus dem wienerwald
CHAX 426 LX 1274/LDX 12/LFX 1014/LVX 137
CHAX 427
lp: toshiba EAC 30110/emi RLS 7714/1C137 54370-54373M
cd: emi 476 8792/763 3262/566 3962/566 4832/512 0382/
warner 2564 633618

038/30 november 1948/columbia session in vienna musikvereinssaal

wiener philharmoniker/*producer walter legge*

johann strauss die fledermaus overture

CHAX 434   LX 1546/LDX 11/LFX 989/LVX 152/GQX 11435
CHAX 435
45: SCD 2101
lp: toshiba EAC 30110
cd: emi 566 3952/566 4832/512 0382/warner 2564 633618

puccini manon lescaut intermezzo

CHAX 385   LX 1208/GQX 11322
45: SCB 109/SCBW 108/SCBQ 5013/SCD 2084
lp: toshiba EAC 30112
cd: emi 566 3932/566 4832/511 9732/warner 2564 633618
*this was a re-make of the recording first made on 12 december 1947
(session no. 028)*

039/november 1948/film soundtrack recording in vienna
wiener philharmoniker/wiener singverein/elisabeth schwarzkopf/elisabeth höngen/walther ludwig/hans braun/karl schmitt-walter/raoul aslan (narrator)/
film director ernst marischka

bach matthäus-passion, abridged version
*this recording, which accompanied a pictorial description of the
passion narrative, remains unpublished in any format; according
to information from angelo scottini, an italian-language version
was also made earlier in 1948 in rome cinecitta with the orchestra
and chorus of santa cecilia but with different vocal soloists and a
different conductor*

040/28 december 1948 and 2 january 1949/stage
recordings from wiener staatsoper guest performances
in milan teatro alla scala
orchester der wiener staatsoper/elisabeth schwarzkopf
(28 december)/maria cebotari (2 january)/irmgard
seefried/sena jurinac/giuseppe taddei/walter höfermayer
mozart le nozze di figaro: fragmentary excerpts
lp: melodram MEL 087/MEL 088/MEL 089
cd: di stefano GDS 1206
each of the issues contains a different selection of fragments;
GDS 1206 is incorrectly attributed to salzburg august 1948

041/21 january 1949/columbia session in vienna
musikvereinssaal
wiener philharmoniker/*producer walter legge*
johann strauss perpetuum mobile
CHA 1017　　　　　LB 128/LW 62/GQ 7251
45: SCD 2111
lp: toshiba EAC 30110/emi RLS 7714/1C137 54370=54373M
cd: emi 476 8792/763 3262/566 3952/566 4832/512 0382/
warner 2564 633618

mascagni cavalleria rusticana intermezzo
CHAX 455　　　　　LX 1208/GQX 11322
45: SCD 2084/SCB 109/SCBW 108/SCBQ 3013
cd: emi 566 3932/566 4832/511 9732/warner 2564 633618

042/14 august 1949/concert recording in salzburg festspielhaus

wiener philharmoniker/wiener singverein/hilde zadek/ margarete klose/helge rosvaenge/boris christoff

verdi messa da requiem

lp: cetra LO 524/discocorp RR 391/rodolphe RP 12403-12404/ dei della musica DMV 34-35

cd: datum DAT 12323/preiser 90445/audite 22 415

043/5 october 1949/concert recording in stockholm konserthuset

stockholms konsertförenings orkester

sibelius symphony no 5: third movement

cd: bis BISCD 424

044/18 october-10 november 1949/columbia sessions in vienna musikvereinssaal

wiener philharmoniker/producer walter legge

brahms symphony no 2 in d op 73

CHAX 473	LVX 125/GQX 11441
CHAX 474	
CHAX 482	LVX 125/GQX 11442
CHAX 483	
CHAX 484	LVX 126/GQX 11443
CHAX 485	
CHAX 486	LVX 127/GQX 11444
CHAX 487	
CHAX 495	LVX 128/GQX 11445
CHAX 496	

lp: FCX 285/angel 35007/toshiba EAC 30106

cd: emi 476 8772/763 3262/566 3902/566 4832/512 0382/ warner 2564 633618

044/18 october-10 november 1949/columbia
sessions in vienna musikvereinssaal/concluded
mozart symphony no 39 in e flat K543

CHAX 477	LX 1375/LWX 398/GQX 11405
CHAX 478	
CHAX 493	LX 1376/LWX 399/GQX 11406
CHAX 494	
CHAX 520	LX 1377/LWX 400/GQX 11407
CHAX 492	

lp: FCX 145/QCX 145/columbia (usa) RL 3068/toshiba EAC 30107
cd: emi 476 8762/566 3882/566 4832/512 0382/deutsche
grammophon 476 8762/warner 2564 633618
*78rpm discs were also published in automatic coupling with
the numbers LX 8785-8787*
johann strauss wiener blut waltz

CHAX 490	LX 1321/LFX 1023/LVX 167/GQX 11436
CHAX 491	

45: SEL 1503/SCD 2075/EW 22/ESBF 109/GQX 11436
lp: toshiba EAC 30111
cd: emi 763 3262/522 0492/567 1772/566 3962/566 4832/
512 0382/deutsche grammophon 459 7342/warner 2654 633618

045/18-24 october 1949/columbia sessions in vienna
musikvereinssaal
wiener philharmoniker/*producer walter legge*
josef strauss sphärenklänge waltz

CHAX 475	LX 1250/LFX 1027/columbia (usa) M 15175
CHAX 476	

45: SEL 1505/SELW 1505/C 50143/EW 55/SEBQ 107
cd: emi 476 8792/763 3262/566 3952/566 4832/512 0382/
deutsche grammophon 435 3352/warner 2564 633618

045/18-24 october 1949/columbia sessions in
vienna musikvereinssaal/concluded

johann strauss tritsch-tratsch polka
CHA 1088   LB 128/LW 62/GQ 7251
45: SCD 2111
lp: toshiba EAC 30110/emi RLS 7714/1C137 54370-54373M
cd: emi 476 8792/763 3262/562 8692/567 1772/566 3962/
566 4832/512 0382/warner 2564 633618

johann strauss unter donner und blitz
CHA 1089   unpublished
lp: preiser LV 15
cd: emi 476 8792/763 3262/764 2992/764 2942/567 1772/
566 3952/566 4832/512 0382/deutsche grammophon 459 7342/
warner 2564 633618

josef strauss transaktionen waltz
CHAX 479   LX 1257/LFX 1022
CHAX 480
45: SEL 1505/SELW 1505/C 50143/EW 53/SEBQ 107
cd: emi 476 8792/763 3262/566 3962/566 4832/512 0382/
warner 2564 633618

johann strauss wein weib und gesang waltz
CHAX 481   LX 1402/LCX 145/LFX 1013/LWX 402/
                   GQX 11437/M 15141
45: SCD 2075/SCB 112/SCBQ 3017
lp: toshiba EAC 30111
cd: emi 476 8792/763 3262/566 3952/566 4832/512 0382/
warner 2564 633618

josef strauss delirienwalzer
CHAX 488   LX 1303/LVX 142
CHAX 489
lp: toshiba EAC 30111/emi RLS 7714/1C137 54370-54373M
cd: emi 476 8792/763 3262/566 3962/566 4832/512 0382/
warner 2564 633618

046/2-3 november 1949/columbia sessions in vienna musikvereinssaal

wiener philharmoniker/chor der wiener staatsoper/
producer walter legge

wagner tannhäuser: freudig begrüssen wir die edle halle

CHAX 497 LX 1347/LFX 1021/LVX 154/GQX 11463/M 15154
CHAX 498

lp: toshiba EAC 30109

cd: emi 566 4832/511 9732/warner 2564 633618

wagner lohengrin: act three prelude; treulich geführt

CHAX 499 LX 1360/LFX 1029/LVX 171/GQX 11471
CHAX 500

lp: toshiba EAC 30109

cd: emi 566 4832/511 9732/warner 2564 633618

wagner die meistersinger von nürnberg: wach auf!;
da zu dir der heiland kam

CHAX 501 LX 1258
CHAX 502

lp: toshiba EAC 30109

cd: emi 566 4832/511 9732/warner 2564 633618

wagner der fliegende holländer: steuermann lass die wacht!

CHAX 503 LX 1440

lp: toshiba EAC 30109

cd: emi 566 4832/511 9732/warner 2564 633618

047/7-8 november 1949/columbia sessions in vienna brahmssaal des musikvereins

wiener philharmoniker/leopold wlach/*producer walter legge*

mozart clarinet concerto in a K622

CHAX 510	LWX 445/GQX 11484
CHAX 511	
CHAX 512	LWX 446/GQX 11485
CHAX 513	
CHAX 514	LWX 447/GQX 11486
CHAX 515	
CHAX 516	LWX 448/GQX 11487

lp: toshiba EAC 30108
cd: emi 764 2942/764 2952/566 3882/566 4832/512 0382/
warner 2564 633618

048/18-30 november 1949/columbia sessions in london kingsway hall

philharmonia orchestra/producer walter legge

balakirev symphony no 1 in c

CAX 10651	LX 1323
CAX 10652	
CAX 10653	LX 1324
CAX 10654	
CAX 10655	LX 1325
CAX 10656	
CAX 10657	LX 1326
CAX 10658	
CAX 10659	LX 1327
CAX 10660	
CAX 10661	LX 1328
CAX 10662	

lp: 33CX 1002/FCX 170/QCX 170/toshiba EAC 37020-37038/
emi XLP 60001/RLS 7715/1C137 54364-54367M
cd: emi 763 3162/566 5952/512 0382/warner 2564 633620
*78rpm discs were also published in automatic coupling
with the numbers LX 8746-8751*

048/18-30 november 1949/columbia sessions in
london kingsway hall/concluded

roussel symphony no 4 in a op 53

CAX 10669	LX 1349/LFX 976
CAX 10670	
CAX 10671	LX 1350/LFX 977
CAX 10672	
CAX 10673	LX 1351/LFX 978
CAX 10674	

lp: FCX 163/QCX 163/toshiba EAC 37020-37038/emi XLP 60003
cd: emi 763 3162/566 5952/512 0382/warner 2564 633621

bartok music for strings percussion and celesta

CAX 10677	LX 1371
CAX 10678	
CAX 10675	LX 1372
CAX 10676	
CAX 10681	LX 1373
CAX 10682	
CAX 10679	LX 1374
CAX 10680	

lp: FC 1012/QC 5032/columbia (usa) ML 4456/
toshiba EAC 37020-37038
cd: emi 763 4642/566 5962/512 0382/warner 2564 633621
*78rpm discs were also published in automatic coupling with
the numbers LX 8781-8784; 512 0382 and 2564 633621
also include rehearsal extract from the bartok sessions*

049/28 november 1949/hmv session in london kingsway hall

philharmonia orchestra/boris christoff/*producer walter legge*

verdi don carlo: ella giammai m'amo
2EA 14330   DB 21007
2EA 14331
45: 7RF 262
lp: emi RLS 735/1C147 03336-03337M
cd: emi 565 5002/566 6032/511 9732/warner 2564 633621

mussorgsky boris godunov: in the town of kazan (varlaam's song)
2EA 14332   DB 21097/victor M 1436
45: 7RF 156/victor EHA 11
lp: BLP 1003/WBLP 1003/emi RLS 735/1C147 03336-03337M
cd: emi 764 2522/566 6032/511 9732/warner 2564 633620

gounod faust: vous qui faites l'endormie
2EA 14333   unpublished
cd: emi 566 6032/511 9732/warner 2564 633621

050/9 june 1950/concert recording in vienna musikvereinssaal

wiener symphoniker/wiener singverein/wiener sängerknaben/irmgard seefried/kathleen ferrier/ walther ludwig/paul schöffler/otto edelmann
bach matthäus-passion BWV 244
lp: foyer FO 1046
cd: foyer 3CF 2013/arkadia CDKAR 211/verona 27070-27072/ gala GL 100 612/andante 1170

051/14 june 1950/columbia test recording from a
rehearsal in vienna musikvereinssaal
wiener symphoniker/elisabeth schwarzkopf/kathleen ferrier
bach mass in b minor: christe eleison; laudamus te; qui sedes;
agnus dei; et in unum dominum
cd: emi 763 6552/763 7902/769 7412/567 2072/586 8382/
511 9732/warner 2564 633629

052/15 june 1950/concert recording in vienna
musikvereinssaal
wiener symphoniker/wiener singverein/elisabeth
schwarzkopf/kathleen ferrier/walther ludwig/
alfred poell/paul schöffler
bach mass in b minor BWV 232
cd: foyer 2CF 2022/arkadia CDKAR 212/verona 27073-27074/
guild GHCD 2260-2266/archipel ARPCD 0031

053/17-21 june and 23-31 october 1950/columbia
sessions in vienna musikvereinssaal
wiener philharmoniker/chor der wiener staatsoper/
elisabeth schwarzkopf/irmgard seefried/sena jurinac/
rosl schwaiger/anny felbermayer/hilde czeska/elisabeth
höngen/erich kunz/george london/erich majkut/wilhelm
felden/marjan rus/*producer walter legge*
mozart le nozze di figaro (recitatives omitted)

CHAX 534	LWX 410
CHAX 535	
CHAX 536	LWX 411
CHAX 563	
CHAX 537	LWX 412
CHAX 607	
CHAX 000	LWX 413
CHAX 000	
CHAX 539	LWX 414
CHAX 564	

053/17-21 june and 23-31 october 1950/columbia
sessions in vienna musikvereinssaal/concluded

CHAX 000	LWX 415
CHAX 000	
CHAX 000	LWX 416
CHAX 000	
CHAX 544	LWX 417
CHAX 545	
CHAX 546	LWX 418
CHAX 547	
CHAX 548	LWX 419
CHAX 549	
CHAX 000	LWX 420
CHAX 000	
CHAX 000	LWX 421
CHAX 000	
CHAX 609	LWX 422
CHAX 610	
CHAX 561	LWX 423
CHAX 555	
CHAX 556	LWX 424
CHAX 557	
CHAX 558	LWX 425
CHAX 559	

lp: 33CX 1007-1009/FCX 174-176/QCX 10002-10004/VCX 503-505/
C 90292-90294/WCX 1007-1009/columbia (usa) SL 114/emi
1C147 01751-01753M/2C165 01751-01753M/1C197 54200-208M
cd: emi 769 6392/567 0682/567 1422/336 7792/511 9732/
membran 222 157

*according to alan sanders in his walter legge discography, matrix
numbers CHAX 534-573 were assigned for the german columbia
78rpm edition, despite the fact that it was made on tape; however
matrix numbers CHAX 568-573 were used for the zauberflöte recording
in session no. 0054, and as the deutsche nationalbibliothek seems to
have some of the figaro discs missing from its archive, it is not possible
to asceratain the actual numbers for LWX 413, 415-416 and 420-421*

48

054/23 august 1950/concert recording in lucerne
kunsthaus
schweizerisches festspielorchester/dinu lipatti
mozart piano concerto no 21 in c K467
lp: 33C 1064/QC 5046/C 80964/C 60714/WS 545/
angel 35931/emi RLS 749/1C197 53780-53786M/
1C047 01469M/2C051 03713/155 0963
cd: emi 476 8842/769 7922/767 1632/512 0382/
warner 2564 633625/207 3182

055/2-21 november 1950/columbia sessions in vienna
musikvereinssaal
wiener philharmoniker/wiener singverein/irmgard
seefried/wilma lipp/emmy loose/sena jurinac/friedl
riegler/else schürhoff/anton dermota/peter klein/
erich majkut/erich kunz/ludwig weber/george london/
ljubomir pantscheff/herald pröglhöf/*producer
walter legge*
mozart die zauberflöte (spoken dialogue omitted)

CHAX 580	LWX 426
CHAX 581	
CHAX 591	LWX 427
CHAX 592	
CHAX 584	LWX 428
CHAX 583	
CHAX 603	LWX 428
CHAX 589	
CHAX 590	LWX 430
CHAX 568	
CHAX 598	LWX 431
CHAX 600	
CHAX 601	LWX 432
CHAX 602	

055/2-21 november 1950/columbia sessions in
vienna musikvereinssaal/concluded

CHAX 569	LWX 433
CHAX 573	
CHAX 608	LWX 434
CHAX 606	
CHAX 597	LWX 435
CHAX 588	
CHAX 596	LWX 436
CHAX 604	
CHAX 593	LWX 437
CHAX 595	
CHAX 570	LWX 438
CHAX 586	
CHAX 575	LWX 439
CHAX 585	
CHAX 571	LWX 440
CHAX 572	
CHAX 576	LWX 441
CHAX 577	
CHAX 578	LWX 442
CHAX 579	
CHAX 582	LWX 443
CHAX 594	
CHAX 599	LWX 444
CHAX 587	

lp: 33CX 1013-1015/FCX 150-152/QCX 159-152/VCX 508-510/
C 90296-90298/WCX 1013-1015/columbia (usa) SL 115/emi
SLS 5052/1C147 01663-01665M/1C197 54200-54208M/
2C163 01663-01665/3C153 01663-01665
cd: emi 769 6332/567 0712/511 9732/membran 222 157

056/3 february 1951/concert recording in vienna
musikvereinssaal
wiener symphoniker/wiener singverein/carla martinis/
nell rankin/hilde forer/lorenz fehenberger/giovanni
malaspina/mario petri/fritz sperlbauer/alois pernerstorfer
verdi aida
cd: arkadia CDKAR 205/walhall WLCD 0057

057/6-13 june 1951/columbia sessions in london
kingsway hall

philharmonia orchestra/walter gieseking/*producer*
walter legge

grieg piano concerto in minor op 16

CAX 11123	LX 1503
CAX 11124	
CAX 11125	LX 1504
CAX 11126	
CAX 11127	LX 1505
CAX 11128	
CAX 11129	LX 1506

lp: 33C 1003/FC 1008/FC 25075/FCX 284/QCX 10239/VC 801/C 70083/
WC 1003/columbia (usa) ML 4885/ML 4431/emi 1C047 00770M/
1C047 01363M/3C153 52425-52431M/toshiba EAC 37001-37018
cd: emi 566 5972/512 0382/warner 2564 633625/265 0812
automatic coupling numbers LX 8888-8891

franck variations symphoniques pour piano et orchestra

CAX 11130	LCX 5000
CAX 11131	
CAX 11132	LCX 5001
CAX 11133	

lp: columbia (usa) ML 4536/ML 4885/toshiba EAC 37001-37018/
emi 1C047 01363M
cd: emi 566 5972/512 0382/philips 456 8112/
warner 2564 633625/265 0812
automatic coupling numbers LX 8937-8938

057/6-13 june 1951/columbia sessions in london kingsway hall/continued

beethoven piano concerto no 5 in e flat op 73 "emperor"

CAX 11134	LCX 5008
CAX 11142	
CAX 11135	LCX 5009
CAX 11141	
CAX 11136	LCX 5010
CAX 11140	
CAX 11137	LCX 5011
CAX 11139	
CAX 11139	LCX 5012

lp: 33CX 1010/FCX 135/QCX 135/VCX 507/C 90295/WCX 1010/
columbia (usa) ML 4623/3216 0029/toshiba EAC 37001-37018/
emi 3C153 52425-52431M
cd: 566 6042/512 0382/philips 456 8112/warner 2564 633625/
265 0812

beethoven piano concerto no 4 in g op 58

CAX 11155	LX 1443/GQX 11493
CAX 11156	
CAX 11157	LX 1444/GQX 11494
CAX 11158	
CAX 11159	LX 1445/GQX 11495
CAX 11160	
CAX 11161	LX 1446/GQX 11496
CAX 11162	

lp: 33C 1007/FC 1014/QC 1012/QCX 10499/VC 804/C 91244/
C 70085/WCX 598/WC 1007/columbia (usa) ML 4535/RL 3092/
3216 0371/toshiba EAC 37001-37018/emi 1C153 52425-52431M
cd: emi 566 6042/512 0382/philips 456 8112/pristine PASC 390/
warner 2564 633625/265 0812
*78rpm discs were also published in automatic coupling with the
numbers LX 8831-8834*

057/6-13 june 1951/columbia sessions in london
kingsway hall/concluded

mozart piano concerto no 23 in a K488

CAX 11163	LX 1510
CAX 11164	
CAX 11165	LX 1511
CAX 11166	
CAX 11167	LX 1512
CAX 11168	
CAX 11169	LX 1513

lp: 33C 1012/FCX 30003/FC 1013/FC 25072/QC 5009/C 70087/
WC 1012/columbia (usa) ML 4536/3216 0371/toshiba
EAC 37001-37018/emi 3C153 52425-52431M
cd: emi 763 7092/512 0382/warner 2564 633625/265 0812
*78rpm discs were also published in automatic coupling with the
numbers LX 8894-8897*

53

058/27 july-21 august 1951/live columbia recording taken from dress rehearsal and public performances in bayreuth festspielhaus

orchester der bayreuther festspiele/chor der bayreuther festspiele/elisabeth schwarzkopf/ira malaniuk/hans hopf/ gerhard unger/otto edelmann/friedrich dalberg/erich kunz/ werner faulhaber/erich majkut/hans berg/heinrich pflanzl/ josef janko/karl mikorey/gerhard stolze/heinz tandler/ heinz borst/arnold van mill/*producer walter legge*

wagner die meistersinger von nürnberg

CAX 11303	LX 1465
CAX 11304	
CAX 11305	LX 1466
CAX 11306	
CAX 11307	LX 1467
CAX 11308	
CAX 11309	LX 1468
CAX 11310	
CAX 11311	LX 1469
CAX 11312	
CAX 11313	LX 1470
CAX 11314	
CAX 11315	LX 1471
CAX 11316	
CAX 11317	LX 1472
CAX 11318	
CAX 11319	LX 1473
CAX 11320	
CAX 11321	LX 1474
CAX 11322	
CAX 11323	LX 1475
CAX 11324	
CAX 11325	LX 1476
CAX 11326	
CAX 11327	LX 1477
CAX 11328	

058/27 july-21 august 1951/live columbia recording in bayreuth festspielhaus/continued

CAX 11329	LX 1478
CAX 11330	
CAX 11331	LX 1479
CAX 11332	
CAX 11333	LX 1480
CAX 11334	
CAX 11335	LX 1481
CAX 11336	
CAX 11337	LX 1482
CAX 11338	
CAX 11339	LX 1483
CAX 11340	
CAX 11341	LX 1484
CAX 11342	
CAX 11343	LX 1485
CAX 11344	
CAX 11345	LX 1486
CAX 11346	
CAX 11347	LX 1487
CAX 11348	
CAX 11349	LX 1488
CAX 11350	
CAX 11351	LX 1489
CAX 11352	
CAX 11353	LX 1490
CAX 11354	
CAX 11355	LX 1491
CAX 11356	
CAX 11357	LX 1492
CAX 11358	
CAX 11359	LX 1493
CAX 11360	
CAX 11361	LX 1494
CAX 11362	

058/27 july-21 august 1951/live columbia recording
in bayreuth festspielhaus/concluded

CAX 11363	LX 1495
CAX 11364	
CAX 11365	LX 1496
CAX 11366	
CAX 11367	LX 1497
CAX 11368	
CAX 11369	LX 1498

lp: 33CX 1021-1025/FCX 128-132/VCX 523-527/C 90275-90279/
WCX 501-505/angel seraphim 6030/emi RLS 7708/RLS 143 3903/
1C151 43390-43394M
cd: emi 763 5002/511 9732/naxos 8.110872-110875
automatic coupling numbers LX 8851-8888

059/5 august 1951/radio broadcast in bayreuth
festspielhaus
orchester der bayreuther festspiele/chor der bayreuther
festspiele/elisabeth schwarzkopf/ira malaniuk/hans hopf/
gerhard unger/otto edelmann/friedrich dalberg/erich kunz/
werner faulhaber/erich majkut/hans berg/heinrich pflanzl/
josef janko/karl mikorey/gerhard stolze/heinz tandler/
heinz borst/arnold van mill
wagner die meistersinger von nürnberg
cd: arkadia CDKAR 224/urania URN 22226/membran documents 221 473

060/11 august 1951/radio broadcast in bayreuth
festspielhaus

orchester der bayreuther festspiele/ira malaniuk/paula
brivkalne/elisabeth schwarzkopf/lore wissmann/herta
topper/rut siewert/paul kuen/walter fritz/wolfgang
windgassen/sigurd björling/werner faulhaber/heinrich
pflanzl/ludwig weber/friedrich dalberg

wagner das rheingold

lp: melodrama MEL 516

cd: melodrama MEL 25107/urania URN 22206/
walhall WLCD 0034/myto HO 54

also recorded by columbia, whose tapes remain unpublished

061/12 august 1951/live columbia recording in bayreuth festspielhaus

orchester der bayreuther festspiele/astrid varnay/ leonie rysanek/ira malaniuk/günther treptow/sigurd björling/arnold van mill/brünnhild friedland/lieselotte thomamüller/elfriede wild/rut siewert/eleanor lausch/ herta töpper/hanna ludwig/*producer walter legge*
wagner die walküre acts one and two
these recordings remain unpublished

wagner die walküre act three

CAX 11287	LX 1447
CAX 11288	
CAX 11289	LX 1448
CAX 11290	
CAX 11291	LX 1449
CAX 11292	
CAX 11293	LX 1450
CAX 11294	
CAX 11295	LX 1451
CAX 11296	
CAX 11297	LX 1452
CAX 11298	
CAX 11299	LX 1453
CAX 11300	
CAX 11301	LX 1454
CAX 11302	

lp: columbia 33CX 1005-1006/C 90280-90281/WCX 1005-1006/ WCX 506-507/FCX 111-112/QCX 111-112/VCX 501-502/ columbia (usa) SL 116/emi 1C181 03035-03036M
cd: emi 764 7042/511 9732/380 0242
78rpm discs were also published in automatic coupling with the numbers LX 8835-8842

062/13 august 1951/radio broadcast in bayreuth festspielhaus

orchester der bayreuther festspiele/astrid varnay/ wilma lipp/rut siewert/bernd aldenhoff/paul kuen/ sigurd björling/heinrich pflanzl/friedrich dalberg

wagner siegfried

lp: melodram MEL 518/foyer FO 1004

cd: melodram MEL 46106/arkadia CDKAR 219/myto HO 55/ walhall WLCD 0096

also recorded by columbia, whose tapes remain unpublished

063/15 august 1951/live columbia recording in bayreuth festspielhaus

orchester der bayreuther festspiele/chor der bayreuther festspiele/astrid varnay/martha mödl/ rut siewert/elisabeth schwarzkopf/lore wissmann/ herta topper/ira malaniuk/bernd aldenhoff/hermann uhde/ludwig weber/heinrich pflanzl

wagner götterdämmerung

this recording remains unpublished

064/24 sepember 1951/concert recording in rome

wiener symphoniker/wiener singverein/elfriede trötschel/sieglinde wagner/ernst haefliger/ heinz rehfuss

beethoven missa solemnis in d op 123

this recording remains unpublished

065/28 november-1 december 1951 and
29 april-8 may 1952/columbia sessions in london
kingsway hall
philharmonia orchestra/_producer walter legge_
beethoven symphony no 7 in a op 92
reel-to-reel tape: CAT 282
lp: 33CX 1035/FCX 160/QCX 10007/VCX 519/C 90504/
WCX 1035/angel 35003/world records SM 143-149/toshiba
EAC 37001-37018/emi SLS 5053/1C181 01830-01836Y
cd: emi 763 3102/512 0382/515 8632/major classics
M3CD 309/ warner 2564 633735

handel water music suite arranged by harty; sibelius
symphony no 5: third movement
these recordings remain unpublished

066/3-4 december 1951/columbia sessions in london kingsway hall

philharmonia orchestra/_producer walter legge_

strauss don juan

CAX 11542	GQX 8039
CAX 11543	
CAX 11544	GQX 8040
CAX 11545	

lp: 33CX 1001/FCX 159/QCX 159/VCX 532/C70425/WC 528/
toshiba EAC 37020-37038/emi RLS 7715/2M055 43228/
1C137 54364-54367M/
cd: emi 763 3162/512 0382/urania URN 22260/testament
SBT 1383/warner 2564 633623

78rpm discs were also published in automatic coupling with the numbers LX 8920-8921; URN 22260 is incorrectly described as a performance in turin on 31 october 1954

strauss till eulenspiegels lustige streiche

CAX 11546	GQX 8037/LVX 173
CAX 11547	
CAX 11548	GQX 8038/LVX 174
CAX 11549	

lp: 33CX 1001/FCX 159/QCX 159/C 70425/WC 528/toshiba
EAC 37020-37038/emi RLS 7715/1C137 54364-54367M/
2M055 43228
cd: emi 763 3162/512 0382/testament SBT 1383/
warner 2564 633623

78rpm discs were also published in automatic coupling with the numbers LX 8908-8909

61

067/26 january 1952/stage recording in milan
teatro alla scala

orchestra e coro del teatro alla scala/elisabeth
schwarzkopf/sena jurinac/lisa della casa/jarmila
barton/else schürhoff/luisa villa/maria amadini/
ilva ligabue/pina carrillo/antonio pirino/erich majkut/
hugues cuenod/otto edelmann/erich kunz/giuseppe
nessi/bruno fichtinger/luciano della pergola/gino del
signore/attilio barbesi/paolo pedani/joszi trojan regar/
franco taino/enrico campi
strauss der rosenkavalier
cd: legato classics LCD 197

068/1-5 may 1952/columbia sessions in london
kingsway hall
philharmonia orchestra/*producer walter legge*
stravinsky jeu de cartes
lp: FCX 163/QCX 163/toshiba EAC 37020-37038/emi XLP 60003
cd: emi 763 3162/566 6012/512 0382/warner 2564 633620

mozart divertimento no 15 in b flat K287
this recording remains unpublished

069/5-7 may and 25-31 july 1952/columbia sessions
in london kingsway hall
philharmonia orchestra/*producer walter legge*
brahms symphony no 1 in c minor op 68
reel-to-reel tape: CAT 251
lp: 33CX 1053/FCX 162/QCX 10044/C 90132/WCX 1053/
angel 35001/toshiba EAC 37020-37038
cd: emi 763 4362/512 0382/warner 2564 633623

070/23 july 1952/stage recording in bayreuth festspielhaus

orchester der bayreuther festspiele/männerchor der bayreuther festspiele/martha mödl/ira malaniuk/ramon vinay/hans hotter/ludwig weber/hermann uhde/gerhard stolze/gerhard unger/werner faulhaber

wagner tristan und isolde

lp: discocorp IGI 291/cetra LO 47/foyer FO 1008/melodram MEL 525

cd: arkadia CD 528/myto MCD 962 149/walhall WLCD 0096/ membran 221 800/urania DS 037 502/orfeo C603 033D

071/25-31 july 1952/columbia sessions in london kingsway hall

philharmonia orchestra/*producer walter legge*

sibelius symphony no 5 in e flat op 82

reel-to-reel tape CAT 255

lp: 33CX 1047/FCX 192/QCX 10019/VCX 520/C 90308/WCX 1047/ angel 35002/toshiba EAC 37020-37038

cd: emi 566 6002/512 0382/warner 2564 633621

handel water music suite arranged by harty

CAX 11744	LX 8945
CAX 11747	
CAX 11746	LX 8946
CAX 11745	

lp: 33CX 1033/FCX 164/QCX 164/angel 35004/ toshiba EAC 37001-37019

cd: emi 763 4642/512 0382/opus kura OPK 7020/ warner 2564 633621

071/25-31 july 1952/columbia sessions in london kingsway hall/concluded

sibelius finlandia

CAX 11813	LX 1593/GQX 11536/LOX 831
CAX 11814	

45: SCD 2115
reel-to-reel tape: CAT 255
lp: 33CX 1047/FCX 192/QCX 10019/VCX 520/C 90308/
WCX 1047/angel 35002/toshiba EAC 37020-37038
cd: emi 763 4642/566 6002/512 0382/warner 2564 633621
tchaikovsky casse noisette ballet suite; symphony no 5
these recordings remain unpublished and probably incomplete

072/29 september 1952/concert recording in perugia basilica san pietro
wiener symphoniker/wiener singverein/rita streich/ dagmar hermann/ernst haefliger/hans braun
bruckner te deum
cd: arkadia CD 705/urania URN 22210

073/25 october 1952/concert recording in vienna musikvereinssaal
wiener symphoniker/clara haskil
beethoven piano concerto no 4 in g op 58
cd: tahra TAH 601-603

074/2-7 november 1952/columbia sessions in vienna musikvereinssaal
wiener symphoniker/wiener singverein/*producer walter legge*
bach mass in b minor: choruses only
orchestra described on this recording as orchester der gesellschaft der musikfreunde; for full details of the complete recording see session no. 076

075/19 november-1 december 1952/columbia sessions in london kingsway hall

philharmonia orchestra/_producer walter legge_
tchaikovsky casse noisette ballet suite
lp: 33CX 1033/FCX 164/QCX 164/VCX 528/angel 35004/
toshiba EAC 37020-37038
cd: emi 476 8992/763 4602/512 0382/warner 2564 633620
beethoven symphony no 3 in e flat op 55 "eroica"
reel-to-reel tape: CAT 278
lp: 33CX 1046/FCX 204/QCX 10013/C 90307/WCX 1046/SHZE 133/
angel 35000/world records SM 143-149/toshiba EAC 37001-37019/
emi SLS 5053/1C181 01830-01836Y
cd: emi 763 3102/512 0382/515 8632/major classics M3CD 309/
naxos 8.111339/warner 2564 633735
tchaikovsky swan lake ballet suite; sleeping beauty ballet suite
reel-to-reel tape: CAT 252/TC-CX 1065
lp: 33CX 1065/FCX 202/FCX 30002/QCX 202/C 90317/WCX 1065/
angel 35006/toshiba EAC 37020-37028
cd: emi 476 8992/763 4602/512 0382/warner 2564 633620
mozart symphony no 35 in d K385 "haffner"
cd: warner 2564 633623 (previously unpublished)

076/23-28 november 1952 and 16 july 1953/
columbia sessions in london abbey road studios
philharmonia orchestra/elisabeth schwarzkopf/
marga höffgen/nicolai gedda/heinz rehfuss/
producer walter legge
bach mass in b minor: arias only
lp: 33CX 1121-1123/FCX 291-293/C 90337-90339/WCX 1121-1123/
QCX 10055-10057/angel 3500/world records T 854-856/emi
RLS 746/EX 29 09743/1C181 01791-01793
cd: emi 763 5052/511 9732/warner 2564 633629
these recordings were combined with those in session. 074
to form complete performance of the mass

077/28-29 november 1952 and 21-22 july 1953/
columbia sessions in london kingsway hall
philharmonia orchestra/_producer walter legge_
bartok concerto for orchestra
lp: 33CX 1054/FCX 199/QCX 10052/C 90313/WCX 1054/
angel 35003/toshiba EAC 37020-37038
cd: emi 763 4642/566 5962/512 0382/warner 2564 633621

078/6 december 1952/concert recording in rome
auditorium del foro italico
orchestra sinfonica di roma della rai/marcelle meyer
pizzetti preludio a un altro giorno; mozart piano concerto no 23;
brahms symphony no 2
these recordings remain unpublished

079/20 december 1952/concert recording in rome
auditorium del foro italico
orchestra sinfonica e coro di roma della rai/magda
laszlo/nicolai gedda/mario petri/nestore catalane/
aldo bertocci/arnoldo foa (narrator)
stravinsky oedipus rex
cd: datum DAT 12311/urania URN 22210

080/24 december 1952/concert recording in rome
auditorium del foro italico
orchestra sinfonica di roma della rai
beethoven symphony no 4; beethoven symphony no 7
these recordings remain unpublished

081/20 february 1953/concert recording in turin
rai auditorium
orchestra sinfonica e coro di torina della rai/elisabeh
schwarzkopf/elsa cavelti/nicolai gedda/mario petri
tippett a child of our time
this recording remains unpublished

082/27 february 1953/concert recordings in turin
rai auditorium
orchestra sinfonica di torino della rai
honegger symphony no 2; strauss tod und verklärung
these recordings remain unpublished

tchaikovsky symphony no 5 in e minor op 64
lp: cetra LAR 46
cd: cetra ARCD 2054/urania URN 22260/dynamic CDS 712

083/26 march 1953/concert recording in rome
auditorium del foro italico
orchestra sinfonica di roma della rai
brahms symphony no 2 in d op 73
cd: tahra TAH 611-613

084/10-11 april 1953/concert recordings in turin
rai auditorium
orchestra sinfonica di torino della rai
beethoven symphony no 2; bartok concerto for orchestra
these recordings remain unpublished

sibelius finlandia
cd: dynamic CDS 712

085/24 april 1953/concert recordings in turin
rai auditorium
orchestra sinfonica di torino della rai/*kurt leimer
*kurt leimer piano concerto for the left hand
cd: private edition vienna

mozart symphony no 41;   britten frank bridge variations
these recordings remain unpublished

086/5 june 1953/concert recording in vienna
musikvereinssaal
wiener symphoniker/wiener singverein/martha mödl/
elisabeth schwarzkopf/wolfgang windgassen/rudolf
schock/otto edelmann/josef metternich/hans braun/
erich majkut/hans schwaiger
beethoven fidelio
cd: walhall WLCD 0063
*final minutes of act one are missing and replaced by that section
from a vienna recording with wilhelm furtwängler*

087/19 june 1953/columbia sessions in london
kingsway hall
philharmonia orchestra/*producer walter legge*
tchaikovsky symphony no 5 in e minor op 64
lp: 33CX 1133/QCX 10098/C 90347/WCX 1133/angel 35055/
toshiba EAC 37020-37038
cd: emi 763 4602/512 0382/warner 2564 633620

088/20 june and 13-15 july 1953/columbia sessions
in london kingsway hall
philharmonia orchestra/*producer walter legge*
beethoven egmont overture; beethoven leonore no 3 overture
lp: 33CX 1136/FCX 250/FC 25107/QCX 10099/C 70363/WC 511/
SHZE 169/angel 35097/toshiba EAC 37001-37019/emi SLS 5053/
1C181 01830-01836Y
cd: emi 763 3102/512 0382/515 8632/warner 2564 633735/
naxos 8.558087-558090 (egmont)/

beethoven coriolan overture
lp: 33CX 1227/FCX 420/FC 25107/QCX 10185/C 90407/WCX 1227/
WC 511/angel 35196/toshiba EAC 37001-37019/emi SLS 5053/
1C181 01830-01836Y
cd: emi 763 3102/512 0382/515 8632/warner 2564 633735

089/27 june-2 july 1953/columbia sessions in london
kingsway hall
philharmonia orchestra/loughton and bancroft's school
choirs/elisabeth schwarzkopf/elisabeth grümmer/anny
felbermayer/maria von ilosvay/else schürhoff/josef
metternich/*producer walter legge*
humperdinck hänsel und gretel
reel-to-reel tape: CAT 276-277
lp: 33CX 1096-1097/FCX 286-287/QCX 10048-10049/C 90327-90328/
WCX 1096-1097/angel 3506/world records OC 187-188/
emi SLS 5145/EX 769 2931
cd: emi 763 2932/567 0612/511 9732/naxos 8.110897-110898

090/2-7 july 1953/columbia sessions in london kingsway hall
philharmonia orchestra/*producer walter legge*
strauss tod und verklärung
lp: emi RLS 7715/1C137 54364-54367M/2M055 43228
cd: emi 763 3162/512 0382/testament SBT 1383/
warner 2564 633623

sibelius symphony no 4 in a minor op 63; tapiola op 112
lp: 33CX 1125/FCX 280/QCX 10078/C 90341/WCX 1225/
angel 35082/toshiba EAC 37020-37038
cd: emi 476 8832 (symphony)/763 4642/566 6002/562 8692/
512 0382/membran 232 779/warner 2564 633621

091/4-16 july 1953/columbia sessions in london kingsway hall
philharmonia orchestra/*producer walter legge*
tchaikovsky symphony no 4 in f minor op 36
reel-to-reel tape: CAT 273
lp: 33CX 1139/FCX 274/QCX 10106/angel 35099/
toshiba EAC 37020-37038
cd: emi 763 4602/512 0382/warner 2564 633620

beethoven symphony no 6 in f op 68 "pastoral"
reel-to-reel tape: CAT 269
lp: 33CX 1124/FCX 234/QCX 10093/C 90340/WCX 1124/
SHZE 196/angel 35080/world recods SM 143-149/toshiba
EAC 37001-37019/emi SLS 5053/1C181 01830-01836Y
cd: emi 763 3102/512 0382/515 8632/opus kura
OPK 7016/membran 232 779/warner 2564 633734

092/16-17 july 1953/columbia sessions in london kingsway hall

philharmonia orchestra/*producer walter legge*

ravel rapsodie espagnole
reel-to-reel tape: CAT 257
lp: 33CX 1099/FCX 298/QCX 10097/angel 35081/toshiba EAC 37020-37038
cd: emi 763 4642/512 0382/warner 2564 633621

chabrier espana
45: SEL 1528/SEBQ 129
lp: 33CX 1335/FCX 512/QCX 10198/C 80464/WSX 528/ angel 35327/toshiba EAC 37020-37038
cd: emi 512 0382/opus kura OPK 7020/warner 2564 633621

093/20-22 july 1953/columbia sessions in london kingsway hall

philharmonia orchestra/*producer walter legge*

debussy la mer
reel-to-reel tape: CAT 257
lp: 33CX 1099/FCX 298/QCX 10059/angel 35081/ toshiba EAC 37020-37038
cd: emi 763 4642/512 0382/warner 2564 633621

waldteufel les patineurs waltz
45: SEL 1628/SEBQ 129/EW 72
lp: 33CX 1335/FCX 30103/QCX 10198/C 80464/WSX 528/ angel 35327/toshiba EAC 37020-37038
cd: emi 512 0382/opus kura OPK 7020/warner 2564 633621

sousa stars and stripes forever march; el capitan march
these recordings remain unpublished

094/24-25 august 1953/columbia sessions in london kingsway hall

philharmonia orchestra/walter gieseking/*producer walter jellinek*

schumann piano concerto in a minor op 54
reel-to-reel tape: CBT 552
lp: 33C 1033/FCX 284/FCX 322/QCX 10239/QC 5020/QC 10222/
C 91324/C 70091/WC 1033/angel 35321/emi 1C047 01401M/
3C153 52425-52431M/toshiba EAC 37001-37019
cd: emi 566 5972/512 0382/warner 2564 633625/265 0812

mozart piano concerto no 24 in c minor K491
lp: 33CX 1526/FCX 30004/FC 25117/QCX 10323/C 91396/WCX 1526/
angel 35501/emi 3C153 52425-52451M/toshiba EAC 37001-37019
cd:emi 476 8842/763 7092/512 0382/philips 456 8112/
warner 2564 633625/265 0812

095/26-28 august 1953/columbia sessions in london kingsway hall

philharmonia orchestra/*producers walter jellinek and walter legge*
beethoven symphony no 5 in c minor op 67
this recording remains unpublished

096/8 september 1953/concert recording in berlin titania palast

philharmonisches orchester berlin
beethoven symphony no 3 in e flat op 55 "eroica"
lp: maestri del secolo APE 1205/wg records WG 30003/
joker SM 1337
cd: artemis 710 000/710 003/audite 23 414

097/10-11 november 1953/columbia sessions in
london abbey road studios
philharmonia orchestra/_producer walter legge_
britten frank bridge variations; vaughan williams tallis fantasia
these recordings remain unpublished

098/12-13 november 1953/columbia sessions in
london kingsway hall
philharmonia orchestra/dennis brain/
producer walter legge
mozart horn concerti: no 1 K412; no 2 K427; no 3 K447
reel-to-reel tape: CAT 270/TC-CX 1140
lp: 33CX 1140/FCX 251/QCX 10100/C 90354/WCX 1140/
angel 35092/toshiba EAC 37001-37019/emi ASD 1140/
1C063 00414/2C051 00414/3C053 00414
cd: emi 761 0132/566 8982/566 0872/512 0382/
membran 232 779/warner 2564 633625/206 0102

099/13-16 november 1953/columbia sessions in
london kingsway hall
philharmonia orchestra/_producer walter legge_
beethoven symphony no 4 in b flat op 60
lp: 33CX 1278/QCX 10149/C 90447/WCX 1278/angel 35023/
toshiba EAC 37001-37019/world records SM 143-149/
emi SLS 5053/1C181 01830-01836Y
cd: emi 763 3102/512 0382/515 8632/major classics
M3CD 309/warner 2564 633735

beethoven symphony no 8 in f op 93
this recording remains unpublished and probably incomplete

100/13 and 23 november 1953/columbia sessions in
london kingsway hall
philharmonia orchestra/*producer walter legge*
beethoven symphony no 2 in d op 36
lp: 33CX 1227/FCX 420/QCX 10185/C 90407/WCX 1227/
angel 35196/toshiba EAC 37001-37019/world records
SM 143-149/emi SLS 5053/1C181 01830-01836Y
cd: emi 763 3102/512 0382/515 8632/major classics
M3CD 309/warner 2564 633735

101/17-18 november 1953/columbia sessions in
london abbey road studios
philharmonia orchestra/sidney sutcliffe/bernard
walton/cecil james/dennis brain/*producer walter legge*
mozart sinfonia concertante in e flat K297b
lp: 33CX 1178/FCX 308/QCX 10101/C 90376/WCX 1178/
angel 35098/toshiba EAC 37001-37019/emi XLP 60004/
RLS 7715/1C137 54364-54367M
cd: emi 763 3162/512 0382/warner 2564 633625

102/18 and 21 november 1953/columbia sessions in london kingsway hall

philharmonia orchestra/_producer walter legge_

mozart serenade no 13 in g K525 "eine kleine nachtmusik"
45: C 50643/SELW 1812
lp: 33CX 1178/FCX 308/FC 25107/QCX 1010/C 90376/C 70391/
WCX 1178/WC 537/angel 35098/toshiba EAC 37001-37019
cd: emi 763 4562/512 0382/warner 2564 633623

beethoven symphony no 1 in c op 21
lp: 33CX 1136/FCX 250/QCX 10099/C 70367/WC 515/angel 35097/
toshiba EAC 37001-37019/world records SM 143-149/emi SLS 5053/
1C181 01830-01836Y
cd: emi 763 3102/512 0382/515 8632/major classics M3CD 309/
warner 2564 633735

103/23 november 1953/columbia sessions in london kingsway hall

philharmonia orchestra/*dennis brain/_producer walter legge_

*mozart horn concerto no 4 K495
reel-to-reel tape: CAT 270/TC-CX 1140
lp: 33CX 1140/FCX 251/QCX 10101/C 90354/WCX 1140/
angel 35092/toshiba EAC 37001-37019/emi ASD 1140/
1C063 00414/2C051 00414/3C053 00414
cd: emi 761 0132/566 8982/566 0872/512 0382/membran
232 779/warner 2564 633625/206 0102

britten frank bridge variations; vaughan williams tallis fantasia
lp: 33CX 1159/QCX 10109/angel 35142/toshiba EAC 37020-37038/
emi XLP 60002/1C053 03827M
cd: emi 476 8802/763 5162/566 6012/512 0382/
warner 2564 633621

104/5 december 1953/concert recordings in rome
auditorium del foro italico
orchestra sinfonica di roma della rai/*bruno giuranna
william walton symphony no 1
cd: emi 562 8692

*ghedini musica da concerto per viola ed archi
cd: private edition vienna

weber euryanthe overture
this item remains unpublished

105/11 december 1953/concert recordings in rome
auditorium del foro italico
orchestra sinfonica di roma della rai
beethoven symphony no 4;   beethoven symphony no 5
these recordings remain unpublished

106/19 december 1953/concert recording in rome
auditorium del foro italico
orchestra sinfonica e coro di roma della rai/elisabeth
schwarzkopf/rita streich/alda noni/carla schiehan/ester
orelli/anna maria rota/bruna rizzoli/gilda capozzi/
nicolai gedda/antonio pirino/giuseppe taddei/mario
petri/nino del sole/plinio clabassi
mozart die zauberflöte/*sung in italian and with dialogues*
spoken by actors
cd: myto MCD 89007/urania URN 22237/walhall WLCD 0017

107/21 december 1953/concert recordings in rome
auditorium del foro italico
orchestra sinfonica e coro di roma della rai/elisabeth
schwarzkopf/oralia dominguez/nicolai gedda/
giorgio tadeo
bach magnificat BWV 243
cd: archipel ARPCD 0237

heinrich sutermeister messa da requiem
*this recording was advertised as a download obtainable
from opera-club.net*

108/18 january 1954/stage recording in milan
teatro alla scala
orchestra e coro del teatro alla scala di milano/maria
callas/luisa villa/giuseppe di stefano/giuseppe zampieri/
rolando panerai/giuseppe modesti/mario carlin
donizetti lucia di lammermoor
lp: historical recording enterprises HRE 291
cd: standing room only SRO 831/melodram MEL 26040/
istituto discografico italiano IDIS 6419-6420

109/4 february 1954/stage recording in milan
teatro alla scala
orchestra e coro del teatro alla scala di milano/
elisabeth schwarzkopf/irmgard seefried/sena jurinac/
luisa villa/mariella adani/mario petri/rolando panerai/
antonio pirino/silvio maionica
mozart le nozze di figaro
lp: cetra LO 70
cd: melodram MEL 37075/arkadia CDKAR 225/myto HO 82/
walhall WLCD 0083/istituto discografico italiana IDIS 6428-6429

110/6 february 1954/concert recording in milan
sala grande del conservatorio
orchestra sinfonica e coro di milano della rai/
elisabeth schwarzkopf/sena jurinac/rita streich/
vittoria palombini/bruna ronchini/rolando panerai
humperdinck hansel und gretel/*sung in italian*
cd: datum DAT 12314/urania URN 22266/walhall WLCD 0080

111/12 february 1954/concert recordings in turin
rai auditorium
orchestra sinfonica di torino della rai/*geza anda
*bartok piano concerto no 3
cd: tahra TAH 611-613/membran 232 779

hilding rosenberg concertino for strings
cd: private edition vienna

beethoven symphony no 6 "pastoral"
this recording remains unpublished

112/15 february 1954/concert recordings in turin
rai auditorium
orchestra sinfonica di torino della rai
beethoven egmont overture;   symphony no 1;
tchaikovsky symphony no 6 "pathetique"
these recordings remain unpublished

113/19 february 1954/concert recordings in turin
rai auditorium
orchestra sinfonica e coro di torino della rai/
janine micheau
mozart symphony no 41 in c K551 "jupiter"
cd: tahra TAH 611-613

handel concerto grosso op 6 no 12; florent schmitt psaume 47
these recordings remain unpublished

114/21 april 1954/concert recording in tokyo nhk hall
nhk symphony orchestra
tchaikovsky symphony no 6 in b minor op 74 "pathetique"
cd: deutsche grammophon (japan) POCG 10175/445 6402

114a/april 1954/brief rehearsal extract (in english)
in takarazuka or nagoya
nhk symphony orchestra
beethoven symphony no 9 in d minor op 125

115/30 june-7 july 1954/columbia sessions in london
kingsway hall
philharmonia orchestra/elisabeth schwarzkopf/
irmgard seefried/rita streich/anny felbermayer/lisa
otto/grace hoffman/rudolf schock/gerhard unger/
helmut krebs/hugues cuenod/hermann prey/karl
dönch/otakar kraus/fritz ollendorff/alfred
neugebauer/erich strauss/*producer walter legge*
strauss ariadne auf naxos
lp: 33CX 1292-1294/FCX 506-508/QCX 10168-10170/
C 90458-90460/WCX 1292-1294/angel 3532/emi RLS 760/
EX 769 2961/1C153 03520-03522/2C153 03520-03522
cd: emi 769 2962/567 0772/567 1562/511 9732/
naxos 8.111033-111034

116/7-9 and 21 july 1954/columbia sessions in london kingsway hall
philharmonia orchestra/*producer walter legge*
berlioz symphonie fantastique
reel-to-reel tape: CAT 264
lp: 33CX 1206/FCX 396/QCX 10136/C 90393/WCX 1206/angel 35202/world records TP 625/toshiba EAC 37001-37019/ emi RLS 7715/1C137 54364-54367M
cd: emi 763 3162/566 5982/512 0382/warner 2564 633621

117/13 july and 6 november 1954/columbia sessions in london kingsway hall (13 july) and abbey road studios
philharmonia orchestra/chorus/elisabeth schwarzkopf/ nan merriman/lisa otto/leopold simoneau/rolando panerai/sesto bruscantini/*producer walter legge*
mozart cosi fan tutte
lp: 33CX 1262-1264/FCX 484-486/QCX 10416-10418/C 90432-90434/ WCX 1262-1264/angel 3522/world records SOC 195-197/emi RLS 7709/1C147 01748-01750M/1C197 54200-54208M/ 2C153 01748-01750/3C153 01748-01750
cd: emi 769 6352/567 0642/511 9732/regis 3010/naxos 8.111232-11134/membran 232 779

118/22-24 july 1954/columbia sessions in london kingsway hall
philharmonia orchestra/*producer walter legge*
weinberger schwanda der dudelsackpfeifer: polka
lp: 33CX 1335/FCX 30103/QCX 10198/C 80464/WSX 528/ angel 35327/toshiba EAC 37020-37038
cd: emi 512 0382/opus kura OPK 7020/warner 2564 633621

118/22-24 july 1954/columbia sessions in london kingsway hall/concluded

bizet carmen: act four prelude; massenet thais: meditation; offenbach les contes d'hoffmann: barcarolle
45: SEL 1547/SEBQ 149/SCD 2130 (carmen and hoffmann)/ SCBQ 3055 (hoffmann)
reel-to-reel tape: CAT 268
lp: 33CX 1265/FCX 407/FC 25106 (thais)/QCX 10150/C 90435/ WCX 1265/angel 35207/toshiba EAC 37020-37038
cd: emi 512 0382/opus kura OPK 7032/warner 2564 633621
manoug parikian was violin soloist in thais meditation

granados goyescas: intermezzo; leoncavallo i pagliacci: intermezzo; verdi la traviata: act three prelude; mascagni cavalleria rusticana: intermezzo
45: SEL 1551/SEBQ 152 (goyescas, pagiacci and traviata)/ SCBQ 3049 (cavalleria)
reel-to-reel tape: CAT 268
lp: 33CX 1265/FCX 407/FC 25106 (goyescas)/QCX 10150/ C 90435/WCX 1265/angel 35207/toshiba EAC 37020-37038
cd: emi 512 0382/opus kura OPK 7032/warner 2564 633621
dennis brain was organ soloist in cavalleria intermezzo

mascagni amico fritz: intermezzo; mussorgsky khovantschina: act four prelude; puccini manon lescaut: intermezzo; kodaly hary janos: intermezzo
45: SEBQ 255 (khovantschina)
reel-to-reel tape: CAT 268
lp: 33CX 1265/FCX 407/QCX 10150/WCX 1265/angel 35207/ toshiba EAC 37020-37038
cd: emi 512 0382/opus kura OPK 7032/warner 2564 633621
bizet carmen: acts two and three preludes
these recordings remain unpublished
beethoven die weihe des hauses overture
this recording remains unpublished and probably incomplete

119/20 september 1954/columbia session in
watford town hall
philharmonia orchestra/elisabeth schwarzkopf/
producer walter legge
beethoven fidelio: abscheulicher wo eilst du hin?
lp: 33CX 1266/FCX 454/FCX 30093/QCX 10186/C 90436/
WCX 1266/angel 35231/toshiba EAC 37001-37019/emi
RLS 7715/154 6133/1C137 54364-54367M
cd: emi 763 2012/511 9732/warner 2564 633629

beethoven ah perfido!, concert aria
lp: 33CX 1278/QCX 10149/C 90447/WCX 1278/angel 35023/
toshiba EAC 37001-37019/emi RLS 7715/154 6133/
1C137 54364-54367M
cd: emi 763 2012/511 9732/warner 2564 633629

120/2 october 1954/concert recording in vienna
musikvereinssaal
wiener symphoniker
bruckner symphony no 5 in b flat
cd: orfeo C231 901A

121/8 october 1954/concert recording in vienna
musikvereinssaal
wiener symphoniker/wiener singverein/kinderchor
der stadt wien/giulietta simionato/hilde güden/
graziella sciutti/luisa ribacchi/nicolai gedda/michel
roux/gino del signore/mario carlin/enzo sordello/
frederick guthrie
bizet carmen
lp: great opera performances GOP 026-028
cd: melodram MEL 27022/gala GL 100 603/bongiovanni
HOC 23-24/walhall WLCD 0082/andante 3100

122/5-8 november 1954/columbia sessions in
london kingsway hall
philharmonia orchestra/_producer walter legge_
verdi aida: act two ballet music; wagner tannhäuser:
venusberg music; borodin prince igor: dance of polovtsian
maidens and polovtsian dances
lp: 33CX 1327/QCX 10192/C 90484/WCX 1327/angel 35307/
toshiba EAC 37020-37038
cd: emi 566 6032/512 0382/testament SBT 1383 (wagner)/
warner 2564 633621

ponchielli la gioconda: dance of the hours; mussorgsky
khovantschina: dance of the persian slaves
45: SCD 2171 (ponchielli)/SEBQ 256 (ponchielli)/
SEBQ 255 (mussorgsky)
lp: 33CX 1327/FC 25106 (ponchielli)/QCX 10192/C 90404/
WCX 1327/angel 35307/toshiba EAC 37020-37038
cd: emi 566 6032/512 0382/warner 2564 633621

123/6 november 1954 and 28-29 may 1955/
columbia sessions in london abbey road studios
philharmonia orchestra/_producer walter legge_
mozart symphony no 35 in d K385 "haffner"
lp: 33CX 1511/C 91305/WCX 1511/angel 35562/
toshiba EAC 37001-37019
cd: emi 763 4562/512 0382/warner 2564 633623

124/8-10 november 1954/columbia sessions in
london kingsway hall
philharmonia orchestra/*producer walter legge*
beethoven symphony no 5 in c minor op 67
lp: 33CX 1266/FCX 454/FCX 30093/QCX 10186/C 70369/WC 517/
SHZE 169/angel 35231/world records SM 143-149/toshiba
EAC 37001-37019/emi SLS 5053/1C181 01380-01386Y
cd: emi 763 3102/512 0382/515 8632/warner 2564 633735

125/11-12 november 1954/columbia sessions in
london kingsway hall
philharmonia orchestra/kurt leimer/*producer*
walter legge
leimer piano concerto;   leimer concerto for the left hand
lp: C 90282/WCX 508/emi SME 91793
cd: emi 512 0382/warner 2564 633625

126/17 november 1954/concert recordings in
vienna musikvereinssaal
wiener symphoniker
handel concerto grosso op 6 no 12; tchaikovsky symphony no 4
cd: orfeo C275 821B

honegger symphony no 3
this recording remains unpublished

127/27 november 1954/concert recording in
vienna musikvereinssaal
wiener symphoniker/wiener singverein/
antonietta stella/oralia dominguez/nicolai gedda/
giuseppe modesti
verdi messa da requiem
cd: orfeo C728 082B

128/4 december 1954/concert recording in rome
auditorium del foro italico
orchestra sinfonica e coro di roma della rai/teresa
stich-randall/hilde rössl-majdan/waldemar kmentt/
gottlob frick
beethoven symphony no 9 in d minor op 125 "choral"
cd: urania RM 11915/tahra TAH 611-613/membran 232 779

129/9 december 1954/concert recording in rome
auditorium del foro italico
orchestra sinfonica di roma della rai
schumann symphony no 2 in c minor op 61
cd: urania RIT 55203

130/11 december 1954/concert recordings in rome
auditorium del foro italico
orchestra sinfonica e coro di roma della rai/geza anda/
antonio pirino/mario borriello
bartok cantata profana
cd: as-disc NAS 2508
recording incorrectly dated 1949

brahms piano concerto no 2 in b flat op 83
lp: replica RPL 2467/joker SM 1332
cd: tahra TAH 611-613/membran 232 779

131/15 december 1954/concert recordings in rome
auditorium del foro italico
orchestra sinfonica di roma della rai
mozart symphony no 39; honegger symphony no 3
these recordings remain unpublished

132/19 december 1954/concert recording in rome
auditorium del foro italico
orchestra sinfonica e coro di roma della rai/elisabeth
schwarzkopf/christiane gayraud/graziella sciutti/ernst
haefliger/michel roux/mario petri/franco calabrese
debussy pelleas et melisande
lp: cetra ARK 6/rodolphe RP 12393-12395
cd: arkadia CDKAR 218

133/15 january 1955/concert recordings in turin
rai auditorium
orchestra sinfonica e coro di torino della rai/
ernst haefliger
handel concerto grosso op 6 no 12; kodaly psalmus
hungaricus; prokofiev symphony no 5
these recordings remain unpublished

134/16 january 1955/concert recordings in turin
rai auditorium
orchestra sinfonica di torino della rai
stravinsky symphony in three movements
cd: private edition vienna

strauss tod und verklärung
this recordings remain unpublished

135/18 january 1955/stage recording in milan
teatro alla scala
orchestra e coro del teatro alla scala/giulietta
simionato/rosanna carteri/graziella sciutti/luisa
ribacchi/giuseppe di stefano/michel roux/enzo
sordello/giuseppe modesti/mario carlin/
gino del signore
bizet carmen
lp: cetra LO 22/morgan MOR 5502/discocorp RR 470/
vox THS 65160-65162
cd: myto H 101/great opera performances GOP 66327

136/22 february 1955/concert recording in berlin
titania palest
philharmonisches orchester berlin
wagner tristan und isolde: prelude and liebestod
this recording remains unpublished

137/27 february 1955/concert recordings in washington constitution hall

philharmonisches orchester berlin

mozart symphony no 35 in d K385 "haffner"
lp: cetra LO 506/maestri del secolo APE 1201/wg records
WG 30004/movimento musica 01.003/joker SM 1315
cd: joker 44 122/artemis 710 005/virtuoso 269 7054/classical collection CDCLC 6000

strauss till eulenspiegels lustige streiche
lp: cetra LO 506/foyer FO 1034

brahms symphony no 1 in c minor op 68
lp: cetra LO 506/maestri del secolo APE 1202/wg records
WG 30001/joker SM 1346
cd: classical collection CDCLC 6000

138/26-30 april 1955/columbia sessions in london kingsway hall

philharmonia orchestra/chorus/elisabeth schwarzkopf/ rita streich/luise martini/nicolai gedda/rudolf christ/ helmut krebs/erich majkut/erich kunz/karl dönch/ franz boheim/*producer walter legge*

johann strauss die fledermaus
reel-to-reel tape: CAT 286-287
lp: 33CX 1309-1310/QCX 10183-10184/C 80512-80513/ WSX 533-534/angel 3539/emi RLS 728/1C149 00427-00428/ 2C181 00427-00428
cd: emi 769 5312/567 0742/511 9732

139/17-20 may 1955/columbia sessions in london
kingsway hall
philharmonia orchestra/_producer walter legge_
brahms haydn variations op 56a
lp: 33CX 1349/FCX 594/QCX 10281/C 90494/WCX 1349/angel
35299/toshiba EAC 37001-37019/emi 3C065 01574
cd: emi 763 4562/512 0382/warner 2564 633623
2564 633623 also contains previously unpublished
stereo version of the variations
schubert symphony no 8 in b minor D759 "unfinished"
lp: 33CX 1349/FCX 594/QCX 10281/C 70390/WC 536/angel
35299/toshiba EAC 37001-37019/emi SXLP 30513/1C053 43052/
1C047 01441M/2C059 43355/3C053 01574
cd: emi 769 2272/512 0382/warner 2564 633623
beethoven symphony no 8 in f op 93
lp: 33CX 1392/FCX 449/QCX 10191/C 90516/C 70364/WCX 1392/
WC 512/angel 3544/toshiba EAC 37001-37019/world records
SM 143-149/emi SLS 5053/1C181 01830-01836Y
cd: emi 763 3102/512 0382/515 8632/major classics M3CD 309/
warner 2564 633735
toshiba lp edition contained both mono and stereo versions
johann and josef strauss pizzicato polka
this recording remains unpublished
140/21-27 may 1955 and 18 june 1956/columbia sessions in
london kingsway hall
philharmonia orchestra/_producer walter legge_
tchaikovsky symphony no 6 in b minor op 74 "pathetique"
lp: 33CX 1377/FCX 576/toshiba EAC 37020-37038/
emi SXLP 30534/1C037 00935
cd: emi 763 4602/252 1432/512 0382/warner 2564 633620
140a/28-29 may 1955/columbia sessions in london abbey
road studios
philharmonia orchestra/_producer walter legge_
mozart divertimento no 15 in b flat K287
lp: 33CX 1511/FCX 735/angel 35562/toshiba EAC 37001-37019
cd: 763 4562/512 0382/warner 2564 633623

141/24-26 may 1955/columbia sessions in london kingsway hall

philharmonia orchestra/_producers walter legge and walter jellinek_

brahms symphony no 2 in d op 73
lp: 33CX 1355/FCX 586/QCX 10231/C 90408/WCX 1355/angel 35218/toshiba EAC 37020-37038/emi SXLP 30513/1C053 43052
cd: emi 769 2272/512 0382/warner 2564 633623
brahms symphony no 4 in e minor op 98
reel-to-reel tape: CAT 285
lp: 33CX 1362/FCX 538/QCX 10201/C 90501/WCX 1362/angel 35298/toshiba EAC 37020-37038/emi SXLP 30505/1C053 03604
cd: emi 476 8812/769 2282/476 8812/512 0382/
warner 2564 633623

142/25 may and 7 july 1955/columbia sessions in london kingsway hall

philharmonia orchestra/_producer walter legge_

johann strauss künstlerleben waltz
reel-to-reel tape: CAT 294
lp: 33CX 1393/FCX 531/FCX 30105/QCX 10205/C 80463/
WSX 527/angel 35342/toshiba EAC 37020-37038
cd: emi 763 4562/512 0382/warner 2564 633623

143/25 june 1955/concert recording in vienna musikvereinssaal

wiener symphoniker/wiener singverein/lisa della casa/ hilde rössel-majdan/waldemar kmentt/otto edelmann
beethoven symphony no 9 in d minor op 125 "choral"
cd: orfeo C729 081B

144/4-6 july 1955/columbia sessions in london kingsway hall

philharmonia orchestra/*producer walter legge*

sibelius symphony no 6 in d minor; symphony no 7 in c

lp: 33CX 1341/QCX 10195/angel 35316/toshiba EAC 37020-37038/

emi SXLP 30430 (no 7)/1C053 03791 (no 7)

cd: emi 763 4642/566 6022/512 0382/warner 2564 633621

145/6-9 july 1955/columbia sessions in london kingsway hall

philharmonia orchestra/*producer walter legge*

josef strauss delirienwalzer; johann strauss kaiserwalzer;

zigeunerbaron overture; an der schönen blauen donau;

johann and josef pizzicato polka

45: SEL 1568 (pizzicato)/SEBQ 171 (pizzicato)

lp: 33CX 1393/FCX 531/FCX 30105/QCX 10205/C 80463/

WSX 527/angel 35342/toshiba EAC 37020-37038

cd: emi 763 4562/512 0382/warner 2564 633623

johann strauss tritsch-tratsch polka; unter donner und blitz;

johann strauss father radetzky march

45: SEL 1568/SEBQ 171

lp: 33CX 1335/FCX 512/FCX 30103/QCX 10198/C 80464/

WSX 528/angel 35327/toshiba EAC 37020-37038

cd: emi 512 0382/opus kura OPK 7020/warner 2564 633623

offenbach orfee aux enfers overture

lp: 33CX 1335/FCX 512/FCX 30103/QCX 10198/C 80464/

WSX 528/angel 35327/toshiba EAC 37020-37038

cd: emi 566 6032/512 0382/opus kura OPK 7020/

warner 2564 633623

suppe leichte kavallerie overture; chabrier joyeuse marche

45: SEL 1557 (suppe)/SEBQ 162 (suppe)/ESBF 135 (chabrier)

lp: 33CX 1335/FCX 512/FCX 30103/QCX 10198/C 80464/

WSX 528/angel 35327/toshiba EAC 37020-37038

cd: emi 512 0382/opus kura OPK 7020/warner 2564 633623

reel-to-reel tape CAT 294 contained all the items from this session

146/9-10 july 1955/columbia sessions in london abbey road studios

philharmonia orchestra/bernard walton/elisabeth schwarzkopf/tito gobbi/*producer walter legge*
mozart clarinet concerto in a K622
lp: 33CX 1361/FCX 740/QCX 10256/C 90500/WCX 1361/angel 35323/toshiba EAC 37001-37038/emi XLP 60004
cd: emi 763 3162/512 0382/membran 232 779/ warner 2564 633625
mozart don giovanni: la ci darem la mano; le nozze di figaro: non piu andrai; reznicek donna diana overture
these recordings remain unpublished
mozart symphony no 39 in e flat K543; minuet from divertimento no 17 K334
these recordings remain unpublished and probably incomplete

147/24-29 july 1955/columbia sessions in vienna musikvereinssaal

philharmonia orchestra/wiener singverein/elisabeth schwarzkopf/marga höffgen/ernst haefliger/otto edelmann/*producer walter legge*
beethoven symphony no 9 in d minor op 125 "choral"
lp: 33CX 1391-1392/FCX 448-449/QCX 10190-10191/ C 90515-90516/WCX 1391-1392/HZE 107/angel 3544/world records SM 143-149/toshiba EAC 37001-37019/emi SLS 5053/ 1C063 01200M/3C053 01200/1C181 01830-01836Y
cd: emi 763 3102/512 0382/515 8632/warner 2564 633735
warner 2564 633735 includes previously unpublished stereo version of the symphony in addition to the familiar mono one

mozart ave verum corpus K618
lp: 33CX 1741/SAX 2389/FCX 887/SAXF 206/QCX 10416/ SAXQ 7316/angel 35948/emi SLS 839/SXLP 30161/YKM 5002/ 1C177 02348-02352/1C047 02350/3C053 00520
cd: emi 511 9732/warner 2564 633629

148/1-6 august 1955/columbia sessions in milan
teatro alla scala
orchestra e coro del teatro alla scala/maria callas/
lucia danieli/luisa villa/nicolai gedda/mario borriello/
renato ercolani/mario carlin/plinio clabassi/enrico
campi/*producer walter legge*
puccini madama butterfly
lp: 33CX 1296-1298/FCX 472-474/QCX 10156-10158/
C 90462-90464/WCX 1296-1298/angel 3523/emi SLS 5015/
EX 29 12653/1C153 00424-00426/2C163 00424-00426/
3C163 00424-00426
cd: emi 747 9598/556 2982/511 9732/
pristine OACO 068/naxos 8.111026-111027

149/27 august 1955/concert recordings in lucerne
kunsthaus
schweizerisches festspielorchester/*wolfgang
schneiderhan
beethoven coriolan overture; *violin concerto; symphony no 7
cd: private edition vienna/archipel ARPCD 0433

150/29 september 1955/stage recording in berlin
theater des westerns
rias-sinfonie-orchester/coro del teatro alla scala di
milano/maria callas/luisa villa/giuseppe di stefano/
giuseppe zampieri/rolando panerai/nicola zaccaria/
mario carlin
donizetti lucia di lammermoor
lp: limited edition society LER 101/bjr records BJR 133/morgan
MOR 5401/cetra LO 18/ARK 5/vox THS 65144-65145/replica
ARPL 32495/paragon DSV 52004/rodolphe RPV 32667-32668/
movimento musica 02.001
cd: melodram MEL 26004/arkadia CD 502/CDHP 502/
movimento musica 012.010/verona 2709-2710/virtuoso
269 7232/palette PAL 2009-2010/rodolphe RPL 32518/
emi 763 5312/566 4412/511 9732

151/10-11 october 1955/columbia sessions in
london kingsway hall
philharmonia orchestra/_producer walter legge_
mozart symphony no 39 in e flat K543
lp: 33CX 1361/FCX 740/QCX 10526/C 90500/C 90633/C 91304/
WCX 1361/angel 35323/35739/toshiba EAC 37001-37019
cd: emi 763 4562/512 0382/warner 2564 633623
2564 633623 also contains previously unpublished stereo
version of the symphony in addition to the familiar mono one

152/11 october 1955 and 18 june 1956/columbia
sessions in london kingsway hall
philharmonia orchestra/_producer walter legge_
mussorgsky-ravel pictures at an exhibition
lp: 33CX 1421/SAX 2261/FCX 518/SAXF 131/QCX 10266/
SAXQ 7271/C 90532/STC 90532/WCX 1421/SAXW 2261/
angel 35430/emi SLS 5019/SXLP 30445/1C037 01390/
1C181 25307-25311/2C053 01169
cd: emi 762 8602/562 8692/512 0382/laserlight 16 206/
warner 2564 633620

153/21 january 1956/concert recordings in
berlin-zehlendorf gemeindehaus
philharmonisches orchester berlin/*wilhelm kempff
*mozart piano concerto no 20 in d minor K466
lp: cetra LO 531/foyer FO 1034/longanesi CGL 14
cd: natise HVK 105/joker 44 122/arkadia CDKAR 231/
artemis 710 005/audite 95 602

mozart symphony no 41 in c K551 "jupiter"
lp: cetra LO 531/maestri del secolo APE 1201/movimento
musica 01.003/wg records WG 30004/joker SM 1315
cd: natise HVK 105/joker 44 122/arkadia CDKAR 231/
artemis 710 005/audite 95 602

154/28 january 1956/concert recording in salzburg
grosser saal des mozarteums
philharmonia orchestra/*clara haskil
mozart divertimento no 15; *piano concerto no 20;
symphony no 39
cd: private edition vienna (symphony)/internationale stiftung
mozarteum ISN 56-4 (symphony and concerto)/archipel
ARPCD 0433 (symphony)/belvedere edition 10152
*performance of the divertimento omitted second and
third movements*

155/7 march 1956/concert recording in milan
rai auditorium
orchestra sinfonica di milano della rai
mussorgsky-ravel pictures at an exhibition
cd: urania RIT 55 203

156/20 june 1956/concert recordings in london
royal festival hall
philharmonia orchestra/*elisabeth schwarzkopf
*strauss vier letzte lieder
cd: emi 763 6552/763 7902/511 9732/urania URN 22296/
warner 2564 633629
beethoven symphony no 2; brahms symphony no 4
these recordings remain unpublished

157/21-29 june 1956/columbia sessions in london
kingsway hall
philharmonia orchestra/chorus/elisabeth schwarzkopf/
nan merriman/anna moffo/fedora barbieri/tito gobbi/
luigi alva/tomaso spataro/renato ercolani/rolando
panerai/nicola zaccaria/*producer walter legge*
verdi falstaff
reel-to-reel tape: BTA 115-117
lp: 33CX 1410-1412/SAX 2254-2256/QCX 10244-10246/
C 90524-90526/WCX 1410-1412/angel 3552/emi SLS 5037/
SLS 5211/1C165 02125-02127/1C153 00442-00443/
2C167 03951-03952/3C153 00442-00443
cd: emi 769 6682/567 0832/511 9732

158/3-9 august 1956/columbia sessions in milan
teatro alla scala
orchestra e coro del teatro alla scala/maria callas/
fedora barbieri/luisa villa/giuseppe di stefano/renato
ercolani/rolando panerai/giulio mauri/nicola zaccaria/
producer walter legge
verdi il trovatore
reel-to-reel tape: CBT 563-565
lp: 33CX 1483-1485/FCX 763-765/QCX 10267-10269/
C 90561-90563/WCX 1483-1485/angel 3554/emi SLS 869/
1C153 00454-00456/2C163 00454-00456/3C165 00454-00456/
749 3471
cd: emi 749 3472/556 3332/511 9732/377 3652/
naxos 8.111280-111281

159/10 december 1956/concert recording in berlin
hochschule für musik
philharmonisches orchester berlin/elisabeth
schwarzkopf
strauss ariadne auf naxos: ein schönes war/es gibt ein reich
cd: andromeda ANDRCD 5151

160/12-22 december 1956/columbia sessions in london kingsway hall

philharmonia orchestra/chorus/elisabeth schwarzkopf/christa ludwig/teresa stich-randall/ ljuba welitsch/anny felbermayer/ kerstin meyer/ otto edelmann/eberhard wächter/nicolai gedda/ erich majkut/paul kuen/gerhard unger/karl friedrich/ harald pröglhöf/franz bierbach/*producer walter legge*

strauss der rosenkavalier

reel-to-reel tape: BTA 126-129

lp: 33CX 1492-1495/SAX 2269-2272/FCX 750-753/CVB 750-753/ C 90566-90569/WCX 1492-1495/SAXW 2269-2272/angel 3563/ emi SLS 810/EX 29 00453/1C191 00459-00462/2C165 00459-00462/ 3C165 00459-00462/749 3541

cd: emi 749 3542/556 2422/556 1132/567 6052/511 9732

the cd issue on 556 1132 was described as using original mono tapes which included some different takes

161/22 december 1956 and 28 april 1957/columbia sessions in london kingsway hall (december) and abbey road studios (april)

philharmonia orchestra/peter ustinov/*producer walter legge*

prokofiev peter and the wolf

lp: 33CX 1559/SAX 2375/FCX 30531/FC 25108/SAXF 130531/ QCX 10339/C 70081/WC 506/SHZE 243/angel 35638/ emi 1C063 01361/2C053 01169/3C053 00868

cd: emi 769 2392/252 2012/512 0382/warner 2564 633620

peter ustinov's narration was recorded in november-december 1957 in capitol studios hollywood; spoken narrations were added at a later date for the french, italian and german versions

162/7-8 january and 18-19 february 1957/columbia
sessions in berlin grunewaldkirche
philharmonisches orchester berlin/*producer fritz ganss*
wagner tannhäuser overture;   tristan prelude and liebestod;
meistersinger overture
lp: 33CX 1496/FCX 689/QCX 10321/C 90286/WCX 512/
angel 35482/emi 1C137 54360-54363/2C069 02603
cd: emi 763 3212/512 0382/warner 2564 633623

163/13 february 1957/concert recordings in vienna
musikvereinssaal
wiener symphoniker
hindemith mathis der maler symphony;   beethoven symphony no 7
cd: orfeo C232 901A
incorrectly dated 18 february 1957

164/2 april 1957/stage recording in vienna staatsoper
orchester der wiener staatsoper/birgit nilsson/leonie
rysanek/jean madeira/ludwig suthaus/hans hotter/
gottlob frick/ljuba welitsch/gerda scheyrer/judith hellwig/
christa ludwig/margareta sjöstedt/marta rohs/rosette
anday/hilde rössel-majdan/lotte rysanek/dorothea frass
wagner die walküre
cd: lyric distribution 447/private edition vienna

165/17 april 1957/concert recording in vienna
musikvereinssaal
wiener philharmoniker
bruckner symphony no 8 in c minor
this recording remains unpublished

166/25 april 1957/concert recording in berlin
hochschule für musik
philharmonisches orchester berlin/chor der
hedwigskathedrale/elisabeth grümmer/marga
höffgen/ernst haefliger/gottlob frick
beethoven symphony no 9 in d minor op 125 "choral"
lp: maestri del secolo APE 1209/movimento musica 08.001/
replica SRPL 22400/wg records WG 30009/joker SM 1340
cd: artemis 710 001/audite 23 414

167/25-26 april 1957/columbia sessions in berlin
grunewaldkirche
philharmonisches orchester berlin/*producer*
fritz ganss
schumann symphony no 4 in d minor op 120
lp: 33C 1056/FC 1070/QC 5043/C 70080/WC 504/emi RLS 768/
F669.711-713/1C047 01441M/1C137 54095-54097
cd: emi 476 8812/CDF 3000 122/763 3212/476 8812/
512 0382/warner 2564 633623

168/28 april 1957/columbia session in london
abbey road studios
philharmonia orchestra/*producer walter legge*
leopold mozart cassation in g/*also known as haydn toy symphony*
45: ESBF 17079
lp: 33CX 1559/SAX 2375/FCX 30531/CVD 2076/QCX 10339/
C 70391/C 70461/WC 537/SBOW 8504/SMC 50600/SMC 80975/
SHZE 243/angel 35638/emi SLS 839/SXLP 30161/1C047 02350/
1C177 02348-02352/1C063 00737/1C063 01361/2C053 00725/
3C053 00868/143 5643
cd: emi 769 2392/252 1522/512 0382/laserlight 24 426/
warner 2564 633623

169/23-25 may 1957/columbia sessions in berlin
grunewaldkirche
philharmonisches orchester berlin/*producers*
walter legge and fritz ganss
bruckner symphony no 8 in c minor
lp: 33CX 1586-1587/C 90972-90973/STC 90972-90973/
WCX 1586-1587/SAXW 9501-9502/angel 3576/world
records T 772-773/ST 772-773/emi SXDW 3024/
CFP 41 44343/1C187 00763-00764
cd: emi 476 9012/763 4692/569 0922/566 1092/512 0382/
warner 2564 633623

170/26 may 1957/concert recordings in berlin
hochschule für musik
philharmonisches orchester berlin/*glenn gould
*beethoven piano concerto no 3 in c minor op 37
cd: nuova era 013.6362/NE 2351-2356/music and arts CD 678/
virtuoso 269 7062/membran 232 779/sony-bmg 88697 287222

sibelius symphony no 5 in e flat op 82
cd: sony-bmg 88697 287222

171/27 july 1957/stage recording in salzburg
felsenreitschule
wiener philharmoniker/chor der wiener staatsoper/
christel goltz/sena jurinac/giuseppe zampieri/
waldemar kmentt/paul schöffler/otto edelmann/
nicola zaccaria/erich majkut/walter berry
beethoven fidelio
lp: melodram MEL 040
cd: arkadia CDKAR 222/claque GM 2007-2008

172/28 july 1957/concert recording in salzburg
festspielhaus
wiener philharmoniker
bruckner symphony no 8 in c minor
cd: orfeo C773 084L

173/29 july 1957/concert recordings in salzburg
grosser saal des mozarteums
philharmonisches orchester berlin/*geza anda
mozart symphony no 35 "haffner"; *piano concerto no 21;
symphony no 41 "jupiter"
cd: deutsche grammophon 453 1992/orfeo C773 084L

174/10 august 1957/stage recording in salzburg
festspielhaus
wiener philharmoniker/chor der wiener staatsoper/
elisabeth schwarzkopf/anna moffo/giulietta simionato/
anna maria canali/luigi alva/tito gobbi/rolando panerai/
tomaso spataro/renato ercolani/mario petri
verdi falstaff
cd: arkadia CDKAR 226/walhall WLCD 0212/andante 3080

175/13 august 1957/concert recordings in salzburg
grosser saal des mozarteums
philharmonisches orchester berlin/*gerty herzog
berger sinfonia parabolica; *von einem piano concerto;
honegger symphony no 3
cd: orfeo C773 084L

176/17 august 1957/concert recording in lucerne
kunsthaus
schweizerisches festspielorchester/nathan milstein
brahms violin concerto in d op 77
cd: tahra TAH 692

177/22 august 1957/concert recording in salzburg
felsenreitschule
wiener philharmoniker/wiener singverein/lisa della
casa/dietrich fischer-dieskau
brahms ein deutsches requiem
cd: emi 566 8792/orfeo C773 084L

178/28 october and 28-29 november 1957/columbia
sessions in berlin grunewaldkirche
philharmonisches orchester berlin/*producer walter legge*
hindemith mathis der maler symphony
lp: 33CX 1783/SAX 2432/FCX 917/SAXF 235/QCX 10502/angel
35949/emi SXLP 30536/1C063 00547/1C137 54360-54363
cd: emi 769 7422/566 1092/512 0382/warner 2564 633623

179/3 november 1957/televised concert in tokyo
nhk concert hall
philharmonisches orchester berlin
wagner meistersinger overture; strauss don juan;
beethoven symphony no 5; bach suite no 3: air
dvd: nhk classical NSDS 9479/dynamic 33644

180/4 november 1957/concert recording in tokyo
nhk concert hall
philharmonisches orchester berlin
brahms symphony no 2 in d op 73
cd: nhk karajan centenary set NSDX 12264

181/6 november 1957/concert recording in tokyo
nhk concert hall
philharmonisches orchester berlin
beethoven symphony no 3 in e flat op 55 "eroica"
cd: nhk karajan centenary set NSDX 12264

schubert symphony no 8 in b minor D759 "unfinished"
this recording remains unpublished

182/29 november 1957 and 6-7 january 1958/
columbia sessions in berlin grunewaldkirche
philharmonisches orchester berlin/*producer
walter legge*
dvorak symphony no 9;   reger variations on a theme of mozart
these recordings remain unpublished and probably incomplete

183/9-10 january 1958/columbia sessions in london kingsway hall

philharmonia orchestra/*producer walter legge*
berlioz carnaval romain overture
reel-to-reel tape: BTA 132
lp: 33CX 1548/CVD 2073/QCX 10328/C 90985/WCX 1548/
angel 35613/emi SLS 5019/SXLP 30450/1C181 25307-25311/
1C053 03929/2C053 00703/143 5643
cd: emi 769 4662/252 1592/566 5982/512 0382/
warner 2564 633621

liszt-müller berghaus hungarian rhapsody no 2 in c sharp minor
45: SCBQ 3054
lp: 33CX 1571/SAX 2302/FCX 824/SAXF 160/CVD 2073/
QCX 10359/SAXQ 7260/C 70486/STC 70486/SBOW 8518/
SHZE 150/angel 35614/37231/emi SLS 5019/SXDW 3048/
1C181 25307-25311/143 5643/1C137 03059-03060/
2C053 01414
cd: emi 762 8692/512 0382/laserlight 16 206/24 426/
warner 2564 633623

184/10-13 january 1958/columbia sessions in london kingsway hall

philharmonia orchestra/*producer walter legge*
respighi i pini di roma
reel-to-reel tape: BTA 132
lp: 33CX 1548/QCX 10328/C 90985/WCX 1548/angel 35613/
emi SLS 5019/SXLP 30450/1C181 25307-25311/1C053 03929
cd: emi 769 4662/252 1592/512 0382/royal classics ROY 6474/
disky HR 700 062/warner 2564 633621

185/13-18 january 1958/columbia sessions in london
kingsway hall
philharmonia orchestra/*producer walter legge*
bizet l'arlesienne: suites 1 and 2
lp: 33CX 1608/SAX 2289/FCX 775/SAXF 133/C 91094/STC 91094/
WCX 1608/SAXW 2289/angel 35618/world records T 1044/
ST 1044/emi SLS 5019/EMX 2028/1C181 25307-25311/
1C053 00995/1C137 03059-03060/2C059 00995/3C065 00995
cd: emi 762 8532/512 0382/warner 2564 633621

bizet carmen: suite
lp: 33CX 1608/SAX 2289/FCX 775/SAXF 133/C 91094/STC 91094/
WCX 1608/SAXW 2289/angel 35618/world records T 1044/
ST 1044/emi SLS 839/SXDW 3048/EMX 2028/1C177 02348-02352/
1C053 00995/2C053 00724/2C059 00995/3C053 00995
cd: emi 769 4672/252 1592/762 8532/512 0382/royal
classics ROY 6474/disky HR 700 062/warner 2564 633621

sibelius valse triste
lp: 33CX 1571/SAX 2302/FCX 824/SAXF 160/CVD 2074/QCX 10359/
SAXQ 7260/SHZE 150/angel 35614/emi SLS 5019/2C053 00726/
1C181 25307-25311/143 5643/1C137 03059-03060
cd: emi 769 4672/252 1592/522 0492/512 0382/royal classics
ROY 6475/disky HR 700 062/warner 2564 633621

tchaikovsky ouverture solennelle 1812
lp: 33CX 1571/SAX 2302/FCX 824/SAXF 160/CVD 2071/QCX 10359/
SAXQ 7260/C 70486/STC 70486/SBOW 8518/SHZE 150/angel 35614/
37232/emi SLS 839/SXDW 3048/1C177 02348-02352/1C053 01413
cd: emi 769 4662/252 1592/512 0382/royal classics ROY 6474/
disky HR 700 062/warner 2564 633620

185/13-18 january 1958/columbia sessions in london kingsway hall/continued

berlioz la damnation de faust: marche hongroise
lp: 33CX 1571/SAX 2302/FCX 824/SAXF 180/CVD 2072/QCX 10359/
SAXQ 7360/SHZE 150/angel 35614/37231/emi SLS 5019/
2C053 00724/1C181 25307-25311/1C137 03059-03060
cd: emi 769 4672/252 1592/566 5982/512 0382/royal
classics ROY 6475/disky HR 700 062/warner 2564 633621

weber-berlioz aufforderung zum tanz
lp: 33CX 1571/SAX 2302/FCX 824/SAXF 180/CVD 2075/QCX 10359/
SAXQ 7360/C 70497/STC 70497/WC 573/SBOW 8525/SHZE 150/
angel 35614/37550/emi SLS 5019/1C181 25307-25311/
2C053 00724/1C137 03059-03060/2C059 43355/143 5643
cd: emi 769 4672/252 1592/252 1352/512 0382/royal classics
ROY 6473/disky DCL 703 262/HR 700 062/warner 2564 633621

liszt les preludes
45: C 50545/SELW 1545
reel-to-reel tape: BTA 132
lp: 33CX 1548/CVD 2075/QCX 10328/C 90985/C 70426/WCX 1548/
WC 529/angel 35613/37231/emi 1C063 00737/2C053 01414/
2C059 43355
cd: emi 769 2282/762 8602/512 0382/laserlight 16 206/
warner 2564 633621

offenbach gaite parisienne: ballet suite arranged by rosenthal
reel-to-reel tape: BTB 307
lp: 33CX 1588/SAX 2274/FCX 789/SAXF 134/QCX 10362/
SAXQ 7286/angel 35607/world records T 1084/ST 1084/emi
SLS 5019/SXLP 30224/1C181 25307-25311/2C059 03054
cd: emi 769 0412/512 0382/warner 2564 633621

185/13-18 january 1958/columbia sessions in london kingsway hall/concluded

rossini guillaume tell: pas de trois et choeur tyrolien
lp: 33CX 1588/SAX 2274/FCX 789/SAXF 134/QCX 10326/
SAXQ 7286/angel 35607/37231/world records T 1084/ST 1084
cd: emi 769 1132/512 0382/warner 2564 633621

gounod faust: ballet music
lp: 33CX 1588/SAX 2274/FCX 789/SAXF 134/QCX 10326/
SAXQ 7286/C 70484/STC 70484/SHZE 216/angel 35607/world
records T 1084/ST 1084/emi SLS 839/SXLP 30224/
1C177 02348-02352/2C059 02352/2C053 00724/
3C065 00996/1C137 03059-03069
cd: emi 769 0412/512 0382/warner 2564 633621

strauss der rosenkavalier: orchestral suite; josef strauss
sphärenklänge waltz
these recordings remain unpublished

186/23 january 1958/austrian newsreel film from philharmoniker ball in vienna staatsoper
wiener philharmoniker

johann strauss kaiserwalzer: fragment only

187/29 april 1958/stage recording in milan
teatro alla scala
orchestra del teatro alla scala/birgit nilsson/leonie
rysanek/jean madeira/ludwig suthaus/hans hotter/
gottlob frick/lotte rysanek/gerda scheyrer/christa
ludwig/margareta sjöstedt/judith hellwig/rosette
anday/marta rohs/hilde rössel-majdan
wagner die walküre
cd: istituto discografico italiano IDIS 6549-6551

188/7 may 1958/concert recording in brussels
palais des beaux arts
wiener philharmoniker/männergesangverein/
hilde güden
johann strauss die fledermaus overture; kaiserwalzer;
annen polka; unter donner und blitz; frühlingsstimmen
waltz; pizzicato polka; auf der jagd; an der schönen blauen
donau; johann strauss father radetzky march
lp: movimento musica 01.039
cd: movimento musica 051.030/arkadia CDKAR 215/
natise HVK 102

189/18-20 may 1958/columbia sessions in berlin grunewaldkirche

philharmonisches orchester berlin/*producers*

walter legge and fritz ganss

dvorak symphony no 9 in e minor op 95 "from the new world"
lp: 33CX 1642/SAX 2272/FCX 814/SAXF 144/CVB 814/QCX 10348/
SAXQ 7263/C 91003/C 91255/STC 91003/STC 91255/WCX 1642/
SAXW 2272/SHZE 160/angel 35613/emi ASD 2863/SLS 839/100 4911/
1C177 02348-02352/1C063 02348/2C065 02348/2C059 02348/
3C063 00491/1C037 02940
cd: emi 252 1342/512 0382/warner 2564 633621

smetana ma vlast: the moldau
45: SEDQ 686/C 50546/SELW 1816
lp: 33CX 1642/SAX 2272/FCX 814/SAXF 144/CVB 814/QCX 10348/
SAXQ 7263/C 91003/C 70426/WCX 1642/WC 529/STC 91003/
SAXW 2275/angel 35613/37232/emi SLS 839/ASD 2863/SXDW 3048/
100 4911/1C177 02348-02352/1C063 02348/1C063 00737/
1C053 01414/2C059 02348/143 5643/2C069 02348/3C065 02348
cd: emi 769 4652/252 1522/252 1592/569 4582/512 0382/laserlight
24 426/disky DCL 705 872/HR 700 062/warner 2564 633621

schubert symphony no 5 in b flat D485
lp: emi 1C137 54360-54363
cd: emi 763 3212/512 0382/warner 2564 633623

frank martin studies for string orchestra
this recording remains unpublished and probably incomplete

190/26 july 1958/stage recording in salzburg felsenreitschule

wiener philharmoniker/chor der wiener staatsoper/ sena jurinac/giulietta simionato/anneliese rothenberger/ eugenio fernandi/ettore bastianini/cesare siepi/marco stefanoni/nicola zaccaria/norbert balatsch/carlo schmidt/norman foster

verdi don carlo

lp: ed rosen records ERR 119/cetra LO 73/foyer FO 1023

cd: arkadia CDKAR 220/deutsche grammophon 447 6552/479 4640

191/21 august 1958/concert recording in salzburg felsenreitschule

wiener philharmoniker/wiener singverein/leonie rysanek/christa ludwig/giuseppe zampieri/cesare siepi

verdi messa da requiem

cd: emi 566 8802

192/12-17 september 1958/columbia sessions in
vienna musikvereinssaal

philharmonia orchestra/wiener singverein/elisabeth
schwarzkopf/christa ludwig/nicolai gedda/nicola zaccaria
beethoven missa solemnis op 123
lp: 33CX 1634-1635/FCX 828-829/SAXF 177-178/QCX 10369-10370/
SAXQ 7317-7318/C 91019-91020/STC 91019-91020/WCX 1634-1635/
angel 3595/eternal 820 558-559/world records T 914-915/ST 914-915/
emi SLS 5198/1C191 00627-00628/1C137 00627-00628/
2C181 00627-00628/3C153 00627-00628
cd: testament SBT 2126/warner 2564 633629
testament edition includes rehearsal extracts and recollections
of the sessions by elisabeth schwarzkopf

mozart symphony no 38 in d K504 "prague"
lp: 33CX 1703/SAX 2356/FCX 810/SAXF 810/QCX 10401/SAXQ 7296/
C 91069/STC 91069/WCX 523/SAXW 2356/angel 35739/world
records T 1032/ST 1032/emi 1C037 00635/1C137 54095-54099
cd: emi 252 1462/512 0382/testament SBT 2126/
warner 2564 633623

193/15 november 1958/concert recordings in
new york carnegie hall
new york philharmonic symphony orchestra
webern five pieces op 5;   mozart symphony no 41 "jupiter"
cd: pristine audio PASC 224

strauss ein heldenleben
cd: pristine audio PASC 225

194/22 november 1958/concert recordings in
new york carnegie hall
new york philharmonic symphony orchestra/
westminster choir/leontyne price/maureen
forrester/leopold simoneau/norman scott
beethoven symphony no 1 in c op 21
cd: pristine audio PASC 224

beethoven symphony no 9 in d minor op 125 "choral"
cd: pristine audio PASC 222

195/30 november-1 december 1958/columbia
sessions in berlin grunewaldkirche
philharmonisches orchester berlin/hans
richter-haaser/*producer walter legge*
brahms piano concerto no 2 in b flat op 83
lp: 33CX 1680/SAX 2328/QCX 10492/sAXQ 7369/C 91052/
STC 91052/WCX 1680/SAXW 2328/angel 35796/eterna 825 433/
world records T 1090/ST 1090/emi 1C053 01973
cd: emi 566 0932/512 0382/disky DCL 705 732/EH 701 542/
warner 2564 633625

196/1-6 january 1959/columbia sessions in london
kingsway hall

philharmonia orchestra/_producer walter legge_
tchaikovsky swan lake ballet suite; sleeping beauty ballet suite
lp: SAX 2306/FCX 832/SAXF 139/CVC 832/SAXQ 7297/SGHX 10507/
angel 35740/emi SLS 839/SXLP 30200/EMX 41 220671/
1C063 00409/2C053 00409/2C059 00409/3C053 00409/
1C177 02348-02352
cd: emi 252 1432/252 2012 (swan lake)/512 0382/
warner 2564 633620

sibelius finlandia
lp: 33CX 1750/SAX 2392/SAXQ 7328/angel 35922/37232/
emi SLS 5019/1C053 00523/1C181 25307-25311
cd: emi 769 4672/252 1592/512 0382/royal classics ROY 6475/
disky DCL 705 872/HR 700 062/warner 2564 633621

mascagni amico fritz intermezzo; puccini manon lescaut
intermezzo; schmidt notre dame intermezzo
lp: SAX 2294/FCX 830/SAXF 142/QCX 10366/SAXQ 7259/STC 91059/
SAXW 2294/angel 35793/emi SLS 5019/1C037 00422/
1C181 25307-25311
cd: emi 769 4672 (puccini)/762 8532 (schmidt)/252 1592 (puccini)/
512 0382/warner 2564 633623

leoncavallo pagliacci intermezzo; mussorgsky
khovantschina entr'acte
lp: SAX 2294/FCX 830/SAXF 142/CVD 2072/QCX 10366/SAXQ 7259/
STC 91065/SAXW 2294/angel 35793/emi SLS 5019/SXDW 3048/
1C181 25307-25311/1C037 00724/1C053 00724
cd: emi 762 8532/512 0382/warner 2564 633623

196/1-6 january 1959/columbia sessions in london
kingsway hall/concluded
berlioz les troyens: royal hunt and storm
lp: SAX 2294/FCX 830/SAXF 142/QCX 10366/SAXQ 7259/
angel 35793/emi SLS 5019/1C037 00422/1C181 25307-25311
cd: emi 769 4652/252 1592/566 5982/512 0382/royal classics
ROY 6473/disky HR 700 062/warner 2564 633621
verdi la traviata: act three prelude; granados goyescas;
offenbach les contes d'hoffmann: barcarolle
lp: SAX 2294/FCX 830/SAXF 142/CVD 2072/QCX 10366/SAXQ 7259/
STC 91065/SAXW 2294/angel 35793/emi SLS 5019/1C037 00422/
1C181 23507-23511/1C137 03059-03060/1C053 00724/143 5643
cd: emi 769 4672/252 1592/562 8692 (offenbach)/512 0382/disky
HR 700 062/royal classics ROY 6475 (granados and offenbach)/
laserlight 24 426 (offenbach)/disky DCL 705 872 (offenbach)/
DCL 703 262 (offenbach)
mascagni cavalleria rusticana intermezzo;
kodaly hary janos intermezzo
these recordings remain unpublished

197/2-4 march 1959/dg sessions in berlin
jesus-christus-kirche
berliner philharmoniker/*producers hans ritter and
werner wolf*
strauss ein heldenleben
lp: LPM 18 550/SLPM 138 025/2535 194/2740 111
cd: 429 7172/449 7272/479 0055

198/9-10 march 1959/decca sessions for rca victor
in vienna sofiensäle
wiener philharmoniker/*producer john culshaw*
beethoven symphony no 7 in a op 92
lp: LM 2548/LD 6407/LSC 2548/LDS 6407/RB 16212/SB 2087/
decca ADD 232/SDD 232
cd: decca 448 0422/478 0155

199/23 march-9 april 1959/decca sessions in
vienna sofiensäle
wiener philharmoniker/_producer john culshaw_
strauss also sprach zarathustra
lp: LXT 5524/SXL 2164/ADD 175/SDD 175/JB 27/london (usa)
LLP 3130/CM 9235/CS 6219/STS 15083/JL 41017
cd: 417 7202/433 3302/433 3392/440 2772/448 0422/
448 5882/466 3882/478 0155

200/23 march-9 april 1959/decca sessions for
rca victor in vienna sofiensäle
wiener philharmoniker/_producer john culshaw_
brahms symphony no 1 in c minor op 68
lp: LM 2537/LM 6411/LD 6407/LSC 2537/LSC 6411/
LDS 6407/RB 16211/ SB 2086/decca ADD 283/SDD 283/
VIV 35/london (usa) STS 15194
cd: decca 417 7392/440 2602/448 0422/478 0155

haydn symphony no 104 in d "london"; mozart
symphony no 40 in g minor K550
lp: LM 2535/LD 6407/LSC 2535/LDS 6407/RB 16219/SB 2092/
decca ADD 233/SDD 233/VIV 55/london (usa) STS 15106
cd: decca 417 6952 (mozart)/436 5192 (mozart)/448 0422/
455 4972 (mozart)/461 5062 (haydn)/478 0155

johann strauss fledermaus overture; zigeunerbaron
overture; annen polka; auf der jagd; g'schichten aus dem
wienerwald; josef strauss delirienwalzer
lp: LM 2346/LD 6407/LSC 2346/LDS 6407/RB 16216/SB 2091/
decca ADD 259/SDD 259/london (usa) STS 15163
cd: decca 417 7742/448 0422/478 0155
selections from these recordings also issued on deutsche
grammophon cds devoted to wiener philharmoniker
and to the strauss dynasty

201/30 april 1959/stage recording in milan
teatro alla scala
orchestra e coro del teatro alla scala/birgit nilsson/
hilde rössel-majdan/wolfgang windgassen/hans
hotter/gustav neidlinger/anton dermota/claude
heater/murray dickie/constantino ego
wagner tristan und isolde
cd: myto MCD 00181/golden melodram GM 10080

202/2 july 1959/concert recordings in hollywood bowl
los angeles philharmonic orchestra
the star-spangled banner; wagner meistersinger overture;
ives the unanswered question; mozart symphony no 35
"haffner"; strauss ein heldenleben
cd: pristine audio PASC 227/private edition vienna

203/5 august 1959/stage recording in salzburg
felsenreitschule
wiener philharmoniker/chor der wiener staatsoper/
giulietta simionato/sena jurinac/graziella sciutti
gluck orfeo ed euridice
lp: legendary recordings LR 132/replica RPL 2436-2437
cd: nuova era NE 2215-2216/memories HR 4382-4383/deutsche
grammophon 439 1012/479 4640

204/19 august 1959/concert recording in salzburg festspielhaus

wiener philharmoniker/wiener singverein/leontyne price/christa ludwig/nicolai gedda/nicola zaccaria
beethoven missa solemnis op 123
lp: melodram MEL 704/joker SM 1343
cd: nuova era NE 2262-2263/emi 566 8672
emi edition also includes rehearsal extracts recorded on
18 august in the felsenreitschule (actual concert was
transferred to festspielhaus due to inclement weather)

205/2-15 september 1959/decca sessions in vienna sofiensäle

wiener philharmoniker/wiener singverein/renata tebaldi/giulietta simionato/eugenia ratti/carlo bergonzi/cornell macneil/arnold van mill/fernando corena/piero de palma/*producer john culshaw*
verdi aida
lp: LXT 5539-5541/SXL 2169-2171/414 0871/
london (usa) A4345/OSA 1313
cd: 414 0872/460 8782/deutsche grammophon 479 4640

206/4 september 1959/dg session in berlin jesus-christus-kirche

berliner philharmoniker/*producers elsa schiller*
and werner wolf
brahms hungarian dances nos 1, 3, 5, 6, 17, 18, 19 and 20;
dvorak slavonic dances op 46 nos 1, 3 and 7 and op 72
nos 10 and 16
lp: LPM 18 610/SLPM 138 080/2543 046 (brahms)/
2543 509 (dvorak)/2720 112 (brahms)/2726 516 (dvorak)
cd: 423 2062 (dvorak)/423 2072 (brahms)/423 5552/
435 5902 (dvorak)/447 4342/479 0055

207/27 october 1959/televised concert in tokyo
nhk concert hall
wiener philharmoniker
brahms symphony no 1; johann strauss an der schönen
blauen donau
dvd: nhk classical NSDS 9480
picture missing in first movement of the symphony and in
strauss waltz, where it is replaced by still photographs or
newsreel footage

mozart symphony no 40 ; japanese and austrian anthems
cd: nhk karajan centenary set NSDX 12264

208/29 october 1959/televised concert in tokyo
nhk concert hall
wiener philharmoniker
beethoven symphony no 5: fragments only
dvd: nhk classical NSDS 9480

209/6 november 1959/televised concert in tokyo
nhk concert hall
wiener philharmoniker
schubert symphony no 8 "unfinished"; brahms symphony no 4
dvd: nhk classical NSDS 9480
picture missing in part of final movement of brahms, part
of first movement and entire second movement of schubert,
where it is replaced by still photographs

theodor berger legende vom prinzen eugen
cd: nhk karajan centenary set NSDX 12264

210/30-31 december 1959/columbia sessions in berlin grunewaldkirche

berliner philharmoniker/*producers walter legge and christfried bickenbach*

mozart serenade no 13 "eine kleine nachtmusik";
handel-harty water music suite
lp: 33CX 1741/SAX 2389/FCX 887/SAXF 206/CVD 2076/
QCX 10416/SAXQ 7316/C 70461 (mozart)/STC 70461 (mozart)/
WC 544 (mozart)/SBOW 8504 (mozart)/SHZE 303 (mozart)/
angel 35948/emi SLS 839/SXLP 30161/1C047 02350 (mozart)/
1C177 02348-02352/1C063 00737 (mozart)/2C053 00723/
3C053 00520/143 5643 (mozart)
cd: emi 769 4652/252 1522 (mozart)/252 1592/769 8822
(mozart)/569 4582 (mozart)/royal classics ROY 6473/
disky DCL 705 872 (mozart)/HR 700 062/warner 2564 633621
(handel)/2564 633623 (mozart)

211/6-9 january and 22-30 june 1960/decca sessions in vienna sofiensäle

wiener philharmoniker/*producer john culshaw*

tchaikovsly romeo and Juliet fantasy overture
lp: LXT 5629/SXL 2269/SPA 119/london (usa) CM 9278/
CS 6209/JL 41021
cd: 417 7222/448 0422/455 4972/460 6552/478 0155

strauss don juan
lp: LXT 5629/SXL 2269/SPA 119/JB 27/london (usa) CM 9280/
CS 6211/JL 41017
cd: 417 7202/417 7882/440 2772/448 0422/
448 5822/478 0155

212/29 february-1 march 1960/columbia sessions in berlin grunewaldkirche

berliner philharmoniker/*producers walter legge and christfried bickenbach*

mozart symphony no 29 in a K201
lp: 33CX 1703/SAX 2356/FCX 810/SAXF 810/QCX 10401/
SAXQ 7296/C 91061/STC 91061/WCX 523/SAXW 2356/angel
35739/6062/world records T 1032/ST 1032/emi RLS 768/
F669.711-715/1C037 00653/1C137 54095-54099/
1C053 00726/2C053 00726
cd: emi CDF 300 0122/764 3272/476 8902/566 0982/
252 1462/769 8822/566 1132/512 0382/warner 2564 633623

tchaikovsky symphony no 4 in f minor op 36
lp: 33CX 1704/SAX 2357/QCX 10398/SAXQ 7295/C 91068/
STC 91068/WCX 522/SAXW 9507/angel 35885/world records
T 872/ST 872/emi SXLP 30433/1C037 00648/1C053 00648/
2C053 01413/3C053 00648
cd: emi 769 8832/512 0382/warner 2564 633620

213/9 march 1960/stage recording in vienna staatsoper

orchester der wiener staatsoper/chor der wiener staatsoper/hilde zadek/christa ludwig/hans hotter/ anton dermota/gerhard stolze/kurt equiluz/claude heater/edmund hurshell/paul schoeffler/walter berry/walter kreppel

pizzetti assassinio nella cattedrale/*sung in german*
cd: deutsche grammophon 457 6712

214/26-30 march 1960/columbia sessions in london abbey road studios

philharmonia orchestra/_producer walter legge_

rossini overtures: il barbiere di siviglia; la scala di seta
45: C 41336/STC 41366/SEGW 7964/ESLW 7508
lp: 33CX 1729/SAX 2378/FCX 798/FC 25507/SAXF 132/
SBOF 125507/QCX 10412/SAXQ 7309/angel 35890/
emi SLS 5019/SXDW 3048/SXLP 30203/1C063 00512/
1C181 25307-25311/2C053 00512/2C059 00512/
1C187 03059-03060
cd: emi 763 1132/763 5572/512 0382/warner 2564 633621

rossini overtures: la gazza ladra; semiramide; guillaume tell;
italiana in algeri
lp: 33CX 1729/SAX 2378/FCX 798/FC 25507 (gazza and
italiana)/SAXF 132/SBOF 125507 (gazza and italiana)/
QCX 10412/SAXQ 7309/angel 35890/emi SLS 5019/
SXLP 30203/1C181 25307-25311/1C053 00512/2C053 00512/
2C059 00512
cd: emi 763 1132/512 0382/warner 2564 633621

215/28-29 march 1960/columbia sessions in london kingsway hall

philharmonia orchestra/_producer walter legge_

sibelius symphony no 2 in d op 43
lp: 33CX 1730/SAX 2379/QCX 10409/SAXQ 7305/C 91093/
STC 91093/WCX 1730/SAXW 2379/angel 35981/
emi SXLP 30414
cd: emi 476 8822/566 5992/512 0382/warner 2564 633621

216/12-20 june 1960/decca sessions in vienna sofiensäle

wiener philharmoniker/chor der wiener staatsoper/ hilde güden/erika köth/regina resnik/hedwig schubert/ waldemar kmentt/giuseppe zampieri/peter klein/ eberhard waechter/erich kunz/walter berry/*producers john culshaw and christopher raeburn*

johann strauss die fledermaus

lp: MET 201-203/LXT 6015-6016/SET 201-203/SXL 6015-6016/ D247 D3/london (usa) A 4347/OSA 1319

cd: 421 0462/deutsche grammophon 479 4640/ pristine PACO 068

original lp issue included a gala sequence not conducted by karajan; ballet music also omitted from most re-issues

217/14 june 1960/stage recording in vienna staatsoper

orchester der wiener staatsoper/chor der wiener staatsoper/leontyne price/giulietta simionato/flaviano labo/ettore bastianini/nicola zaccaria/ludwig weber/ gerda scheyrer/ermanno lorenzi

verdi aida

this poor-quality in-house recording remains unpublished

218/22-30 june and september 1960/decca sessions
in vienna sofiensäle

wiener philharmoniker/*producer john culshaw*
strauss till eulenspiegels lustige streiche
lp: LXT 5620/SXL 2261/ADD 211/SDD 211/HZT 501/JB 27/
london (usa) CM 9280/CS 6211/JL 41017
cd: 417 7222/440 2772/448 0422/448 5822/
466 3882/478 0155

strauss tod und verklärung
lp: LXT 5620/SXL 2261/ADD 211/SDD 211/london (usa)
CM 9278/CS 6209
cd: 417 7202/448 0422/478 0155

strauss salome: dance of the seven veils
lp: LXT 5620/SXL 2261/ADD 211/SDD 211/LXT 6282-6284/
SXL 6282-6284/london (usa) CM 9280/CS 6211
cd: 417 7882/445 5822/448 0422/466 3882/478 0155

219/26 july 1960/stage recording in salzburg
grosses festspielhaus

wiener philharmoniker/chor der wiener staatsoper/
lisa della casa/sena jurinac/hilde güden/judith
hellwig/hilde rössel-majdan/giuseppe zampieri/
renato ercolani/otto edelmann/erich kunz/erich
majkut/alois pernerstorfer/siegfried rudolf frese/
josef knapp/fritz sperlbauer/lieselotte maikl/evelyn
labruce/ute frey
strauss der rosenkavalier
cd: arkadia CDKAR 213/gala GL 100 606/
deutsche grammophon 453 2002/479 4640

220/3 august 1960/stage recording in salzburg
altes festspielhaus
wiener philharmoniker/chor der wiener staatsoper/
elisabeth schwarzkopf/leontyne price/graziella sciutti/
cesare valletti/eberhard waechter/walter berry/
rolando panerai/nicola zaccaria
mozart don giovanni
lp: historical recording enterprises HRE 274/
movimento musica 03.001
cd: movimento musica 013.012/curcio OP 6/
arkadia CDKAR 225/paragon DSV 52010

221/24 august 1960/concert recordings in salzburg
grosses festspielhaus
wiener philharmoniker/wiener singverein/leontyne
price/ hilde rössel-majdan/fritz wunderlich/eberhard
waechter/walter berry
mozart requiem mass K626
lp: historical recording enterprises HRE 317/
movimento musica 01.203
cd: priceless D 16573/claque GM 2003-2004/foyer CDS 16001

bruckner te deum
cd: emi 566 8802

222/27-30 august 1960/film and soundtrack sessions
for the rank organisation in salzburg grosses festspielhaus/
film director paul czinner
wiener philharmoniker/chor der wiener staatsoper/
elisabeth schwarzkopf/sena jurinac/anneliese
rothenberger/judith hellwig/hilde rössel-majdan/
giuseppe zampieri/renato ercolani/otto edelmann/
erich kunz/erich majkut/alois pernerstorfer/siegfried
rudolf frese/josef knapp/fritz sperlbauer/lieselotte maikl/
evelyn labruce/ute frey
strauss der rosenkavalier
cd: celestial audio CA 185
vhs video: rank 7015E/gig 555 019/kultur 1268
laserdisc: king (japan) 485L 2501-2502
dvd: rca-bmg 74321 840379/park circus PC 0021
blu-ray disc: kultur BD 4684

223/16-19 september 1960/columbia sessions in
berlin grunewaldkirche
berliner philharmoniker/producer walter legge
wagner der fliegende holländer overture; lohengrin prelude;
weber freischütz overture; nicolai die lustigen weiber von
windsor overture
lp: 33CX 1791/SAX 2439/C 70496/STC 70496/WC 573/
SBOW 8525/SGHX 10508/angel 35950/world records
T 639/ST 639/emi SXLP 30210/EMX 41 20521/143 5643/
1C137 54360-54363/1C053 01143 (lohengrin)
cd: 476 9012/763 3212/569 5632 (holländer)/569 4582
(weber and nicolai)/512 0382/warner 2564 633623
mendelssohn hebrides overture
lp: 33CX 1791/SAX 2439/SGHX 10508/CVD 2073/angel
35950/world records T 639/ST 639/emi SXLP 30210/
SXDW 3048/EMX 41 20521/1C053 01143
cd: emi 476 9012/769 4662/764 6292/252 1592/569 4582/
512 0382/royal classics ROY 6474/disky DCL 705 872/
HR 700 062/warner 2564 633623

223a/18 april 1960/concert recording in berlin
hochschule für musik
berliner philharmoniker/leontyne price
handel giulio cesare: v'adoro pupille
lp: legendary recordings LR 139

224/20-23 september 1960/columbia sessions in
london kingsway hall
philharmonia orchestra/*producer walter legge*
sibelius symphony no 5 in e flat op 82
lp: 33CX 1750/SAX 2392/SAXQ 7328/C 70480/STC 70480/WC 558/
angel 35922/emi SXLP 30430/1C053 00523/1C053 03791
cd: emi 476 8822/566 5992/512 0382/warner 2564 633621
verdi aida: act two ballet; borodin prince igor: dance of polovtsian
maidens and polovtsian dances; ponchielli la gioconda: dance of
the hours; wagner tannhäuser: venusberg bacchanale
reel-to-reel tape: TC-CX 1774
lp: 33CX 1774/SAX 2421/FCX 898/SAXF 210/CVD 2071/QCX 10192/
SAXQ 7344/SHZE 216/angel 35925/37232/emi SLS 5019/
SXDW 3048/SXLP 30445/1C181 25307-25311/1C037 01390/
2C053 01413/143 5643
cd: emi 769 0412/512 0382/warner 2564 633621
mussorgsky khovantschina: dance of the persian slaves
reel-to-reel tape: TC-CX 1774
lp: 33CX 1774/SAX 2421/FCX 898/SAXF 210/CVD 2071/QCX 10192/
SAXQ 7344/angel 35925/emi SLS 839/EMX 41 26071/SXLP 30200/
SXLP 30445/1C177 02348-02352/1C053 03870/2C053 01413
cd: emi 769 3502/512 0382/warner 2564 633621
suppe leichte kavallerie overture
45: C 41152/SMC 41152/SEGW 7909
lp: 33CX 1758/SAX 2404/FCX 894/SAXF 216/CVD 2073/angel 35926/
37931/world records T 838/ST 838/emi SLS 5019/CFP 40368/
1C037 00765/1C177 02348-02352/1C137 03059-03060/
2C053 00703/143 5643
cd: emi 769 4662/252 1592/512 0382/royal classics ROY 6474/
disky HR 700 062/warner 2564 633621

224/20-23 september 1960/columbia sessions in london kingsway hall/concluded

chabrier joyeuse marche
lp: 33CX 1758/SAX 2404/FCX 894/SAXF 216/CVD 2074/angel
35926/37250/world records T 838/ST 838/emi SLS 5019/
CFP 40368/1C037 00765/1C181 25307-25311/2C053 00726
cd: emi 769 4672/252 1592/562 8692/512 0382/royal classics
ROY 6475/laserligh 24 426/disky HR 700 062/
warner 2564 633621

waldteufel les patineurs waltz
lp: 33CX 1758/SAX 2404/FCX 894/SAXF 216/CVD 2074/angel
35926/37250/world records T 838/ST 838/emi SLS 839/
SXLP 30224/SXDW 3048/CFP 40368/1C177 02348-02352/
1C137 03059-03060/1C037 00765/2C053 00726/2C059 03054
cd: emi 769 4652/252 1592/562 8692/512 0382/royal classics
ROY 6471/laserlight 24 426/disky HR 700 062/
warner 2564 633621

weinberger schwanda der dudelsackpfeifer polka;
offenbach orfee aux enfers overture
lp: 33CX 1758/SAX 2404/FCX 894/SAXF 216/angel 35926/world
records T 838/ST 838/emi SLS 5019 (weinberger)/SLS 839
(offenbach)/CFP 40368/1C181 25307-25311 (weinberger)/
1C177 02348-02352 (offenbach)/ 1C037 00765/2C053 00793
(offenbach)/143 5643 (offenbach)
cd: emi 769 4672/252 1592/512 0382/562 8692 (weinberger)/
royal classics ROY 6475 (weinberger)/ROY 6473 (offenbach)/
laserlight 24 426/disky DCL 703 332 (offenbach)/HR 700 062/
warner 2564 633621

225/24 september 1960/columbia session in london abbey road studios

philharmonia orchestra/*producer walter legge*

chabrier espana

lp: 33CX 1758/SAX 2404/FCX 894/SAXF 216/CVD 2075/angel 35926/world records T 838/ST 838/emi SLS 839/SXDW 3048/ CFP 40368/1C037 00765/1C177 02348-02352/ 1C137 03059-03060/2C053 01414/143 5643

cd: emi 769 4672/252 1592/512 0382/522 0492/562 8692/ royal classics ROY 6475/laserlight 24 426/disky DCL 705 872/ HR 700 062/warner 2564 633621

johann strauss tritsch-tratsch polka; unter donner und blitz; johann strauss father radetzky march

lp: 33CX 1758/SAX 2404/FCX 894/SAXF 216/CVD 2074/angel 35926/37232 (radetzky)/world records T 838/ST 838/ emi CFP 40368/1C037 00765/1C137 02059-02060 (tritsch-tratsch)/143 5643 (radetzky)/2C053 00726

cd: emi 769 4672 (radetzky)/252 1592 (radetzky)/512 0382/ laserlight 24 426/royal classics ROY 6475 (radetzky)/ disky HR 700 062 (radetzky)/warner 2564 633621

226/29 september-8 october 1960/decca sessions in vienna sofiensäle

wiener philharmoniker/*producer john culshaw*

brahms symphony no 3 in f op 90

lp: MET 231/SET 231/ADD 284/SDD 284/london (usa) CM 9318/ CS 6249/JL 41035

cd: 417 7442/433 3302/433 3392/448 0422/478 0155

227/9-11 november 1960/columbia sessions in berlin grunewaldkirche

berliner philharmoniker/*producers walter legge and christfried bickenbach*

bartok music for strings, percussion and celesta
lp: 33CX 1783/SAX 2432/FCX 917/SAXF 235/QCX 10502/angel 35949/emi SXLP 30536/1C063 00547/1C137 54360-54363
cd: emi 476 8972/769 2422/512 0382/warner 2564 633621

mozart deutsche tänze K600 no 3 and K602 no 3
lp: 33CX 1741/SAX 2389/FCX 887/SAXF 206/CVD 2076/QCX 10416/ SAXQ 7316/SHZE 303/angel 35948/emi 2C053 00723/3C053 00620
cd: emi 763 3262/512 0382/warner 2564 633623

mozart deutscher tanz K605 no 3
lp: 33CX 1741/SAX 2389/FCX 887/SAXF 206/CVD 2076/QCX 10416/ SAXQ 7316/SHZE 303/angel 35948/emi SLS 839/SXLP 30161/ 1C177 02348-02352/1C047 02350/2C053 00723/2C053 00520
cd: emi 769 4652/769 8822/252 1592/512 0382/royal classics ROY 6573/disky HR 700 062/warner 2564 633623

228/27 november 1960/stage recording in vienna staatsoper

orchester der wiener staatsoper/chor der wiener staatsoper/aase nordmo-lövberg/wilma lipp/wolfgang windgassen/murray dickie/walter kreppel/hans hotter/ otto wiener

beethoven fidelio
cd: golden melodram GM 50053/private edition Vienna

229/12-13 december 1960/dg sessions in berlin
jesus-christus-kirche
berliner philharmoniker/*shura cherkassky/*producers*
elsa schiller and hans ritter
liszt hungarian rhapsody no 5 in e minor
lp: LPM 18 692/SLPM 138 692/135 031
cd: 477 7099/479 0055

*liszt hungarian fantasy for piano and orchestra
lp: LPM 18 692/SLPM 138 692/135 031
cd: 415 9672/419 8622/447 3372/453 1302/479 0055

230/17 december 1960/stage recording in milan
teatro alla scala
orchestra e coro del teatro alla scala/birgit nilsson/
wilma lipp/jon vickers/gerhard unger/gottlob frick/
hans hotter/franz crass/walter gullino/dino mantovani
beethoven fidelio
lp: historical recording enterprises HRE 388
cd: golden melodrama GM 50071/istituto discografico
italiano IDIS 6587-6588
IDIS 6587-6588 is dated 20 december 1960

231/31 december 1960/stage recording in vienna
staatsoper
orchester der wiener staatsoper/chor der wiener
staatsoper/hilde güden/rita streich/giuseppe zampieri/
peter klein/gerhard stolze/eberhard waechter/
erich kunz/elfried ott/josef meinrad
johann strauss die fledermaus
lp: foyer FO 1031
cd: foyer 3CF 2021/arkadia CDKAR 215/rca-bmg 74321 619492/
74321 619532
giuseppe di stefano and walter berry appear as special guests
in this new year's eve performance

232/16-17 february 1961/dg sessions in berlin
jesus-christus-kirche
berliner philharmoniker/*producers elsa schiller,
otto gerdes and hans ritter*
liszt mazeppa
lp: LPM 18 692/SLPM 138 692/2726 517/415 6281
cd: 415 9672/445 2892/447 5502/453 1302/479 0055

liszt hungarian rhapsody no 4 in d minor
lp: LPM 18 692/SLPM 138 692/135 031/415 6281
cd: 419 8622/429 1562/445 2892/447 4152/479 0055

233/1 april 1961/stage recording in vienna
staatsoper
orchester der wiener staatsoper/chor der wiener
staatsoper/elisabeth höngen/christa ludwig/fritz uhl/
eberhard waechter/hans hotter/walter berry/tugomir
franc/lieselotte maikl/margarete sjöstedt/gundula
janowitz/hilde güden/anneliese rothenberger/gerda
scheyrer/hilde rössel-majdan/erich majkut/kurt
equiluz/ermanno lorenzi/kostas paskalis
wagner parsifal
cd: arkadia CDKAR 219/rca-bmg 74321 619502/74321 619532
*the role of kundry was divided in this production between
elisabeth höngen (acts 1 and 3) and christa ludwig (act 2)*

234/17 april 1961/concert recording in london
royal festival hall
berliner philharmoniker
beethoven symphony no 8 in f op 93
cd: arkadia CDKAR 208/curcio CONB 03

235/25-28 april 1961/dg sessions in berlin
jesus-christus-kirche
berliner philharmoniker/*producer hans weber*
chopin-douglas les sylphides
lp: LPEM 19 257/SLPEM 136 257/2535 189/413 9811
cd: 423 2152/423 5552/429 1632/437 4042/
459 4452/479 0055
delibes coppelia ballet suite
lp: LPEM 19 257/SLPEM 136 257/2535 189/413 9811
cd: 457 4042/459 4452/479 0055

236/10-21 may 1961/decca sessions in vienna
sofiensäle
wiener philharmoniker/konzertvereinigung
wiener staatsopernchor/wiener grosstadtkinderchor/
renata tebaldi/ana raquel satre/mario del monaco/
aldo protti/nello romanato/fernando corena/tom
krause/athos cesarini/libero arbace/*producer
john culshaw*
verdi otello
lp: MET 209-211/SET 209-211/411 6181/london (usa)
A 4352/OSA 1324
cd: 411 6182/455 9012
*recording included ballet music, which was omitted from
cd re-issue*

237/3-5 june 1961/decca sessions in vienna
sofiensäle
wiener philharmoniker/wiener grosstadtkinderchor/
leontyne price/*producer john culshaw*
christmas songs by gruber, mendelssohn, willis, bach, schubert,
adam, bach-gounod, mozart and traditional
lp: LXT 5657/SXL 2294/JB 38/london (usa) 5644/OSA 25280
cd: 421 1031/448 9982

238/20 august 1961/concert recording in salzburg
grosses festspielhaus
wiener philharmoniker/wiener singverein/leontyne
price/christa ludwig/nicolai gedda/gerard souzay/
walter berry
bach mass in b minor
lp: movimento musica 03.012

238a/26 august 1961/concert recordings in edinburgh
usher hall
berliner philharmoniker
bach orchestral suite no 2; stravinsky symphony in c;
strauss ein heldenleben
these recordings remain unpublished

239/5-22 september 1961/decca sessions in vienna
sofiensäle
wiener philharmoniker/*damenchor der wiener
staatsoper/*producer john culshaw*
tchaikovsky casse noisette ballet suite
lp: LXT 5673/SXL 2308/JB 16/HZT 501/417 2741/london (usa)
CM 9420/CS 6420/JL 41021
cd: 417 7002/448 0422/448 5922/455 4982/466 3792/478 0155

adam giselle, standard abridged version
lp: LXT 6002/SXL 6002/JB 14/london (usa) CM 9320/CS 6251
cd: 417 7382/448 0422/478 0155

grieg peer gynt, excerpts comprising first suite and scenes
from second suite
lp: LXT 5673/SXL 2308/JB 16/417 6981/London (usa)
CM 9420/CS 6420
cd: 417 7222/448 0422/478 0155

239/5-22 september 1961/decca sessions in
vienna sofiensäle/concluded
*holst the planets
lp: LXT 5669/SXL 2305/SDD 400/JB 30/london (usa) CM 9313/
CS 6244/JL 41005
cd: 417 7092/448 0422/452 3032/478 0155
brahms tragic overture
lp: MET 231/SET 231/ADD 284/SDD 284/london (usa)
CM 9318/CS 6249/JL 41035
cd: 417 7392/417 7882/440 2602/448 0422/478 0155

240/29 september-8 october 1961, october 1962
and september 1963/decca sessions in vienna sofiensäle
wiener philharmoniker/_producer john culshaw_
dvorak symphony no 8 in g op 88
lp: LXT 6169/SXL 6169/SDD 440/JB 71/london (usa) CM 9443/
CS 6443/JL 41043
cd: 417 4772/448 0422/478 0155

241/5-12 october 1961/dg sessions in berlin
jesus-christus-kirche
berliner philharmoniker/wiener singverein/wilma lipp/
hilde rössel-majdan/anton dermota/walter berry/
producer otto gerdes
mozart requiem mass K626
lp: LPM 18 767/SLPM 138 767/2535 257
cd: 423 2132/423 5552/429 1602/439 4322/450 0272/
457 9252/479 0055

242/10 december 1961/stage recording in vienna staatsoper

orchester der wiener staatsoper/chor der wiener staatsoper/regina resnik/hilde güden/lieselotte maikl/ hilde rössel-majdan/dimiter usunow/aldo protti/ ludwig welter/alfred poell/murray dickie/harald pröglhöf/franz klos

bizet carmen
cd: arkadia CDKAR 201
this issue was incorrectly dated 10 december 1962

243/27 december 1961-22 january 1962/dg sessions in berlin jesus-christus-kirche

berliner philharmoniker/*producers elsa schiller and otto gerdes*

beethoven symphony no 1 in c op 21; symphony no 2 in d op 36
lp: KL 1-8/SKL 101-108/LPM 18 801/SLPM 138 801/2542 102/ 2720 007/2720 104/2721 055
cd: 429 0362/453 7002/453 7012/459 2392/463 0882/479 0055

244/6 january 1962/stage recording in vienna staatsoper
orchester der wiener staatsoper/chor der wiener staatsoper/hilde güden/elisabeth höngen/adriana martino/henri gui/eberhard waechter/nicola zaccaria/ alfred poell

debussy pelleas et melisande
cd: private edition vienna

245/23 january 1962/dg sessions in berlin
jesus-christus-kirche
berliner philharmoniker/*producers elsa schiller and
otto gerdes*
beethoven symphony no 8 in f op 93
lp: KL 1-8/SKL 101-108/LPM 18 808/SLPM 138 808/SLPM 139 013/
2720 007/2740 104/2721 055/2725 101/2726 503
cd: 429 0362/431 1592/453 7002/455 7012/459 0242/
459 0682/463 0882/479 0055

246/29 january 1962/stage recording in vienna staatsoper
orchester der wiener staatsoper/chor der wiener
staatsoper/floriana cavalla/dimiter usunow/aldo protti/
erich majkut/ferruccio mazzoli/karl dönch/harald
pröglhöf/ljubomir pantscheff/ein wiener sängerknabe
puccini tosca
cd: arkadia CDKAR 206

247/13-15 february 1962/dg sessions in berlin
jesus-christus-kirche
berliner philharmoniker/*producers elsa schiller and
otto gerdes*
beethoven symphony no 6 in f op 68 "pastoral"
lp: KL 1-8/SKL 101-108/LPM 18 805/SLPM 138 805/2542 106/
2720 007/2720 104/2721 055
cd: 423 2032/423 5552/429 0362/431 1592/453 7002/
453 7012/457 9212/463 0882/479 0055

248/9-14 march 1962/dg sessions in berlin
jesus-christus-kirche

berliner philharmoniker/producers elsa schiller and
otto gerdes

beethoven symphony no 5 in c minor op 67
lp: KL 1-8/SKL 101-108/LPM 18 804/SLPM 138 804/2542 105/
2720 007/2720 104/2721 055
cd: 423 2032/423 5552/429 0362/429 4322/453 7002/
453 7012/457 9212/463 0882/479 0055

beethoven symphony no 7 in a op 92
lp: KL 1-8/SKL 101-108/LPM 18 806/SLPM 138 806/2542 107/
2720 007/2720 104/2721 055
cd: 429 0362/453 7002/453 7012/463 0882/479 0055

249/14 march and 9 november 1962/dg sessions in
berlin jesus-christus-kirche

berliner philharmoniker/producers elsa schiller and
otto gerdes

beethoven symphony no 4 in b flat op 60
lp: KL 1-8/SKL 101-108/LPM 18 803/SLPM 138 803/2542 104/
2720 007/2720 104/2721 055
cd: 423 0362/453 7002/453 7012/463 0882/479 0055

250/6 april 1962/concert recordings in london
royal festival hall
wiener philharmoniker
british and austrian national anthems; mozart symphony no 41;
bruckner symphony no 7
cd: ica classics ICAC 5102

251/25 may 1962/stage recording in vienna staatsoper
orchester der wiener staatsoper/chor der wiener
staatsoper/christa ludwig/gundula janowitz/jon vickers/
waldemar kmentt/walter kreppel/walter berry/eberhard
waechter/kostas paskalis/ljubomir pantscheff
beethoven fidelio
lp: movimento musica 03.014
cd: deutsche grammophon 477 7364

252/26 may 1962/concert recordings in vienna
musikvereinssaal
wiener philharmoniker/wiener singverein/wilma lipp/
elisabeth höngen/nicolai gedda/walter kreppel
bruckner symphony no 9 in d minor; te deum
these recordings remain unpublished

254/30 may 1962/stage recording in vienna theater an der wien

orchester der wiener staatsoper/chor der wiener staatsoper/wilma lipp/ingeborg hallstein/graziella sciutti/gerda scheyrer/grace hoffmann/hilde rössel-majdan/nicolai gedda/paul kuen/eberhard waechter/erich kunz/gottlob frick/ermanno lorenzi/ kostas paskalis/frederick guthrie

mozart die zauberflöte
lp: movimento musica 03.015
cd: movimento musica 015.028

255/31 july 1962/stage recording in salzburg grosses festspielhaus

wiener philharmoniker/chor der wiener staatsoper/ leontyne price/giulietta simionato/laurence dutoit/ franco corelli/ettore bastianini/nicola zaccaria/ siegfried rudolf frese/rudolf zimmer/kurt equiluz

verdi il trovatore
lp: morgan records MOR 6201/hope records HOPE 247/ cetra ARK 7/paragon DSV 52025/historical recording enterprises HRE 287/movimento musica 03.018/ melodram MEL 710
cd: movimento musica 012.001/rodolphe RPC 32482-32483/ arkadia CDKAR 228/curcio OP 8/priceless D 20791/gala GL 100 505/deutsche grammophon 447 6592/479 4640

256/9 august 1962/concert recording in salzburg grosses festspielhaus
berliner philharmoniker/wiener singverein/leontyne price/giulietta simionato/giuseppe zampieri/nicolai ghiaurov
verdi messa da requiem
cd: testament SBT 1491

257/24-26 september 1962/dg sessions in vienna musikvereinssaal
wiener symphoniker/sviatoslav richter/*producers elsa schiller and otto ernst wohlert*
tchaikovsky piano concerto no 1 in b flat minor op 23
lp: LPM 18 882/SLPM 138 882/SKL 922-928/2726 506/2740 126/ 419 0681/eterna 826 502/hungaraton SLPX 12074/supraphon 110 1313/melodiya D 011275-011276/C 0473-0474/ CM 04255-04256/C10 04255 000
cd: 419 0682/429 9182/447 4202/479 0055

258/24 september-6 october 1962/decca sessions for rca victor in vienna sofiensäle
wiener philharmoniker/chor der wiener staatsoper/ leontyne price/giuseppe di stefano/giuseppe taddei/ carlo cava/fernando corena/piero de palma/leonardo monreale/alfredo mariotti/herbert weiss/*producer john culshaw*
puccini tosca
lp: rca victor LD 7022/RE 5507-5508/LDS 7022/SER 5507-5508/ decca 5BB 123-124/london (usa) OSA 1294
cd: 440 4022/440 6342/452 7282/466 3842/ deutsche grammophon 479 4640

259/8-13 october and 9 november 1962/dg sessions
in berlin jesus-christus-kirche
berliner philharmoniker/wiener singverein/gundula
janowitz/hilde rössel-majdan/waldemar kmentt/walter
berry/*producers elsa schiller and otto gerdes*
beethoven symphony no 9 in d minor op 125 "choral"
lp: KL 1-8/SKL 101-108/LPM 18 807-808/SLPM 138 807-808/
2543 030/2720 007/2720 104/2720 111/2720 261/2721 055/
2725 103/2726 503
cd: 423 2042/423 5552/429 0362/447 4012/453 7002/453 7012/
463 0882/479 0055
rehearsal extracts were also published on various promotional
lps and cds

260/16-17 october 1962 and 9-10 april 1963/decca
sessions in vienna sofiensäle
wiener philharmoniker/*producer john culshaw*
mozart symphony no 41 in c K551 "Jupiter"
lp: LXT 6067/SXL 6067/SDD 312/SDD 361/VIV 6/417 6951/
london (usa) CM 9369/CS 6369
cd: 417 6952/436 5192/448 0422/455 4972/478 0155

261/11-15 november 1962/dg sessions in berlin
jesus-christus-kirche
berliner philharmoniker/*producers elsa schiller and*
otto gerdes
beethoven symphony no 3 in e flat op 55 "eroica"
lp: KL 1-8/SKL 101-108/LPM 18 802/SLPM 138 802/2543 103/
2720 007/2720 104/2721 055
cd: 429 0362/453 7002/453 7012/459 0242/459 0682/
459 2392/463 0882/479 0055

141

262/8 january 1963/stage recording in vienna staatsoper

orchester der wiener staatsoper/chor der wiener staatsoper/gre brouwenstijn/christa ludwig/gundula janowitz/hans beirer/ waldemar kmentt/kurt equiluz/ eberhard waechter/gottlob frick/ ludwig welter/ tugomir franc

wagner tannhäuser
lp: melodram MEL 427
cd: nuova era NE 6307-6308/arkadia CDKAR 204/deutsche grammophon 457 6822

263/1 april 1963/stage recording in vienna staatsoper
orchester der wiener staatsoper/chor der wiener staatsoper/sena jurinac/margarita lilowa/gundula janowitz/hilde rössel-majdan/olivera miljakovic/gerda scheyrer/gerhard stolze/otto wiener/carlo cava/ murray dickie/ermanno lorenzi/erich majkut/ siegfried rudolf frese

monteverdi l'incoronazione di poppea
cd: deutsche grammophon 457 6742

264/9-11 april 1963/decca sessions in vienna sofiensäle
wiener philharmoniker/*producer john culshaw*
haydn symphony no 103 in e flat "drum roll"
lp: LXT 6067/SXL 6067/SDD 312/SDD 362/VIV 55/london (usa) CM 9369/CS 6369
cd: 448 0422/461 5062/478 0155

265/5 may 1963/concert recording in munich herkulessaal
berliner philharmoniker
henze antifone per orchestra
this recording remains unpublished

266/22 june 1963/stage recording in vienna
staatsoper
orchester der wiener staatsoper/chor der wiener
staatsoper/hilde güden/leontyne price/graziella
sciutti/fritz wunderlich/eberhard waechter/walter
berry/rolando panerai/walter kreppel
mozart don giovanni
cd: gala GL 100 608/verona 27065-27067

267/31 july 1963/stage recording in salzburg
grosses festspielhaus
wiener philharmoniker/chor der wiener staatsoper/
elisabeth schwarzkopf/sena jurinac/anneliese
rothenberger/Judith hellwig/hetty plümacher/
regolo romani/renato ercolani/otto edelmann/
karl dönch/martin häusler/siegfried rudolf frese/
josef knapp/alois pernerstorfer/fritz sperlbauer
strauss der rosenkavalier
lp: movimento musica 04.004/discocorp RR 659

268/13 august 1963/stage recording in salzburg
grosses festspielhaus
wiener philharmoniker/chor der wiener staatsoper/
kammerchor der salzburger festspiele/leontyne price/
giulietta simionato/laurence dutoit/james mccracken/
ettore bastianini/nicolazaccaria/siegfried rudolf frese/
rudolf zimmer/kurt equiluz
verdi il trovatore
cd: omega opera archive OOA 1591

269/15 august 1963/concert recording in salzburg
grosses festspielhaus
wiener philharmoniker/wiener singverein/gundula
janowitz/christa ludwig/waldemar kmentt/walter berry
beethoven symphony no 9 in d minor op 125 "choral"
cd: private edition Italy

270/10-16 october 1963/dg sessions in berlin
jesus-christus-kirche
berliner philharmoniker/*producers otto gerdes and
hans weber*
brahms symphony no 1 in c minor op 68
lp: KL 33-39/SKL 133-139/LPM 18 924/SLPM 138 924/2542 166/
2543 042/2720 104/2720 112/2721 075/2740 242
cd: 427 2532/431 1612/447 4082/479 0055

brahms symphony no 2 in d op 73
lp: KL 33-39/SKL 133-129/LPM 18 925/SLPM 138 925/2542 167/
2720 104/2721 075/2740 242
cd 429 1532/435 0672/439 4782/479 0055

brahms symphony no 4 in e minor op 98
lp: KL 33-39/SKL 133-139/LPM 18 927/SLPM 138 927/2542 169/
2543 042/2720 104/2720 112/2721 075/2740 242
cd: 423 2052/423 5552/437 6452/445 0092/479 0055

271/15 october 1963/inaugural ceremony to open
the berlin philharmonie
berliner philharmoniker
beethoven leonore no 3 overture
cd: arkadia CDKAR 222
incorrectly described by arkadia as a performance in london in 1961

272/15 october 1963/concert recording in berlin philharmonie

berliner philharmoniker/chor der hedwigskathedrale/ rias-chor/gundula janowitz/sieglinde wagner/luigi alva/otto wiener

beethoven symphony no 9 in d minor op 125 "choral"

cd: stiftung berliner philharmoniker BPH 0606

273/17-19 october 1963 and 10 february 1964/ dg sessions in berlin jesus-christus-kirche

berliner philharmoniker/*producers otto gerdes and hans weber*

stravinsky le sacre du printemps

lp: LPM 18 920/SLPM 138 920

cd: 423 2142/423 5552/429 1622/479 0055

274/2 november 1963/concert recording in vienna musikvereinssaal

wiener symphoniker/wiener singverein/wilma lipp/ hilde rössel-majdan/fritz wunderlich/kieth engen

mozart requiem K626

cd: melodram MEL 18003/arkadia CDKAR 202

melodram issue incorrectly described as a 1960 performance in Salzburg

275/9 november 1963/stage recording in vienna staatsoper

orchester der wiener staatsoper/chor der wiener staatsoper/mirella freni/hilde güden/gianni raimondi/ giuseppe taddei/rolando panerai/ivo vinco/peter klein/ siegfried rudolf frese/kurt equiluz/rudolf zimmer/ herbert zack/rudolf kreuzberger

puccini la boheme

lp: melodram MEL 414/movimento musica 02.020

cd: melodram MEL 27007/rodolphe RPC 32513/curcio OP 1/ arkadia CDMP 477/rca-bmg 74321 577362

276/18-26 november 1963/decca sessions for
rca victor in vienna sofiensäle
wiener philharmoniker/chor der wiener staatsoper/
wiener sängerknaben/leontyne price/mirella freni/
franco corelli/robert merrill/monique linval/genevieve
macaux/jean-christophe benoit/maurice besancon/
frank schooten/bernard demigny/*producer john culshaw*
bizet carmen
lp: LD 6164/LDS 6164/LMDS 6199/LSC 6199/RB 5514-5516/
SER 5600-5602/VLS 45473
cd: GD 86199/74321 394952

277/1 december 1963/stage recording in munich
nationaltheater
orchester und chor der bayerischen staatsoper/
christa ludwig/hanny steffek/fritz uhl/gerhard stolze/
gottlob frick/walter berry/hermann prey/heinrich
weber/hans-bruno ernst
beethoven fidelio
cd: arkadia CDKAR 208

278/february 1964/radio broadcast in paris/france 4
haute fidelite
les symphonies 1 et 2 de brahms analysees au piano par
herbert von karajan
cd: ina memoire IMV 079

279/11-13 february 1964/dg sessions in berlin
jesus-christus-kirche

berliner philharmoniker/*producers otto gerdes and hans weber*

tchaikovsky symphony no 6 in b minor op 74 "pathetique"
lp: LPM 18 921/SLPM 138 921/SKL 922-928/2535 341/
2726 009/2726 514/2740 126
cd: 423 2232/423 5552/479 0055
brahms haydn variations op 56a
lp: KL 33-39/SKL 133-139/LPM 18 926/SLPM 138 926/2542 168/
2543 046/2707 018/2720 112/2726 078/2726 506
cd: 423 2052/423 5552/427 2632/439 4782/445 0092/479 0055

280/4-5 march 1964/dg sessions in berlin
jesus-christus-kirche

berliner philharmoniker/*producers otto gerdes and otto ernst wohlert*

dvorak symphony no 9 in e minor op 95 "from the new world"
lp: LPM 18 922/SLPM 138 922/77 199/2543 053/2720 112/2726 516
cd: 423 2062/423 5552/429 4322/429 6762/435 5902/479 0055

281/9-11 march 1964/dg sessions in berlin
jesus-christus-kirche

berliner philharmoniker/*karl-heinz zöller/
producer otto gerdes

debussy la mer
lp: LPM 18 925/SLPM 138 925/2542 116/2543 058/2720 111
cd: 423 2172/423 5552/427 2592/447 4262/479 0055
ravel daphnis et chloe: second suite
lp: LPM 18 925/SLPM 138 925/2543 058/2720 112
cd: 423 2172/423 5552/427 2502/479 0055
*debussy prelude a l'apes-midi d'un faune
lp: LPM 18 925/SLPM 138 925/2535 621/2542 116/2543 058/
2720 111/77 199
cd: 423 2172/423 5552/427 2502/479 0055

282/4-6 may 1964/dg sessions in berlin
jesus-christus-kirche

berliner philharmoniker/christian ferras/*producers*
otto gerdes and otto ernst wohlert

brahms violin concerto in d op 77
lp: KL 33-39/SKL 133-139/LPM 18 930/SLPM 138 930/
2542 117/2543 045/2720 112/2740 137
cd: 429 5132/479 0055

283/16-18 may 1964/dg sessions in vienna
musikvereinssaal

berliner philharmoniker/wiener singverein/gundula
janowitz/eberhard waechter/*producers otto gerdes*
and hans weber

brahms ein deutsches requiem
lp: KL 33-39/SKL 133-139/2707 018/2726 078/2726 505
cd: 427 2522/479 0055

284/18 may 1964/concert recording in vienna
musikvereinssaal

berliner philharmoniker/wilhelm backhaus

brahms piano concerto no 2 in b flat op 83
cd: cetra CDE 1009/bellaphon 689 22002

285/8 june 1964/dress rehearsal recording in vienna
staatsoper

orchester der wiener staatsoper/chor der wiener
staatsoper/gundula janowitz/gladys kuchta/grace
hoffmann/lucia popp/jess thomas/otto wiener/
walter kreppel/fritz wunderlich/margarita lilowa/
olivera miljakovic/laurence dutoit/Judith hellwig/
liselotte maikl/margherita sjöstedt/ludwig welter/
siegfried rudolf frese/erich majkut

strauss die frau ohne schatten
cd: gala GL 100 607/omega opera archive OOA 4493

286/11 june 1964/stage recording in vienna staaatsoper

orchester der wiener staatsoper/chor der wiener staatsoper/leonie rysanek/christa ludwig/grace hoffmann/lucia popp/jess thomas/walter berry/ walter kreppel/fritz wunderlich/margarita lilowa/ olivera miljakovic/laurence dutoit/judith hellwig/ liselotte maikl/margherita sjöstedt/ludwig welter/ siegfried rudolf frese/erich majkut

strauss die frau ohne schatten
cd: nuova era NE 2288-2290/arkadia CDKAR 207/deutsche grammophon 457 6782

287/1 july 1964/concert recording in amsterdam concertgebouw

wiener philharmoniker

bruckner symphony no 7 in e
this recording remains unpublished and it is possible that only the second movement survives

288/1 august 1964/stage recording in salzburg grosses festspielhaus

wiener philharmoniker/chor der wiener staatsoper/ elisabeth schwarzkopf/sena jurinac/anneliese rothenberger/judith hellwig/hetty plümacher/otto edelmann/willy ferenz/ermanno lorenzi/renato ercolani/richard van vrooman/kurt equiluz/siegfried rudolf frese/alois pernerstorfer/josef knapp/ fritz sperlbauer

strauss der rosenkavalier
cd: arkadia CDKAR 227

289/15 august 1964/concert recordings in salzburg
grosses festspielhaus
berliner philharmoniker/elisabeth schwarzkopf/
lothar koch
strauss oboe concerto
this recording remains unpublished
strauss vier letzte lieder
cd: paragon PCD 84008/nuova era 2251-2252/virtuoso 269 7152/
verona 27075/golden melodram GM 70004/dg-salzburger
festspiele 415 5082
strauss ein heldenleben
cd: paragon PCD 84008/virtuoso 269 7152

290/17-24 august 1964/dg sessions in sankt moritz
viktoriasaal
berliner philharmoniker/michel schwalbe/karlheinz
zöller/matthias rütters/lothar koch/karl steins/adolf
scherbaum/alan civil/shirley hopkins/edith
picht-axenfeld/*producers otto gerdes and hans weber*
bach brandenburg concerti no 1 BWV 1046, no 2 BWV 1047 and
no 3 BWV 1049
lp: LPM 18 976-978/SLPM 138 976-978/LPEM 39 005/SLPEM 139 005/
2535 488/2709 016/2721 198 (no 1)/2726 080/413 1851
cd: 423 7022/423 5552/427 0492/431 1732/437 8892/479 0055

bach brandenburg concerti no 4 BWV 1049 and no 5 BWV 1050
lp: LPM 18 976-978/SLPM 138 976-978/LPEM 39 006/SLPEM 139 006/
2535 489/2543 019 (no 5)/2709 016/2726 080/413 1851
cd: 423 0022 (no 5)/423 5522 (no 5)/431 1732/457 8892/479 0055

bach orchestral suites no 2 BWV 1067 and no 3 BWV 1068
lp: LPM 18 976-978/SLPM 138 976-978/LPEM 39 007/SLPEM 139 007/
2535 138/2543 020/2709 016/2720 111
cd: 423 2022 (no 3)/423 5552 (no 3)/431 1732/457 8892 (no 3)/
474 2872 (no 3)/479 0055

291/17 august 1964/stage recording in salzburg
grosses festspielhaus
wiener philharmoniker/chor der wiener staatsoper/
astrid varnay/martha mödl/hildegard hillebrecht/
james king/eberhard waechter/tugomir franc/richard
van vrooman/siegfried rudolf frese/anja de haan/
hildegard rütgers/judith hellwig/helen watts/margarita
sjöstedt/cvetka ahlin/lisa otto/lucia popp
strauss elektra
lp: estro armonico EA 044/melodram MEL 713
cd: melodram CDM 27044/orfeo C298 922I

292/30 august 1964/concert recordings in salzburg
grosses festspielhaus
wiener philharmoniker/pierre fournier/rudolf streng
strauss don quixote; also sprach zarathustra
cd: andante 2060 (zarathustra)/orfeo C909 151B

293/23 september 1964/concert recording in moscow
bolshoi theatre
orchestra e coro del teatro alla scala di milano/
leontyne price/fiorenza cossotto/carlo bergonzi/
nicolai ghiaurov
verdi messa da requiem
lp: melodiya M10 45785 005/foyer FO 1045
cd: foyer 2CF-2012

294/26 september 1964/stage recording in moscow
bolshoi theatre
orchestra e coro del teatro alla scala di milano/
mirella freni/edda vincenzi/gianni raimondi/gianni
maffeo/rolando panerai/ivo vinco/carlo badioli/franco
calabrese/franco ricciardi/giuseppe morresi/angelo
mercuriali
puccini la boheme
cd: cetra CDE 1010/legato classics LCD 147/
omega opera archive OOA 1471

295/28-30 september 1964/dg sessions in berlin
jesus-christus-kirche
berliner philharmoniker/*producers otto gerdes and
hans weber*
brahms symphony no 3 in f op 90
lp: KL 33-39/SKL 133-139/LPM 18 926/SLPM 138 926/2542 168/
2720 104/2721 075/2740 242
cd: 429 1532/437 6452/479 0055

296/october 1964/sender freies berlin video
recording sessions in berlin ccs studios
ad hoc orchestra
strauss till eulenspiegels lustige streiche
*this recording remains unpublished: information about the
sessions came from peter csobadi*

297/27-30 october 1964/dg sessions in berlin
jesus-christus-kirche
berliner philharmoniker/*christian ferras/producers
otto gerdes and otto ernst wohlert*
*sibelius violin concerto in d minor op 47
lp: LPM 18 961/SLPM 138 961/2543 063/2720 112/
2740 137/2740 255
cd: 419 8712/479 0055

297/27-30 october 1964/dg sessions in berlin
jesus-christus-kirche/concluded
schubert symphony no 8 in b minor D759 "unfinished"
lp: LPEM 39 001/SLPEM 139 001/2543 034/2720 111/2721 198/
77 199/413 9821/415 8481
cd: 415 8482/423 2192/423 5552/429 4322/429 6762/479 0055
sibelius finlandia
lp: LPM 18 961/SLPM 138 961/LPEM 39 016/SLPEM 139 016/
2542 109/2543 062/2720 112/2740 255/643 212/410 9811
cd: 419 8712/423 2082/423 5552/427 2222/427 8082/
449 4182/479 0055
sibelius tapiola
lp: LPM 18 973/SLPM 138 973/LPEM 39 016/SLPEM 139 016/
2740 255
cd: 419 8712/423 2082/423 5552/449 3192/457 7482/479 0055

298/15 december 1964/dress rehearsal recording in
milan teatro alla scala
orchestra e coro del teatro alla scala/mirella freni/romana
righetti/limbania leoni/renato cioni/mario sereni/giorgio
goretti/alfredo giacomotti/silvio maionica/nicola zaccaria/
franco ricciardi/virgilio carbonari/carlo forti
verdi la traviata
cd: paragon PCD 84006-84008/as-disc AS 1015-1016/
arkadia CDKAR 229

299/22 december 1964/stage recording in milan
teatro alla scala
orchestra e coro del teatro alla scala/anna moffo/
romana righetti/limbana leoni/renato cioni/mario sereni/
giorgio goretti/alfredo giacomotti/silvio maionica/nicola
zaccaria/franco ricciardi/virgilio carbonari/carlo forti
verdi la traviata
cd: arkadia CDKAR 230/gala GL 100 506

299a/27-30 december 1964/dg sessions in berlin
jesus-christus-kirche
berliner philharmoniker/*producers otto gerdes
and otto ernst wohlert*
berlioz symphonie fantastique
lp: LPM 18 964/SLPM 138 964/2535 256/2543 036/2720 111
cd: 429 5112/463 0802/479 0055

300/22-27 february 1965/dg sessions in berlin
jesus-christus-kirche
berliner philharmoniker/*michel schwalbe/
*karl-heinz zöller/*producers otto gerdes, hans weber
and otto ernst wohlert*
sibelius symphony no 5 in e flat op 82
lp: LPM 18 973/SLPM 138 973/2542 109/2543 062/2720 067/
2720 112/2740 255
cd: 415 1072/439 9822/449 4182/457 7482/479 0055
sibelius symphony no 4 in a minor op 63
lp: LPM 18 974/SLPM 138 974/2542 128/2720 067/2740 255
cd: 415 1082/439 5272/457 7482/479 0055
bach brandenburg concerto no 6 in b flat BWV 1051
lp: LPM 18 976-978/SLPM 138 976-978/LPEM 39 006/
SLPEM 139 006/2535 489/2709 016/2726 080/413 1851
cd: 431 1732/457 8892/479 0055

301/19 march 1965/decca sessions in vienna sofiensäle
wiener philharmoniker/*producer john culshaw*
tchaikovsky swan lake ballet suite; sleeping beauty ballet suite
lp: LXT 6187/SXL 6187/JB 35/417 2741/london (usa) CM 9452/
CS 6452/JL 41003
cd: 417 7002/448 0422/448 5922/455 4982/466 3792/478 0155

302/3 april 1965/concert recordings in london
royal festival hall
wiener philharmoniker
mozart symphony no 29 in a K201
this recording remains unpublished

bruckner symphony no 8 in c minor
cd: nuova era NE 2251-2252

303/9 april 1965/concert recordings in paris
theatre des champs-elysees
wiener philharmoniker
beethoven symphony no 7; josef strauss delirienwalzer
thesein-house recordings remain unpublished,
and in the case of delirienwalzer incomplete

304/april-may 1965/unitel soundtrack and film
sessions in milan
orchestra e coro del teatro alla scala/mirella freni/
adriana martino/gianni raimondi/gianni maffeo/
rolando panerai/ivo vinco/carlo badioli/franco
ricciardi/giuseppe morrresi/angelo mercuriali/carlo
forti/*film producer franco zeffirelli*
puccini la boheme
vhs video: deutsche grammophon 072 1053
laserdisc: deutsche grammophon 072 1051
dvd: deutsche grammophon 073 0279

305/16 may 1965/concert recordings in helsinki
concert hall
berliner philharmoniker
sibelius symphony no 4; symphony no 5; finlandia
these recordings remain unpublished

306/26 july 1965/stage recording in salzburg
grosses festspielhaus
wiener philharmoniker/chor der wiener staatsoper/
chor der kroatischen nationaloper/kammerchor der
salzburger festspiele/nicolai ghiaurov/sena jurinac/
olivera miljakovic/nadejna dobrianowa/marianne radev/
margarita lilowa/dimiter usunow/gerhard stolze/
eberhard waechter/nicolai ghiuselev/nicolae herlea/
anton diakov/milen paunov/aleksey maslennikov/
tugomit franc/gregor radev/zvonimir prelcec/miljenko
grozdanic/siegfried rudolf frese/paul karolidis
mussorgsky boris godunov
cd: arkadia CDKAR 210
incorrectly dated 26 july 1964

307/19-23 august 1965/dg sessions in sankt moritz
viktoriasaal
berliner philharmoniker/*lothar koch/*producers
otto gerdes, hans weber and otto ernst wohlert*
mozart symphony no 29 K201; symphony no 33 K319
lp: LPEM 39 002/SLPEM 139 002/2535 155
cd: 429 6682/429 6772/429 8002 (no 33)/429 8042 (no 33)/
435 0702 (no 33)/479 0055
mozart serenade no 13 K525 "eine kleine nachtmusik"
lp: LPEM 39 004/SLPEM 139 004/2535 259/2543 026/2720 111/
2726 528/77 199/410 8411
cd: 423 2122/423 5552/429 1702/429 8002/429 8052/479 0055
mozart divertimenti no 10 K247 and *no 11 K251
lp: LPEM 39 013/SLPEM 139 013/2726 031/419 3561
cd: 449 0492/479 0055
mozart divertimenti no 15 K287 and no 17 K334
lp: LPEM 39 004 (no 15)/LPEM 39 008 (no 17)/SLPEM 139 004
(no 15)/SLPEM 139 008 (no 17)/2726 032/2726 528 (no 15)
cd: 449 0422/479 0055

308/29 august 1965/concert recording in salzburg grosses festspielhaus

wiener philharmoniker/wiener singverein/gundula janowitz/fritz wunderlich/hermann prey/kim borg

haydn die schöpfung

cd: arkadia CDKAR 203/bel canto BEL 6013/
deutsche grammophon 474 9552/479 4640

309/12 september 1965/concert recording in epidaurus amphitheatre

berliner philharmoniker/wiener singverein/renata scotto/christa ludwig/carlo bergonzi/nicola zaccaria

verdi messa da requiem

this in-house recording remains unpublished and in poor quality sound

310/20-27 september and 4-9 november 1965/ dg sessions in berlin jesus-christus-kirche

berliner philharmoniker/*christian ferras/*producers otto gerdes, hans weber and otto ernst wohlert*

bartok concerto for orchestra

lp: LPEM 39 003/SLPEM 139 003/2535 202/2543 066/2720 112
cd: 415 3222/479 0055

beethoven fidelio overture

lp: LPEM 39 001/SLPEM 139 001/SLPEM 139 015/2530 414/
2535 310/2542 141/2707 046/2720 011/2721 137/
2726 079/419 0511
cd: 415 2762/419 0512/427 2562/429 0892/429 6772/
445 1122/479 0055

157

310/20-27 september and 4-9 november 1965/
dg sessions in berlin jesus-christus-kirche/concluded
beethoven coriolan overture
lp: LPEM 39 001/SLPEM 139 001/SLPEM 139 015/2530 414/
2542 141/2543 031/2707 046/2720 011/2720 111/
2721 137/2726 079/410 8371/415 8331
cd: 415 2762/415 8332/427 2562/429 0892/429 6772/
445 1122/479 0055

beethoven leonore no 3 overture
lp: LPEM 39 001/SLPEM 139 001/SLPEM 139 015/2530 414/
2542 141/2543 028/2707 046/2720 011/2720 111/
2721 137/2726 079/77 199/419 0491
cd: 419 0492/427 2562/429 0892/429 6772/445 1122/479 0055

sibelius the swan of tuonela
lp: LPM 18 974/LPEM 39 016/SLPM 138 974/SLPEM 139 016/
2535 261/2542 128/2543 063/2720 112/2740 255
cd: 439 9822/445 2882/457 7482/479 0055

tchaikovsky symphony no 5 in e minor op 64
lp: SKL 922-928/SLPEM 139 018/2542 108/2726 009/2740 126
cd: 445 0262/479 0055

mussorgsky-ravel pictures at an exhibition
lp: LPEM 39 010/SLPEM 139 010/2543 047/2720 112/
2726 514/2740 161
cd: 423 2142/423 5552/429 1622/447 4262/479 0055

*tchaikovsky violin concerto
lp: SKL 922-928/SLPEM 139 038/2543 051/2543 529/2720 112/
2726 506/2740 126/2740 137
cd: 423 2242/423 5552/429 1662/479 0055

311/september-october 1965/dg sessions in milan
teatro alla scala
orchestra e coro del teatro alla scala/fiorenza cossotto/
adriana martino/maria gracia allegri/carlo bergonzi/
giangiacomo guelfi/*producers otto gerdes and hans weber*
mascagni cavalleria rusticana
lp: LPEM 39 205-207/SLPEM 139 205-207/2709 020/2726 512/413 2751
cd: 419 2572/457 7642/479 4640

312/september-october 1965/dg sessions in
milan teatro alla scala
orchestra e coro del teatro alla scala/joan carlyle/carlo
bergonzi/ugo benelli/giuseppe taddei/rolando panerai/
giuseppe morresi/franco ricciardi/*producers otto gerdes
and hans weber*
leoncavallo i pagliacci
lp: LPEM 39 205-207/SLPEM 139 205-207/2709 020/413 2751
cd: 419 2572/449 7272/479 4640

313/november-december 1965/cosmotel film sessions
in vienna rosenhügel studios
wiener symphoniker/*film producer henri-georges clouzot*
schumann symphony no 4 in d minor op 120
vhs video: deutsche grammophon 072 1913
laserdisc deutsche grammophon 072 1911
dvd: euroarts 207 2118
dvd edition includes extensive rehearsal sequence

314/27-30 december 1965/dg sessions in berlin
jesus-christus-kirche
berliner philharmoniker/pierre fournier/giusto cappone/
producers otto gerdes and hans weber
strauss don quixote
lp LPEM 39 009/SLPEM 139 009/2535 195/2740 111
cd: 429 1842/457 7252/479 0055

315/january 1966/cosmotel film sessions in vienna
rosenhügel studios
wiener symphoniker/yehudi menuhin/*film producer*
henri-georges clouzot
mozart violin concerto no 5 in a K219
vhs video: deutsche grammophon 072 1913
laserdisc: deutsche grammophon 072 1911
dvd: c major 704 008
dvd edition includes rehearsal sequence and short conversation
between karajan and menuhin

316/january-february 1966/cosmotel film sessions in
berlin union studios
berliner philharmoniker/*film producer*
henri-georges clouzot
dvorak symphony no 9 in e minor op 95 "from the new world"
vhs video: deutsche grammophon 072 1823
laserdisc: deutsche grammophon 072 1821
dvd: c major 704 008
dvd edition includes introductory interview between karajan and
joachim kaiser

beethoven symphony no 5 in c minor op 67
vhs video: deutsche grammophon 072 1823
laserdisc: deutsche grammophon 072 1821
dvd: euroarts 207 2118
blu-ray: euroarts 207 2724
207 2118 includes rehearsal sequence with students and
interview between karajan and joachim kaiser

317/21-28 february 1966/dg sessions in berlin
jesus-christus-kirche

berliner philharmoniker/wiener singverein/gundula
janowitz/christa ludwig/fritz wunderlich/werner krenn/
walter berry/dietrich fischer-dieskau/*producers*
otto gerdes and hans weber

beethoven missa solemnis op 123
lp: KL 95-96/SKL 195-196/2707 030/2720 013/2721 135/
2726 048/410 5351
cd: 423 9132/453 0162/479 0055
haydn die schöpfung
lp: 643 515-516/2707 044/410 9511
cd: 435 0772/449 7612/479 0055
additional sessions were needed in september and november 1968
and april 1969

318/26 february 1966/concert recording in berlin
philharmonie

berliner philharmoniker/wiener singverein/gundula
janowitz/christa ludwig/fritz wunderlich/walter berry
beethoven missa solemnis op 123
cd: arkadia CDKAR 214

319/14-19 march 1966/dg sessions in
berlin jesus-christus-kirche

berliner philharmoniker/*producers otto gerdes, hans*
weber and otto ernst wohlert

bruckner symphony no 9 in d minor
lp: LPEM 39 011/SLPEM 139 011/2542 129/2543 039/2720 111
cd: 429 9042/479 0055
ravel bolero
lp: LPEM 39 010/SLPEM 139 010/2542 116/2543 047/2720 111/
2740 261/77 199/413 9831
cd: 423 2172/423 5552/427 2502/437 4042/447 4262/479 0055

320/12 april 1966/televised recordings in tokyo nhk hall
berliner philharmoniker
japanese and german national anthems; beethoven coriolan
overture; symphony no 6; symphony no 5
these video recordings remain unpublished

321/13 april 1966/concert recordings in tokyo nhk hall
berliner philharmoniker
beethoven symphony no 4; symphony no 7
these recordings remain unpublished

322/14 april 1966/concert recordings in tokyo nhk hall
berliner philharmoniker
beethoven symphony no 1; symphony no 3
these recordings remain unpublished

323/15 april 1966/concert recordings in tokyo nhk hall
berliner philharmoniker
beethoven leonore no 3 overture; symphony no 2; symphony no 8
these recordings remain unpublished

324/16 april 1966/concert recording in tokyo nhk hall
berliner philharmoniker/nhk chorus/gundula janowitz/
nagano/john van kesteren/martti talvela
beethoven symphony no 9
this recording remains unpublished

325/19 april 1966/concert recording in sapporo
berliner philharmoniker
brahms symphony no 2
this recording remains unpublished

326/21 april 1966/televised recording in osaka/
berliner philharmoniker
beethoven coriolan overture
dvd nhk: included with the cd-set NSDX 12264

327/22 april 1966/concert recordings in osaka
symphony hall
berliner philharmoniker
webern six pieces; strauss don juan; brahms symphony no 1
these recordings remain unpublished

328/24 april 1966/concert recordings in yokohama
berliner philharmoniker
dvorak symphony no 8; debussy prelude a l'après-midi
d'un faune; la mer
these recordings remain unpublished

329/28 april 1966/concert recordings in fukuoka
berliner philharmoniker
schubert symphony no 8; dvorak symphony no 9
these recordings remain unpublished

330/29 april 1966/concert recordings in hiroshima
berliner philharmoniker
bach brandenburg concerto no 6; brahms haydn variations
these recordings remain unpublished

331/2 may 1966/concert recording in tokyo nhk hall
berliner philharmoniker
bruckner symphony no 8
this recording remains unpublished

332/3 may 1966/concert recordings in tokyo nhk hall
berliner philharmoniker
mozart divertimento no 15; strauss ein heldenleben
these recordings remain unpublished

333/16 june 1966/concert recording in amsterdam concertgebouw
berliner philharmoniker
brucknersymphony no 8 in c minor
this recording remains unpublished

334/27 july 1966/stage recording in salzburg
grosses festspielhaus
wiener philharmoniker/chor der wiener staatsoper/
grace bumbry/mirella freni/jon vickers/justino diaz/
nadine sautereau/jane berbie/milen paunov/gerard
dunan/anton diakov/roger soyer
bizet carmen
cd: frequenz CBJ 3/omega opera archive OOA 1304

335/13 august 1966/stage recording in salzburg
grosses festspielhaus
wiener philharmoniker/chor der wiener staatsoper/
chor der kroatischen nationaloper/kammerchor und
kinderchor der salzburger festspiele/nicolai ghiaurov/
sena jurinac/gertrude jahn/nadejna dobrianowa/
marianne radev/margarita lilowa/aleksey maslennikow/
gerhard stolze/sabin markov/kim borg/zoltan kelemen/
anton diakov/milen paunov/zvonimir prelcec/miljenco
grozdanic/siegfried rudolf frese/paul karolidis/
tugomir franc/gregor radev
mussorgsky boris godunov
cd: nuova era NE 6351-6353

336/17-23 august 1966/dg sessions in sankt moritz
viktoriasaal

berliner philharmoniker/christian ferras/michel
schwalbe/thomas brandis/emil maas/hanns-joachim
westphal/ottomar borwitzky/karl scheit/friedrich
fischer/fritz helmis/horst göbel/edith picht-axenfeld/
herbert von karajan/*producers otto gerdes and
hans weber*

handel concerti grossi op 6: no 5 in d; no 10 in d minor;
no 12 in b minor
lp: LPEM 39 012/SLPEM 139 012/2543 021 (no 5)/2720 111 (no 5)/
2726 069/2726 520 (nos 5 and 12)/77 199 (no 5)
cd: 435 0412/479 0055

handel concerti grossi op 6: no 1 in g: no 8 in c minor; no 11 in a
lp: 139 042/2535 260 (no 8)/2726 068
cd: 435 0412/479 0055

bach violin concerti BWV 1041 and BWV 1042;
double violin concerto BWV 1043
cd: 445 1952 (BWV 1041 and BWV 1042)/479 0055

337/28 august 1966/concert recordings in salzburg
grosses festspielhaus
wiener philharmoniker
beethoven symphony no 1 in c op 21
cd: andante 2060

bruckner symphony no 7 in e
cd: private edition Italy

338/25 august, september and 30 december 1966/
dg sessions in berlin jesus-christus-kirche
berliner philharmoniker/regine crespin/gundula
janowitz/josephine veasey/jon vickers/thomas
stewart/martti talvela/liselotte rebmann/carlotta
ordassy/ingrid steger/lili brockhaus/daniza mastilovic/
barbro ericson/cvetka ahlin/helga jenckel/*producers
otto gerdes and hans weber*
wagner die walküre
lp: LPEM 39 229-233/SLPEM 139 229-233/2713 002/2720 051/
2740 146/2740 240
cd: 415 1452/435 2112/457 7852/457 7902/479 4640

339/6-15 october 1966/dg sessions in berlin
jesus-christus-kirche
berliner philharmoniker/*don cossack choir/
producers otto gerdes and hans weber
tchaikovsky symphony no 4 in f minor op 36
lp: SKL 922-928/139 017/2535 340/2721 051/2725 005/
2740 126/413 4841
cd: 445 1952/479 0055

tchaikovsky serenade for strings
lp: SKL 922-928/139 030/2543 052/2720 112/2740 126/410 8551
cd: 415 8552/479 0055

tchaikovsky casse noisette: ballet suite
lp: SKL 922-928/139 030/2725 105/2726 509/2740 126/419 4811
cd: 419 1752/423 2252/423 5552/479 0055
additional session for this recording was held on 26 december 1966

339/6-15 october 1966/dg sessions in berlin
jesus-christus-kirche/concluded
tchaikovsky capriccio italien
lp: SKL 922-928/139 028/2543 529
cd: 419 1782/419 8722/423 2252/423 5552/427 2222/
445 0262/463 6142/479 0055

tchaikovsky marche slave
lp: SKL 922-928/139 029/2543 052/2543 532/2720 112/
2721 198/2740 126/419 0661
cd: 419 0662/419 1762/423 2252/423 5552/479 0055

tchaikovsky romeo and juliet fantasy overture
lp: SKL 922-928/139 029/2543 532/2725 105/2726 509/
2740 126/419 4811
cd: 423 2232/423 5552/479 0055

*tchaikovsky ouverture solennelle "1812"
lp: SKL 922-928/139 029/2538 142/2543 052/2543 532/
2720 112/2726 514/2740 126/643 212/415 8551
cd: 415 8552/419 1772/423 2252/423 5552/427 2222/
463 6142/479 0055
*additional session for this recording was held on
29 december 1966*

340/28 november-1 december 1966/dg sessions
in berlin jesus-christus-kirche
berliner philharmoniker/*christoph eschenbach/
producers otto gerdes and hans weber
shostakovich symphony no 10
lp: 139 020
cd: 429 7162/479 0055

*beethoven piano concerto no 1 in c op 15
lp: 139 023/2535 273/2543 031/2720 111/410 8371
cd: 435 0962/479 0055/philips 456 7632

341/28-29 december 1966/dg sessions in berlin
jesus-christus-kirche
berliner philharmoniker/_producers otto gerdes and_
hans weber
johann strauss die fledermaus overture
lp: 139 014/2535 310/2543 533/2563 414/2726 507/
2725 525/77 199
cd: 423 8262/479 0055

johann strauss der zigeunerbaron overture
lp: 139 014/2543 533/2726 507/2726 525
cd: 413 4322/445 2892/470 0055

johann strauss an der schönen blauen donau
lp: 139 014/2538 095/2542 143/2543 040/2720 111/
2726 507/415 8521
cd: 423 2212/423 5552/423 8262/431 6412/437 2552/
447 3372/479 0055

johann strauss kaiserwalzer
lp: 139 014/2543 040/2720 111/2726 507/77 199/415 8521
cd: 423 2212/423 5552/423 8262/431 6412/437 2552/
447 3372/479 0055

johann strauss annen polka; tritsch-tratsch polka
lp: 139 014/2542 143/2563 414 (annen)/2726 507/
415 8321 (annen)
cd: 423 2212/423 5552/423 8262/431 6412/
437 2552/479 0055

johann strauss perpetuum mobile
lp: 139 014/2726 507/77 199
cd: 423 2212/423 5552/423 8262/431 6412/
437 2552/479 0055

341/28-29 december 1966/dg sessions in berlin
jesus-christus-kirche/concluded

josef strauss delirienwalzer
lp: 139 014/2726 507
cd: 423 2212/423 5552/431 6412/437 2552/479 0055

Johann strauss father radetzky march
lp: 139 014/2726 507/77 199/415 8521
cd: 423 8262/429 0742/431 6412/439 3462/479 005

342/1967/cosmotel film sessions in berlin
berliner philharmoniker/karlheinz zöller/
film producer francois reichenbach
bach brandenburg concerto no 3; orchestral suite no 2;
mozart divertimento no 17 K334
these video recordings remain unpublished

343/14-15 january 1967/unitel film sessions in milan
teatro alla scala
orchestra e coro del teatro alla scala/leontyne price/
fiorenza cossotto/ luciano pavarotti/nicolai ghiaurov/
film producer henri-georges clouzot
verdi messa da requiem
cd: melodram MEL 28012/curcio CON 31
vhs video: deutsche grammophon 072 1423
laserdisc: deutsche grammophon 072 1421
dvd: deutsche grammophon 073 0229

344/25-31 january 1967/dg sessions in berlin
jesus-christus-kirche
berliner philharmoniker/*christian ferras/*producers otto gerdes and hans weber*
*beethoven violin concerto in d op 61
lp: 139 021/2726 521/2740 137/419 0521
cd: 437 6442/479 0055

rimsky-korsakov scheherazade
lp: 139 022/2543 036/2720 112/419 0631
cd: 419 0632/463 6142/479 0055

sibelius valse triste
lp: LPEM 39 016/SLPEM 139 016/2538 095/2542 109/
2543 062/2720 112/2740 255/410 9811
cd: 423 2082/423 5552/439 5272/445 2882/449 4182/479 0055

345/19 march 1967/stage recording in salzburg grosses
festspielhaus
berliner philharmoniker/regine crespin/gundula
janowitz/christa ludwig/jon vickers/thomas stewart/
martti talvelva/liselotte rebmann/carlotta ordassy/
ingrid steger/lilo brockhaus/gerda scheyrer/barbro
ericson/cvetka ahlin/helga jenckel
wagner die walküre
cd: memories HR 4107-4121/HR 4107-4110/arkadia CDKAR 223/
private edition vienna
rehearsal sequences were filmed for a documentary by francois reichenbach

346/20 march 1967/concert recordings in salzburg
grosses festspielhaus
berliner philharmoniker/*christian ferras
bach brandenburg concerto no 1; brandenburg concerto no 3
cd: arkadia CDKAR 212

*bach violin concerto BWV 1042
cd: arkadia CDKAR 211

bach orchestral suite no 2
this recording remains unpublished

347/21 march 1967/concert recording in salzburg
grosses festspielhaus
berliner philharmoniker
bruckner symphony no 8 in c minor
cd: arkadia CD 705

348/27 march 1967/stage recording in salzburg grosses
festspielhaus
berliner philharmoniker/nadezna kniplova/gundula
janowitz/christa ludwig/ticho parly/walter berry/martti
talvela/liselotte rebmann/carlotta ordassy/Ingrid steger/
lilo brockhaus/gerda scheyrer/barbro ericson/cvetka
ahlin/helga jenckel
wagner die walküre
cd: private edition vienna

349/april 1967/unitel film sessions in berlin philharmonie
berliner philharmoniker/alexis weissenberg/
film producer ake falck
tchaikovsky piano concerto no 1 in b flat minor op 23
vhs video: deutsche grammophon 072 1413
laserdisc: deutsche grammophon 072 1411

350/14-18 april 1967/dg sessions in berlin
jesus-christus-kirche
berliner philharmoniker/*producers otto gerdes
and hans weber*
sibelius symphony no 6 in d minor op 104
lp: 139 032/2542 137/2720 067/2740 255
cd: 415 1082/439 9822/457 7482/479 0055

smetana ma vlast: the moldau; vysherad
lp: 139 037/2543 037/2543 509 (moldau)/2720 111/
2726 516 (moldau)
cd: 423 2202/423 5552/427 8082 (moldau)/447 4152/
479 0055

liszt les preludes; hungarian rhapsody no 2 in d minor
lp: 139 037/2535 253 (rhapsody)/2543 037/2720 111/
2726 517/643 212/415 6281
cd: 415 9672/419 7352 (rhapsody)/423 2202/423 5552/
427 2222 (preludes)/427 8082 (preludes)/447 4152 (preludes)/
449 7272 (rhapsody)/453 1302 (preludes)/479 0055

351/14-15 may 1967/concert recordings in
florence teatro communale
berliner philharmoniker
bach brandenburg concerto no 3; brahms haydn variations;
beethoven symphony no 4; strauss ein heldenleben
cd: nuova era NE 2282-2283

beethoven symphony no 5
this recording remains unpublished

352/20 may 1967/televised recordings in rome auditorium pio

orchestra sinfonica di roma della rai/coro della rai di roma e di milano/helen donath/tatiana troyanos/ werner krenn/franz crass

mozart coronation mass; verdi te deum

these video recordings remain unpublished

353/june 1967/unitel soundtrack recording in vienna sofiensäle

wiener philharmoniker/chor der wiener staatsoper/ grace bumbry/mirella freni/olivera miljakovic/julia hamari/jon vickers/justino diaz/robert kerns/anton diakov/kurt equiluz/milen paunov

bizet carmen

see session no. 355 below for film sessions for this recording

354/29 july 1967/stage recording in salzburg grosses festspielhaus

wiener philharmoniker/chor der wiener staatsoper/ kammerchor und kinderchor der salzburger festspiele/ grace bumbry/mirella freni/olivera miljakovic/julia hamari/jon vickers/john van kesteren/milen paunov/ anton diakov/robert kerns

bizet carmen

cd: arkadia CDKAR 221/omega opera archive OOA 1306

355/august 1967/unitel film sessions in munich bavaria studios

bizet carmen

vhs video: philips 070 4403

laserdisc: philips 070 4401

dvd: deutsche grammophon 073 4032

soundtrack recording for this film was made in june 1967 (session no. 353 above)

356/16 august 1967/concert recording in salzburg
grosses festspielhaus/jörg demus/christoph
eschenbach/herbert von karajan
cleveland orchestra
mozart concerto for three pianos K242
cd: private edition vienna

prokofiev symphony no 5 in b flat
this recording remains unpublished

357/19-22 august 1967/dg sessions in sankt moritz
viktoriasaal
berliner philharmoniker/leon spierer/emil maas/
ottomar borwitzky/edith picht-axenfeld/horst göbel/
producers otto gerdes and hans weber
handel concerti grossi op 6: no 2 in f; no 4 in a minor; no 6 in g
lp: 139 035/2535 269 (no 4)/2543 021 (nos 4 and 6)/
2720 111 (nos 4 and 6)/2726 068
cd: 435 0412/479 0055

handel concerti grossi op 6: no 3 in e minor; no 7 in b major;
no 9 in f
lp: 139 036/2535 269 (nos 3 and 9)/2543 021 (nos 3 and 9)/
2720 111 (nos 3 and 9)/2726 069
cd: 435 0412/477 0055

358/3 september 1967/concert recordings in
edinburgh usher hall
berliner philharmoniker
mozart divertimento no 15 K287
this recording remains unpublished

tchaikovsky symphony no 4
cd: private edition vienna

359/5 september 1967/concert recordings in
edinburgh usher hall
berliner philharmoniker/scottish festival chorus/helen
donath/josephine veasey/robert tear/gerard souzay
bach magnificat; brahms symphony no 1
these recordings remain unpublished

360/18-25 september 1967/dg sessions in berlin
jesus-christus-kirche
berliner philharmoniker/*geza anda/*producers otto
gerdes and hans weber*
*brahms piano concerto no 2 in b flat op 83
lp: 139 034/2535 263/2543 044/2720 112/410 9771
cd: 431 1622/479 0055

sibelius symphony no 7
lp: 139 032/2542 137/2720 067/2740 255
cd: 415 1072/439 5272/457 7482/479 0055

verdi la traviata: act three prelude; puccini manon lescaut
intermezzo; schmidt notre dame intermezzo; massenet
thais: meditation; giordano fedora intermezzo; cilea adriana
lecouvreur intermezzo; puccini sour angelica intermezzo;
wolf-ferrari gioelli della madonna intermezzo; mascagni
amico fritz intermezzo; mussorgsky khovantschina intermezzo;
mascagni cavalleria rusticana intermezzo; leoncavallo pagliacci
intermezzo
lp: 139 031/2726 512/415 8561
cd: 415 8562/419 2572/479 0055

361/24 september 1967/concert recordings in
berlin philharmonie
berliner philharmoniker
bach brandenburg concerto no 5; shostakovich symphony no 10
these recordings remain unpublished

362/october 1967/unitel film sessions in berlin ccc-film
studios and philharmonie/*film producer hugo niebeling*
berliner philharmoniker
beethoven symphony no 6 in f op 68 "pastoral"
vhs video: deutsche grammophon 072 1303
laserdisc: deutsche grammophon 072 1301
dvd: deutsche grammophon 073 4102/073 4107

363/21 november 1967/stage recording in new york
metropolitan opera house
metropolitan opera orchestra/birgit nilsson/gundula
janowitz/christa ludwig/jon vickers/thomas stewart/
karl ridderbusch/phyllis brill/joann grillo/clarice carson/
carlotta ordassy/rosalind hupp/louise pearl/gwendolyn
killebrew
wagner die walküre
cd: omega opera archive OOA 4725

364/6-28 december 1967/dg sessions in berlin
jesus-christus-kirche
berliner philharmoniker/josephine veasey/oralia
dominguez/simone mangelsdorff/helen donath/edda
moser/anna reynolds/dietrich fischer-dieskau/robert
kerns/donald grobe/gerhard stolze/erwin wohlfahrt/
zoltan kelemen/martti talvela/karl ridderbusch/
producers otto gerdes and hans weber
wagner das rheingold
lp: SKL 104 966-968/2709 023/2720 051/2740 145/2740 240
cd: 415 2562/429 1682/439 4232/437 6892/459 0312/
459 0692/479 4640

365/1 january 1968/televised concert in berlin philharmonie

berliner philharmoniker/chor der deutschen oper/ gundula janowitz/christa ludwig/jess thomas/ walter berry

beethoven symphony no 9 in d minor op 125 "choral"
cd: claque GM 1003/curcio CONB 1
dvd: deutsche grammophon 072 4103/072 4107

365a/6 january 1968/concert recording in berlin philharmonie
berliner philharmoniker
wagner tristan und isolde: prelude
cd: arkadia CDKAR 204/CD 739
this recording is incorrectly dated salzburg 1966

366/29 january 1968/concert recording in berlin philharmonie
berliner philharmoniker
penderecki polymorphia per 18 strumenti
cd: foyer 1CF-2038

367/7 april 1968/stage recording in salzburg grosses festspielhaus
berliner philharmoniker/josephine veasey/oralia dominguez/simone mangelsdorff/helen donath/edda moser/anna reynolds/dietrich fischer-dieskau/robert kerns/donald grobe/gerhard stolze/erwin wohlfahrt/ zoltan kelemen/karl ridderbusch/martti talvela
wagner das rheingold
cd: memories HR 4107-4121/HR 4111-4113/arkadia CDKAR 223

368/8 april 1968/concert recordings in salzburg
grosses festspielhaus
berliner philharmoniker
beethoven coriolan overture
cd: nuova era NE 2235/NE 2399-2404/arkadia CDKAR 224/
CDKAR 222/ curcio CONB 4/natise HVK 101

beethoven symphony no 7 in a op 92
cd: nuova era NE 2235/CONB 4

369/11 april 1968/concert recording in salzburg
grosses festspielhaus
berliner philharmoniker/wiener singverein/gundula
janowitz/dietrich fischer-dieskau
brahms ein deutsches requiem
this recording remains unpublished

370/11 june 1968/stage recording in milan
teatro alla scala
orchestra e coro del teatro alla scala/fiorenza cossotto/
anna di stasio/adriana martino/gianfranco cecchele/
giangiacomo guelfi
mascagni cavalleria rusticana
cd: frequenz 011.044

371/june 1968/unitel soundtrack and film sessions
in milan
orchestra e coro del teatro alla scala/fiorenza cossotto/
anna di stasio/adriana martino/gianfranco cecchele/
giangiacomo guelfi/*film producer ake falck*
mascagni cavalleria rusticana
vhs video: decca 071 4303
laserdisc: decca 071 4301
dvd: deutsche grammophon 073 4389

372/june 1968/unitel soundtrack and film sessions
in milan

orchestra e coro del teatro alla scala/raina kabaiwanska/
jon vickers/peter glossop/sergio lorenzi/rolando panerai/
carlo ricciardi/carlo moresi

leoncavallo i pagliacci
vhs video: decca 071 4303
laserdisc: decca 071 4301
dvd: deutsche grammophon 073 4389

373/26 july 1968/stage recording in salzburg grosses
festspielhaus

wiener philharmoniker/chor der wiener staatsoper/
gundula janowitz/teresa zylis-gara/mirella freni/
alfredo kraus/nicolai ghiaurov/geraint evans/rolando
panerai/martti talvela

mozart don giovanni
lp: great opera performances GOP 53
cd: paragon PCD 84009-84011/nuova era NE 2330-2332

374/14-15 august 1968/concert recordings in salzburg
mozarteum

berliner philharmoniker

bach the six brandenburg concerti BWV 1046-1051
cd: nuova era NE 2312-2313

375/17-22 august 1968/dg sessions in sankt moritz viktoriasaal

berliner philharmoniker/*gerd seifert/*producers otto gerdes and hans weber*

*mozart the four horn concerti K412, K417, K447 and K495
lp: 139 038/2543 025/2720 111/2726 522 (K412 and K495)/
419 0571
cd: 419 0572/429 8002/429 8172/479 0055

rossini string sonatas nos 1, 2, 3 and 6
lp: 139 041/2535 187
cd: 429 5252/457 9142/479 0055

mozart serenata notturna K239; the three string
divertimenti K136-K138
lp: 139 033/2535 253 (K239)/2535 259/2543 026/2720 111/
2726 031/2726 528/410 8411/419 3561
cd: 423 2122/423 5552/429 8002/429 8052/479 0055

376/25 august 1968/concert recordings in salzburg grosses festspielhaus

wiener philharmoniker

schubert symphony no 8 in b minor D759 "unfinished"
cd: deutsche grammophon 439 1042/andante 2060

johann strauss der zigeunerbaron overture; kaiserwalzer;
annen polka; perpetuum mobile; an der schönen blauen
donau; johann strauss father radetzky march; josef strauss
delirienwalzer
cd: deutsche grammophon 439 1042

377/12-24 september 1968/dg sessions in berlin
jesus-christus-kirche
berliner philharmoniker/*mstislav rostropovich/
producers otto gerdes and hans weber
*dvorak cello concerto in b minor op 104
lp: 139 044/2543 054/2720 112/2726 519/2740 262/
supraphon 110 1396
cd: 413 8192/447 4132/479 0055

*tchaikovsky rococo variations for cello and orchestra
lp: 139 044/2543 054/2720 112/2726 506/2740 262
cd: 413 8192/431 6062/447 4132/479 0055

prokofiev symphony no 5 in b flat op 100
lp: 139 040/410 9921
cd: 423 2162/423 5552/437 2532/463 6132/479 0055

schubert symphony no 9 in c D944 "great"
lp: 139 043/2535 290/2543 033/2720 111/419 9801
cd: 423 2192/423 5552/460 1082/479 0055

378/8 november 1968/stage recording in new york
metropolitan opera house
metropolitan opera orhestra/regine crespin/
hildegard hillebrecht/christa ludwig/jon vickers/
thomas stewart/martti talvela/judith de paul/
joann grillo/phyllis brill/carlotta ordassy/shirley
love/louise pearl/marcia baldwin/gwendolyn
killebrew
wagner die walküre
cd: opera lovers WAL 196 803

379/2-12 december 1968 and 3 march 1969/
dg sessions in berlin jesus-christus-kirche
berliner philharmoniker/helga dernesch/oralia
dominguez/catherine gayer/jess thomas/gerhard
stolze/thomas stewart/zoltan kelemen/karl
ridderbusch/*producers otto gerdes and hans weber*
wagner siegfried
lp: 643 536-540/2713 003/2720 051/2740 147/2740 240
cd: 415 1502/435 2112/457 7902/459 0692/479 4640

380/3-6 january 1969/dg sessions in berlin
jesus-christus-kirche
berliner philharmoniker/*gundula janowitz/
*ernst schellow/*producers otto gerdes and hans weber*
beethoven wellingtons sieg
lp: 139 045/643 210/2530 212/2535 125/2538 142/
2538 212/413 2651
cd: 419 6242/447 9122/479 0055

*beethoven egmont: overture and incidental music
lp: 2530 301/2720 011/2721 137
cd: 419 6242/447 9122/479 0055

beethoven die ruinen von athen overture
lp: 2530 414/2542 141/2707 046/2721 011/2721 137/
2726 079/419 8331
cd: 419 0332/427 2562/429 0892/429 6772/445 1122/
447 9072/479 0055

beethoven die geschöpfe des prometheus overture
lp: 2707 046/2720 011/2721 137/2726 079/419 8331
cd: 419 8332/427 2562/429 0892/429 6772/445 1122/479 0055

182

380/3-6 january 1969/dg sessions in berlin
jesus-christus-kirche/concluded
beethoven leonore no 1 overture; leonore no 2 overture
lp: 2707 046/2720 011/2721 137/2726 079
cd: 415 1122 (no 1)/427 2562/479 0055

beethoven könig stephan overture; namensfeier overture;
die weihe des hauses overture
lp: 2707 046/2720 011/2721 137/2726 079
cd: 427 2562/437 6442/445 1122 (weihe)/
447 9572 (könig stephan)/479 0055

381/2 february 1969/concert recording in berlin
philharmonie
berliner philharmoniker
tchaikovsky symphony no 5 in e minor op 64
cd: nuova era NE 2399-2404/natise HVK 103

schoenberg orchestral variations
cd: arkadia CD 587

382/22 february 1969/stage recording in new york
metropolitan opera house
metropolitan opera orchestra/anna reynolds/
lili chookasian/simone mangelsdorff/shirley love/
edda moser/liselotte rebmann/gerhard stolze/
donald grobe/andrea veils/theo adam/sherill milnes/
zoltan kelemen/martti talvela/karl ridderbusch
wagner das rheingold
cd: omega opera archive OOA 3169/private edition vienna

383/1 march 1969/stage recording in new york
metropolitan opera house
metropolitan opera orchestra/birgit nilsson/regine
crespin/josephine veasey/jon vickers/theo adam/
martti talvela/judith de paul/joann grillo/phyllis brill/
carlotta ordassy/shirley love/louise pearl/marcia
baldwin/gwendolyn killebrew
wagner die walküre
cd: nuova era NE 2405-2408/arkadia CDKAR 217/omega opera
archive OOA 3045

384/30 march 1969/stage recording in salzburg
grosses festspielhaus
berliner philharmoniker/helga dernesch/oralia
dominguez/reri grist/jess thomas/gerhard stolze/
thomas stewart/zoltan kelemen/karl ridderbusch
wagner siegfried
cd: memories HR 4107-4121/HR 4114-4117/arkadia
CDKAR 223/private edition vienna

385/31 march 1969/concert recordings in salzburg
grosses festspielhaus
berliner philharmoniker
mozart divertimento no 17 K334; bruckner symphony no 7
these recordings remain unpublished

386/28-29 april 1969/dg sessions in berlin

jesus-christus-kirche

berliner philharmoniker/*producers otto gerdes and*
hans weber

johann strauss leichtes blut; postillon d'amour; josef strauss
sphärenklänge
cd: 449 7682/479 0055

johann strauss persischer marsch; johann and josef strauss
pizzicato polka
lp: 2530 027/2726 507/415 8521
cd: 423 2212 (pizzicato)/423 5552 (pizzicato)/431 6412 (pizzicato)/
437 2552 (pizzicato)/449 7682/470 0055

johann strauss g'schichten aus dem wienerwald; wiener blut
lp: 2530 027/2535 253 (wiener blut)/2543 142/2543 040/
2720 111/2721 198 (g'schichten)/2726 507/415 8521
lp: 413 4322 (wiener blut)/423 2212/423 5552/423 8262
(wiener blut)/431 6412/437 2552/445 1202 (wiener blut)/
447 3372 (wiener blut)/449 7682/479 0055

johann strauss morgenblätter waltz
lp: 2530 027/2543 040/2720 111/2726 507
cd: 413 4322/423 8262/445 2882/449 7682/479 0055

johann strauss auf der jagd; aegyptischer marsch
lp: 2530 027/2563 414/2726 507 (marsch)
cd: 413 4322/423 2212 (auf der jagd)/423 5552 (auf der jagd)/
423 8262/431 8412 (auf der jagd)/437 2552 (auf der jagd)/
449 7682/479 0055

johann strauss unter donner und blitz
lp: 2530 027/2542 143/2563 414/2726 507/415 8521
cd: 423 2212/423 5552/423 8262/431 6412/437 2552/
449 7682/479 0055

387/28 may 1969/concert recordings in moscow
great hall of the conservatory
berliner philharmoniker
beethoven coriolan overture; symphony no 5 in c minor op 67
cd: melodiya MELCD 10 01512

beethoven symphony no 6 in f op 68 "pastoral"
lp: melodiya C10 27621 004
cd: melodiya MELCD 10 01512

388/29 may 1969/concert recordings in moscow
great hall of the conservatory
berliner philharmoniker
bach brandenburg concerto no 1 BWV 1046
lp: melodiya C10 27621 004
cd: melodiya MELCD 10 01513

shostakovich symphony no 10 in e minor op 93
lp: melodiya C10 21277 009
cd: melodiya MELCD 10 01513

389/30 may 1969/concert recordings in moscow
great hall of the conservatory
berliner philharmoniker
mozart divertimento no 17 K334
cd: melodiya MELCD 10 01514

strauss ein heldenleben
lp: melodiya C10 21473 000
cd: jupiter (italy) 2111 9205/melodiya MELCD 10 01514

390/4 june 1969/concert recording in london
royal festival hall
berliner philharmoniker/christoph eschenbach/
justus frantz/herbert von karajan
mozart concerto for three pianos K242
cd: curcio CON 18

prokofiev symphony no 5
this recording remains unpublished

391/6 june 1969/concert recording in london
royal festival hall
berliner philharmoniker
bruckner symphony no 7 in e
cd: arkadia CD 721

392/1 august 1969/stage recording in salzburg
grosses festspielhaus
wiener philharmoniker/chor der wiener staatsoper/
gundula janowitz/teresa zylis-gara/mirella freni/
alfredo kraus/nicolai ghiaurov/geraint evans/
rolando panerai/victor von halem
mozart don giovanni
cd: memories HR 4362-4364/arcadia CDKAR 202/
nuova era NE 2330-2332

393/5-7 august 1969/dg sessions in sankt moritz
französische kirche
berliner philharmoniker/_producers otto gerdes and_
hans weber
mozart adagio and fugue in c minor K546
lp: 2530 066
cd: 449 5152/463 2912/479 0055

albinoni-giazotto adagio; pachelbel-seiffert canon and fugue in d
lp: 2530 247/415 2011/419 0461/419 4881
cd: 415 2012 (albinoni)/419 0462/417 0492 (pachelbel)/479 0055

boccherini quintettino "la ritrata di madrid"; respighi antiche
danze ed arie: third suite
lp: 2530 247
cd: 413 8222 (respighi)/449 7242/457 9142 (boccherini)/479 0055

394/8-24 august 1969/dg sessions in sankt moritz
französische kirche
berliner philharmoniker/_producers otto gerdes and_
hans weber
beethoven-weingartner grosse fuge
lp: 2530 066
cd: belart 450 1082/deutsche grammophon 479 0055

honegger symphony no 2
lp: 2530 068/2535 805
cd: 423 2422/447 4352/479 0055

strauss metamorphosen
lp: 2530 066/2740 111
cd: 423 8882/447 4222/479 0055

stravinsky concerto in d
lp: 2530 267
cd: 423 2522/447 4352/479 0055

395/22 august 1969/concert recording in sankt moritz französische kirche

berliner philharmoniker/sviatoslav richter

bach piano concerto BWV 1053

this recording remains unpublished; information about this recording came from a list of richter's concerts compiled by ates tanin

396/27 august 1969/concert recording in salzburg grosses festspielhaus

wiener philharmoniker

bruckner symphony no 5 in b flat

cd: arkadia CD 720/CDGI 720/andante 2060

397/15-17 september 1969/emi sessions in berlin jesus-christus-kirche

berliner philharmoniker/sviatoslav richter/david oistrakh/mstislav rostropovich/*producer peter andry*

beethoven triple concerto op 56

lp: ASD 2582/1C065 02042/2C069 02042/3C065 02042/ angel 36727/melodiya CM 02021-02022/supraphon SU 11 00898/eternal 826 226

cd: 476 8862/769 0322/764 7442/566 0922/566 1122/ 566 2192/566 9022/512 0382/217 4112/ warner 2564 633624

398/20-25 september 1969/dg sessions in berlin
jesus-christus-kirche
berliner philharmoniker/*lothar koch/*producers*
otto gerdes and hans weber
*strauss oboe concerto
lp: 2530 439/2543 059/2720 112
cd: 423 8882/477 9814/479 0055

honegger symphony no 3 "liturgique"
lp: 2530 068/2535 805
cd: 423 2422/447 4352/479 0055

bartok music for strings, percussion and celesta
lp: 2530 065/2542 143/2543 065/2720 112
cd: 415 3222/457 8902/479 0055

suppe overtures: banditenstreiche; die schöne galathea; leichte
kavallerie; dichter und bauer; pique dame; morgen mittag und
abend in wien
lp: 2530 051/2535 510 (leichte kavallerie)/2535 629 (pique dame)/
2543 533 (banditenstreiche, schöne galathea, leichte kavallerie
and dichter und bauer)/2721 198 (dichter und bauer)/
2726 525 (banditenstreiche, schöne galathea, leichte kavallerie
and dichter und bauer)
cd: 415 3772 (leichte kavallerie, dichter und bauer and morgen
mittag und abend in wien)/419 7352 (dichter und bauer)/
435 7122/445 2862 (banditenstreiche, schöne galathea and
pique dame)/479 0055/479 4640

399/11-23 october and 29 december 1969-6 january
1970/dg sessions in berlin jesus-christus-kirche
berliner philharmoniker/chor der deutschen oper/
helga dernesch/christa ludwig/gundula janowitz/liselotte
rebmann/edda moser/catarina ligendza/anna reynolds/
lili chookasian/helge brilioth/thomas stewart/zoltan
kelemen/karl ridderbusch/*producers otto gerdes
and hans weber*
wagner götterdämmerung
lp: 2716 051/2720 019/2720 051/2740 148/2740 240
cd: 415 1552/435 2112/457 7802/457 7952/479 4640
stravinsky symphony in c
lp: 2530 267/2543 065/2720 112
cd: 423 2522/479 0055

400/25-29 november 1969/emi sessions in paris
salle wagram
orchestre de paris/*producer michel glotz*
franck symphony in d minor
lp: ASD 2552/EG 29 08531/1C065 02034/2C069 02034/3C065 02034
cd: 769 0082/764 7472/512 0382/warner 2564 633593

401/22 january 1970/concert recordings in berlin
philharmonie
berliner philharmoniker/*chor der deutschen oper
bruckner symphony no 9 in d minor; *verdi te deum
cd: arkadia CD 722

402/february 1970/emi sessions in paris salle wagram
orchestre de paris/alexis weissenberg/*producers*
michel glotz and peter andry
tchaikovsky piano concerto no 1 in b flat minor op 23
lp: ASD 2576/1C065 02044/2C069 02044/3C065 02044/
angel 36755
cd: 769 3812/512 0382/warner 2564 622624

403/30 march 1970/stage recording in salzburg
grosses festspielhaus
berliner philharmoniker/chor der wiener staatsoper/
helga dernesch/christa ludwig/gundula janowitz/
liselotte rebmann/edda moser/catarina ligendza/
anna reynolds/lili chookasian/jess thomas/thomas
stewart/zoltan kelemen/karl ridderbusch
wagner götterdämmerung
cd: memories HR 4107-4121/HR 4118-4121/arkadia
CDKAR 223/private edition vienna

404/14 april 1970/dg session in berlin
jesus-christus-kirche
berliner philharmoniker/producers otto gerdes
and hans weber
stravinsky circus polka
lp: 2530 267
cd: 439 4632/479 0055

405/9 june 1970/concert recordings in vienna
musikvereinssaal
berliner philharmoniker
beethoven coriolan overture; symphony no 6; symphony no 7
cd: private edition vienna

406/10 june 1970/concert recordings in vienna musikvereinssaal

berliner philharmoniker

beethoven symphony no 1; symphony no 3 "eroica"

cd: private edition vienna/foyer CF 2038 (no 3)

407/11 june 1970/concert recordings in vienna musikvereinssaal

berliner philharmoniker

beethoven symphony no 4; symphony no 5

cd: private edition vienna

408/12 june 1970/concert recordings in vienna musikvereinssaal

berliner philharmoniker

beethoven symphony no 8; symphony no 2;

leonore no 3 overture

cd: private edition vienna

409/14 june 1970/concert recordings in vienna musikvereinssaal

berliner philharmoniker/wiener singverein/gundula janowitz/anna reynolds/werner hollweg/walter berry

beethoven symphony no 9 "choral"

cd: nuova era NE 2399-2404/private edition vienna

nuova era issue incorrectly dated 17 june 1970

410/25 june 1970/film sessions in paris

orchestre de paris/*film producer roger benamon*

berlioz symphonie fantastique

dvd: emi classic archive 410 1129/410 1139

blu-ray: euroarts classic archive 307 5094

411/27 july 1970/stage recording in salzburg
grosses festspielhaus
wiener philharmoniker/chor der wiener staatsoper/
gundula janowitz/teresa zylis-gara/olivera miljakovic/
stuart burrows/nicolai ghiaurov/geraint evans/
rolando panerai/victor von halem
mozart don giovanni
cd: arkadia CDKAR 231/orfeo C615 033L

412/10 august 1970/stage recording in salzburg
grosses festspielhaus
wiener philharmoniker/chor der wiener staatsoper/
kammerchor der salzburger festspiele/mirella freni/
stefania malagu/jon vickers/ryland davies/peter
glossop/luigi roni/hans wegmann/siegfried rudolf
frese/victor von halem
verdi otello
cd: foyer 2CF 2034/arkadia CDKAR 228

413/12 august 1970/concert recordings in salzburg
grosses festspielhaus
berliner philharmoniker/lothar koch/karl leister/
gerd seifert/günter piesk
mozart sinfonia concertante K297b; strauss also sprach
zarathustra
cd: arkadia CD 587 (zarathustra)/testament SBT 1474

414/19-23 august 1970/dg sessions in sankt moritz
französische kirche
berliner philharmoniker/thomas brandis/emil maas/
dietrich gerhardt/hans priem/ottomar borwitzky/
waldemar döling/wolfgang meyer/*producers*
hans hirsch and hans weber
christmas concerti: corelli concerto grosso op 6 no 6; manfredini
concerto op 3 no 12; torelli concerto a 4 op 8 no 6; locatelli
concerto grosso op 1 no 8
lp: 2530 070/2542 143/415 0271/419 0461/419 4131
cd: 415 0722/415 3012/419 0462/419 4132/427 0492/
449 9242/479 1671
not all editions contain all four items

vivaldi concerti: RV 27 "l'amoroso"; RV 169 "al santo sepolcro";
RV 234 "l'inquietudine"; RV 151 "alla rustica";
RV 129 "madrigalesco"; double concerto RV 523
lp: 2530 094/2726 513/415 0271/419 0461
cd: 419 0462/423 2262/423 5552/429 1672/459 4222/
449 8512/479 1671
not all editions contain all six items

415/26 august 1970/concert recording in salzburg
grosses festspielhaus
wiener philharmoniker/wiener singverein/
gundula janowitz/christa ludwig/carlo bergonzi/
ruggero raimondi
verdi messa da requiem
cd: doremi DHR 7716/gala GL 100 541

416/21-25 september 1970/emi sessions in berlin
jesus-christus-kirche
berliner philharmoniker/_producer michel glotz_
mozart symphony no 35 K385 "haffner"; symphony no 39 K543
lp: SLS 809/ASD 3016/EG 29 12901/1C165 02145-02148/
2C069 02145/3C065 02145/angel 36770
cd: 476 8902 (no 35)/476 8912 (no 39)/769 0122/769 8822/
566 0982/566 1132/512 0382/warner 2564 633627

mozart symphony no 38 K504 "prague";
symphony no 36 K425 "linz"
lp: SLS 809/ASD 2918/1C165 02145-02148/2C069 02146/
3C065 02146/angel 36771
cd: 476 8902 (no 36)/476 8912 (no 38)/769 8822/566 0992/
566 1132/512 0382/warner 2564 633627

mozart symphony no 40 K550; symphony no 41 K551 "Jupiter"
lp: SLS 809/ASD 2732/EG 29 12901/SXLP 30527/1C037 03722/
1C165 02145-02148/2C069 02147/3C065 02147/
2C167 54712-54714/angel 36772
cd: 476 8922/764 3272/769 0122/769 8822/566 1002/
566 1132/512 0382/warner 2564 633627

rehearsal extracts: symphony no 39 (first and second
movements); symphony no 40 (first movement);
symphony no 41 (fourth movement)
lp: SLS 809/1C165 02145-02148
cd: 566 0992 (no 39)/566 1002 (nos 40 and 41)/566 1132/
512 0382/warner 2564 633627

rehearsal extract: symphony no 41 (second movement)
cd: warner 2564 633627
incorrectly described by warner as second movement
of symphony no 40

417/25 september and 6 october 1970/emi
sessions in berlin jesus-christus-kirche
berliner philharmoniker/*producer michel glotz*
brahms tragic overture
lp: SLS 996/SEOM 18/SXLP 30506/CFP 44223/1C047 02831/
1C053 43026/1C157 02580-02581/2C167 02580-02581/
3C165 02580-02581/angel 3838
cd: 763 3212/764 5632/566 1092/512 0382/
warner 2564 633622
bruckner symphony no 4 in e flat "romantic"
lp: SLS 811/RLS 768/EG 29 05661/1C195 02189-02191/
2C167 02189-02191/3C165 02189-02191/1C065 02414/
2C069 02414/3C065 02414/F669.711-715/angel 3779
cd: 476 8872/769 0062/566 0942/CDF 3000 122/
512 0382/warner 2564 633622

418/26 september 1970/concert recording in
berlin philharmonie
berliner philharmoniker
bach brandenburg concerto no 4 BWV1049
cd: foyer 1CF-2038
stravinsky apollon musagete
this recording remains unpublished

419/12-17 october and 15 december 1970/emi
sessions in berlin jesus-christus-kirche
berliner philharmoniker/chor der deutschen oper/
helga dernesch/helen donath/jon vickers/horst
laubenthal/karl ridderbusch/jose van dam/werner
hollweg/siegfried rudolf frese/*producer michel glotz*
beethoven fidelio
lp: SLS 954/SLS 5231/EX 769 2901/1C165 02125-02127/
2C165 02125-02127/3C153 02125-02127/
2C167 43064-43065/angel 3773
cd: 769 2902/511 9732

420/19 october 1970 and 3-4 february 1971/
emi sessions in berlin jesus-christus-kirche
berliner philharmoniker/*producer michel glotz*
bruckner symphony no 7 in e
lp: SLS 811/SLS 5086/EG 29 08581/1C195 02189-02191/
2C167 02189-02191/3C165 02189-02191/
1C165 02467-02468/angel 3779
cd: 476 8882/769 9232/566 0952/512 0382/
warner 2564 633622

421/2-20 november 1970/decca sessions in
vienna sofiensäle
wiener philharmoniker/chor der wiener staatsoper/
sofia radio chorus/wiener sängerknaben/nicolai
ghiaurov/galina vishnevskaya/margarita lilowa/
olivera miljakovic/najejda dobrianova/biserka cvecic/
aleksey maslennikov/sabin markov/martti talvela/
ludovic spiess/zoltan kelemen/anton diakov/gregor
radev/leo heppe/zvonimir prelcec/paul karolidis/
siegfried rudolf frese/*producers ray minshull and
david harvey*
mussorgsky boris godunov
lp: SET 514-517/411 8621/london (usa) OSA 1439
cd: 411 8622/deutsche grammophon 479 4640

422/24 november-1 december 1970/emi-eterna sessions in dresden lukaskirche

sächsische staatskapelle dresden/chor der staatsoper dresden/rundfunkchor leipzig/helen donath/ruth hesse/rene kollo/peter schreier/theo adam/karl ridderbusch/geraint evans/kurt moll/ horst lunow/zoltan kelemen/hans joachim rotzsch/ peter bindszus/horst hiestermann/hermann christian polster/heinz reeh/siegfried vogel/*producers dieter gerhardt worm and ronald kinloch anderson*
wagner die meistersinger von nürnberg
lp: SLS 957/EX 749 6831/1C193 02174-78/1C157 02174-8/
2C165 02174-78/3C165 02174-78/angel 3776/
eterna 826 227-826 231
cd: 769 6832/567 0862/511 9732

423/14-15 december 1970/concert recording in berlin philharmonie

berliner philharmoniker/christa ludwig/horst laubenthal/ludovic spiess
mahler das lied von der erde
cd: arkadia CD 739

424/28-29 december 1970/dg sessions in berlin jesus-christus-kirche

berliner philharmoniker/daniel deffayet/*producers hans hirsch and hans weber*
bizet carmen suite; l'arlesienne suites 1 and 2
lp: 2530 128/2543 041/2720 111/413 9831 (carmen)/419 4691
cd: 431 1602/479 1671

425/29-30 december 1970 and 6-8 january 1971/
dg sessions in berlin jesus-christus-kirche
berliner philharmoniker/_producers hans hirsch_
and hans weber
borodin prince igor: dance of the polovtsian maidens and
polovtsian dances
lp: 2530 200/2721 198/419 0631
cd: 419 0632/423 2072/423 5552/479 1671

tchaikovsky evgeny onegin: polonaise and waltz
lp: 2530 200/415 8351
cd: 415 8352/419 1762/423 5552/423 2252/479 1671

verdi aida: dances of the priestesses and moorish slaves
and ballet music
lp: 2530 200/415 8561
cd: 415 8562/479 1671

verdi otello: ballet music
lp: 2530 200
cd: 457 6892/479 1671

ponchielli la gioconda: dance of the hours
lp: 2530 200/415 8561
cd: 415 8562/445 2882/459 4452/479 1671

426/2-6 january 1971/dg sessions in berlin
jesus-christus-kirche
berliner philharmoniker/*producers hans hirsch*
and hans weber
rossini overtures: la gazza ladra; la scala di seta; semiramide;
il barbiere di siviglia; italiana in algeri; guillaume tell
lp: 2530 144/2726 525/2535 253 (gazza)/2535 310 (tell)
cd: 415 3772/419 7352 (barbiere)/423 2182/423 5552/
429 1642/431 1852/439 4152/445 2862/479 1671

427/4 and 22 january and 17 february 1971/
dg sessions in berlin jesus-christus-kirche
berliner philharmoniker/michel schwalbe/
producers hans hirsch and hans weber
tchaikovsky swan lake and sleeping beauty ballet suites
lp: 2530 195/2725 105/2726 509/419 4811 (sleeping beauty)
cd: 419 1752/437 4042 (sleeping beauty)/459 4452
(sleeping beauty)/479 1671

428/4-8 january and 15 february 1971/dg sessions
in berlin jesus-christus-kirche
berliner philharmoniker/*producers hans hirsch*
and hans weber
schumann symphony no 1 in b flat op 38 "spring"
lp: 2530 169/2720 046/2720 104/2740 129/419 0651
cd: 423 2092/423 5552/429 4322/429 6922/
439 1582/447 4082/477 8005/479 1671

428/4-8 january and 15 february 1971/dg sessions
in berlin jesus-christus-kirche/concluded
schumann symphony no 3 in e flat op 97 "rhenish"
lp: 2530 447/2720 046/2720 104/2740 129
cd: 419 8702/429 6722/429 6772/477 8005/479 1671

schumann symphony no 4 in d minor op 120
lp: 2530 169/2543 034/2720 046/2720 111/2740 129/
419 9021/419 0651
cd: 429 6722/429 6772/445 7182/477 8005/479 1671

429/7-8 january 1971/dg sessions in berlin
jesus-christus-kirche
berliner philharmoniker/*producers hans hirsch and
hans weber*
mendelssohn symphony no 3 in a minor op 56 "scotch";
hebrides overture op 26
lp: 2530 126/2535 253 (overture)/2535 310 (overture)/
2720 068 (symphony)/2720 098 (symphony)/
2720 104 (symphony)/419 4771
cd: 419 4772/429 6642 (symphony)/429 6772 (symphony)/
449 7432/477 8005/479 1671

430/23 january and 15 february 1971/dg sessions
in berlin jesus-christus-kirche
berliner philharmoniker/*producers hans hirsch
and hans weber*
offenbach gaite parisienne: ballet suite arranged by rosenthal
lp: 2530 199/413 9831
cd: 423 2152/423 5552/429 1632/437 4042/
459 4152/479 1671

gounod faust: ballet music
lp: 2530 199/415 8561
cd: 437 4042/459 4452/479 1671

gounod faust: valse
lp: 2530 199/415 8561
cd: 415 8562/447 3372/479 1671

431/14 and 16 february 1971/dg sessions in berlin
jesus-christus-kirche
berliner philharmoniker/*producers hans hirsch
and hans weber*
weber overtures: beherrscher der geister; euryanthe;
abu hassan; peter schmoll
lp: 2530 201/419 0701
cd: 419 0702/479 1671

432/16-17 february 1971/dg sessions in berlin
jesus-christus-kirche
berliner philharmoniker/*producers hans hirsch
and hans weber*
weber overtures: der freischütz; oberon
lp: 2530 201/2535 315/419 0701
cd: 419 0702/479 1671

schumann symphony no 2 in c op 61
lp: 2530 170/2720 046/2720 104/2740 129
cd: 429 6722/429 6772/431 0672/477 8005/479 1671

schumann overture scherzo and finale
lp: 2530 170/2720 046/2740 129
cd: 431 1612/477 8005/479 1671

433/3 april 1971/stage recording in salzburg
grosses festspielhaus
berliner philharmoniker/chor der wiener staatsoper/
kammerchor der salzburger festspiele/helga dernesch/
edith mathis/jon vickers/donald grobe/jose van dam/
zoltan kelemen/karl ridderbusch/werner krenn/
siegfried rudolf frees
beethoven fidelio
this recording remains unpublished

434/4 april 1971/concert recordings in salzburg
grosses festspielhaus
berliner philharmoniker/alexis weissenberg
beethoven piano concerto no 4
this recording remains unpublished

strauss ein heldenleben
cd: live classic best (japan) LCB 129

435/28-29 june 1971/emi sessions in paris
salle wagram
orchestre de paris/*producer michel glotz*
ravel le tombeau de couperin; alborada del gracioso;
la valse; rapsodie espagnole
lp: ASD 2766/SXLP 30446/1C065 02214/2C069 02214/
3C065 02214/1C053 02214/angel 36869
cd: 763 5262/764 3572/512 0382/2564 633593

436/30 july 1971/stage recording in salzburg
grosses festspielhaus
wiener philharmoniker/chor der wiener staatsoper/
kammerchor der salzburger festspiele/mirella
freni/stefania malagu/jon vickers/ryland davies/
peter glossop/hans wegmann/luigi roni/siegfried
rudolf frese
verdi otello
cd: memories HR 4533-4534/private edition vienna

437/15 august 1971/concert recordings in salzburg
grosses festspielhaus
tschechische philharmonie prag/jean bernard
pommier/walter klien/Justus frantz/herbert von karajan
bach concerto for 4 pianos BWV 1065
this recording remains unpublished

dvorak symphony no 9 in e minor op 95 "from the new world"
cd: private edition vienna

438/17-24 august 1971/emi sessions in sankt moritz
französische kirche
berliner philharmoniker/karl steins/lothar koch/karl
leister/james galway/andreas blau/helmut stahr/
gerhard hauptmann/manfred braun/günter piesk/
fritz helmis/*producer michel glotz*
haydn symphony no 83 "la poule"; symphony no 101 "die uhr"
lp: ASD 2817/1C065 02298/2C069 02298/3C065 02298/
angel 36868
cd: 476 8892/769 9612/566 0972/512 0382/warner 2564 633627

mozart sinfonia concertante K297b; oboe concerto K314
lp: SLS 817/ASD 3191/1C165 02238-02240/2C069 02239/
3C065 02239/angel 3783
cd: 476 8922 (oboe)/763 6722/566 1012/512 0382/
warner 2564 633624

mozart clarinet concerto K622; bassoon concerto K191
lp: SLS 817/ASD 2916/EG 29 12841/1C165 02238-02240/
2C065 02240/3C065 02240/angel 3783
cd: 476 8912 (bassoon)/769 0142/763 4722/568 7552/
512 0382/warner 2564 633624

438/17-24 august 1971/emi sessions in sankt moritz
französische kirche/concluded
mozart flute and harp concerto K299; flute concerto K313
lp: SLS 817/ASD 2993/EG 29 03041/1C165 02238-02240/
2C069 02238/3C065 02238/angel 3783
cd: 769 1872/763 4722/568 7552/512 0382/
warner 2564 633624

439/16 and 20-21 september 1971/emi sessions in
berlin jesus-christus-kirche
berliner philharmoniker/*producer michel glotz*
tchaikovsky symphony no 4 in f minor op 36
lp: SLS 833/ASD 2814/1C195 02305-07/2C167 02305-07/
1C065 02305/3C065 02305/angel 36884
cd: 769 2532/512 0382/warner 2564 633593

tchaikovsky symphony no 5 in e minor op 64
lp: SLS 833/ASD 2815/1C195 02305-07/2C167 02305-07/
1C065 02306/3C065 02306/angel 36885
cd: 769 8832/769 2532/512 0382/warner 2564 633593

tchaikovsky symphony no 6 in b minor op 74 "pathetique"
lp: SLS 833/ASD 2816/1C195 02305-07/2C167 02305-07/
1C065 02307/3C065 02307/angel 36886
cd: 769 0432/769 8832/512 0382/warner 2564 633593

440/22-24 september 1971/dg sessions in berlin
jesus-christus-kirche
berliner philharmoniker/_producers hans hirsch_
and hans weber
grieg peer gynt: first & second suites from the incidental music
lp: 2530 243/2543 055/2720 112/410 9811/419 4741
cd: 419 4742/423 2082/423 5552/479 1671

grieg sigurd jorsalfar: three pices from the incidental music
lp: 2530 243/2543 055/2720 112
cd: 419 4742/479 1671

weber-berlioz aufforderung zum tanz
lp: 2530 244/419 0701
cd: 419 0702/447 3372/479 1671

berlioz damnation de faust: danse des sylphs & menuet des follets
lp: 2530 244/415 8561
cd: 415 8562/429 5112/463 0802/479 1671

liszt mephisto waltz no 1
lp: 2530 244/2726 517/415 6281
cd: 415 9672/419 8622/447 3372/479 1671

smetana bartered bride: polka, furiant & dance of the comedians
lp: 2530 244/2543 509/2726 516/415 8561 (polka)
cd: 415 8562 (polka)/423 2072/423 5552/479 1671

dvorak scherzo capriccioso
lp: 2530 244/2543 509
cd: 423 2202/423 5552/447 4342/479 1671

441/25 september 1971/concert recordings in
berlin philharmonie

berliner philharmoniker/*christian ferras

vivaldi concerto al santo sepolcro; stravinsky
le sacre du printemps

these recordings remain unpublished

*sibelius violin concerto in d minor op 47

cd: private edition vienna

441a/october 1971/unitel film session in paris

orchestra de paris/christoph eschenbach/justus
frantz/herbert von karajan/*film producer*

herbert von karajan

mozart concerto for 3 pianos K242

this video recording remains unpublished

442/october 1971/unitel film sessions in berlin
ccc-film studios

berliner philharmoniker/*film producer*

herbert von karajan

beethoven symphony no 3 in e flat op 55 "eroica";
symphony no 7 in a op 92

vhs: deutsche grammophon 072 1323

laserdisc: deutsche grammophon 072 1321

dvd: deutsche grammophon 073 4101 (no 3)/
073 4103 (no 7)/073 4107

443/november 1971/unitel film sessions in berlin
ccc-film studios

berliner philharmoniker/*film producer*

herbert von karajan

beethoven symphony no 2 in d op 36;
symphony no 8 in f op 93

vhs: deutsche grammophon 072 1303

laserdisc: deutsche grammophon 072 1301

dvd: deutsche grammophon 073 4101 (no 2)/
073 4103 (no 8)/073 4107

444/2-10 december 1971 and 10 january 1972/emi
sessions in berlin jesus-christus-kirche
berliner philharmoniker/helga dernesch/christa
ludwig/jon vickers/karl ridderbusch/walter berry/
peter schreier/bernd weikl/martin vantin/
producer michel glotz
wagner tristan und isolde
lp: SLS 963/EX 769 3191/1C193 02293-02297/2C165 02293-02297/
3C165 02293-02297/eternal 826 004-826 008/angel 3777
cd: 769 3192/511 9732

445/14 december 1971, 5-7 january, 24 february,
7-26 june, 1 july and 1 november 1972/dg sessions in
berlin jesus-christus-kirche
berliner philharmoniker/wiener singverein/chor der
deutschen oper/knaben des staats- und domchors/
gundula janowitz/christa ludwig/peter schreier/horst
laubenthal/dietrich fischer-dieskau/walter berry/
anton diakov/michel schwalbe/leon spierer/andreas
blau/Johannes mertens/lothar koch/helmut schlövogt/
heinrich karcher/gerhardt stempnik/gerhard koch/
ottomar borwitzky/*producers hans hirsch
and cord garben*
bach matthäus-passion BWV 244
lp: 2711 012/2720 070
cd: 419 7892/479 1671

446/december 1971/unitel film sessions in berlin
ccc-film studios
berliner philharmoniker/*film producer*
herbert von karajan
beethoven symphony no 1 in c op 21;
symphony no 4 in b flat op 60
vhs: deutsche grammophon 072 1303 (no 1)/072 1313 (no 4)
laserdisc: deutsche grammophon 072 1301 (no 1)/
072 1311 (no 4)
dvd: deutsche grammophon 073 4101 (no 1)/
073 4102 (no 4)/073 4107

447/1 january 1972/concert recordings in berlin
philharmonie
berliner philharmoniker
silvesterkonzert: rossini semiramide overture; bizet
l'arlesienne suite; sibelius valse triste; puccini manon
lescaut intermezzo; massenet thais meditation; mascagni
amico fritz intermezzo; suppe leichte kavallerie overture;
josef strauss delirienwalzer
these recordings remain unpublished

448/2, 8 and 22 january and 17 february 1972/
dg sessions in berlin jesus-christus-kirche
berliner philharmoniker/*producers hans hirsch
and hans weber*
mendelssohn symphony no 4 in a op 90 "Italian"
lp: 2530 416/2543 035/2543 511/2720 068/2720 098/
2720 104/2720 111/415 8481
cd: 423 2092/423 5552/429 1582/429 4322/429 6642/
429 6772/449 7432/477 8005/479 1671

449/3-5 january 1972/dg sessions in berlin
jesus-christus-kirche
berliner philharmoniker/wiener singverein/mirella
freni/christa ludwig/carlo cossutta/nicolai ghiaurov/
producers hans hirsch and hans weber
verdi messa da requiem
lp: 2707 065/415 2151
cd: 415 2152/453 0912/479 1671

450/9 january 1972/concert recording in berlin
philharmonie
berliner philharmoniker
schumann symphony no 2 in c op 61
this recording remains unpublished

451/14-16 february 1972/dg sessions in berlin
jesus-christus-kirche
berliner philharmoniker/elizabeth harwood/teresa
stratas/rene kollo/werner hollweg/donald grobe/
werner krenn/zoltan kelemen/karl renar/*producers*
hans hirsch and hans weber
lehar die lustige witwe
lp: 2707 070/2725 102/2726 501/410 9211
cd: 435 7122/479 4640
recording completed on 2-3 december 1972

mendelssohn symphony no 5 in d op 107 "reformation"
lp: 2530 416/2543 035/2543 511/2720 068/2720 098/2720 104
cd: 419 8702/429 6642/429 6772/477 8005/479 1671

452/17 and 27 february 1972/dg sessions in berlin
jesus-christus-kirche
berliner philharmoniker/*producers hans hirsch and*
hans weber
european anthem arranged by karajan from beethoven and
the national anthems of the 17 member states of the council
of europe: austria, belgium, cyprus, denmark, west germany,
france, iceland, ireland, italy, luxembourg, malta,
netherlands, norway, sweden, switzerland, turkey and
united kingdom
lp: 2530 250
cd: 479 1671

453/february 1972/unitel film sessions in berlin
philharmonie
berliner philharmoniker/*film producer herbert*
von karajan
beethoven symphony no 5 in c minor op 67
vhs: deutsche grammophon 072 1313
laserdisc: deutsche grammophon 072 1311
dvd: deutsche grammophon 073 4102/073 4107

454/25 march 1972/stage recording in salzburg
grosses festspielhaus
berliner philharmoniker/chor der wiener staatsoper/
helga dernesch/christa ludwig/jon vickers/karl
ridderbusch/walter berry/bernd weikl/gerhard
unger/peter schreier
wagner tristan und isolde
cd: private edition vienna

455/26 march 1972/concert recordings in salzburg
grosses festspielhaus
berliner philharmoniker
stravinsky apollon musagete; brahms symphony no 2
these recordings remain unpublished

456/27 march 1972/concert recordings in salzburg
grosses festspielhaus
berliner philharmoniker
debussy prelude a l'apres-midi d'un faune; ravel
daphnis et chloe second suite
these recordings remain unpublished

457/28 march 1972/concert recording in salzburg
grosses festspielhaus
berliner philharmoniker/wiener singverein/tölzer
sängerknaben/gundula janowitz/christa ludwig/
peter schreier/werner krenn/dietrich fischer-dieskau/
anton diakov
bach matthäus-passion BWV244
cd: private edition vienna

458/15 may 1972/concert recordings in london
royal festival hall
berliner philharmoniker
mozart divertimento no 15 K287; stravinsky sacre du printemps
cd: testament SBT 1453

459/16 may 1972/concert recordings in london
royal festival hall
berliner philharmoniker
beethoven symphony no 6; strauss ein heldenleben
cd: testament SBT 1452

460/26 july 1972/stage recording in salzburg
grosses festspielhaus
wiener philharmoniker/chor der wiener staatsoper/
elizabeth harwood/edith mathis/teresa berganza/
evelyn mandac/kerstin meyer/tom krause/walter
berry/michel senechal/paolo montarsolo/zoltan
kelemen/willy caron/gunda spiluttini
mozart le nozze di figaro
this recording remains unpublished
461/30 july 1972/concert recordings in salzburg
grosses festspielhaus
wiener philharmoniker/chor der wiener staatsoper/
edith mathis/johanna simon/horst laubenthal/
jose van dam
mozart coronation mass K317; bruckner te deum
cd: andante 2060
461a/13 august 1972/concert recordings in salzburg
grosses festspielhaus
sächsische staatskapelle dresden/geza anda
bartok piano concerto no 3. schumann symphony no 4
cd: deutsche grammophon 447 6662/as-disc NAS 2508 (bartok)
462/15-23 august 1972/dg sessions in sankt moritz
französische kirche
berliner philharmoniker/michel schwalbe/
producers hans hirsch and hans weber
vivaldi le 4 stagioni: concerti RV269, RV315, RV293 and RV297
lp: 2530 296/2543 018/2720 111/2726 513/415 2011/419 4881
cd: 415 2012/459 4222/474 2872/479 1671
479 1671 also contains additional vivaldi concerti not
conducted by karajan
stravinsky apollon musagete
lp: 2530 066/2542 134
cd: 415 9792/479 0055

463/25 august 1972/concert recording in salzburg
grosses festspielhaus
berliner philharmoniker
schoenberg verklärte nacht
cd: private edition vienna

464/27 august 1972/concert recording in salzburg
grosses festspielhaus
berliner philharmoniker/christa ludwig/rene kollo
mahler das lied von der erde
this recording remains unpublished

465/1 september 1972/concert recordings in
lucerne kunsthaus
berliner philharmoniker
mozart symphony no 39 K543
this recording remains unpublished

stravinsky le sacre du printemps
cd: private edition vienna

466/7-11 september 1972/dg sessions in berlin
jesus-christus-kirche
berliner philharmoniker/chor der deutschen oper/
edith mathis/lieselotte rebmann/werner hollweg/
producers hans hirsch and hans weber
mendelssohn symphony no 1 in c minor op 11;
symphony no 2 in b flat op 52 "lobgesang"
lp: 2707 084/2720 068/2720 098/2720 104
cd: 429 6642/429 6772/431 4712 (no 2)/477 8005/479 1671
recording of symphony no 1 completed on 1 november 1972
and recording of symphony no 2 completed on
23 february 1973

467/21-27 september 1972/emi sessions in berlin
jesus-christus-kirche

berliner philharmoniker/alexis weissenberg/
producer michel glotz

rachmaninov piano concerto no 2 in c minor; franck
variations symphoniques pour piano et orchestra
lp: ASD 2872/EG 29 08531 (franck)/1C065 02374/
2C069 02374/3C065 02374/angel 36905
cd: 769 3802/764 7472 (franck)/769 0082 (franck)/
512 0382/warner 2564 633604

467a/26 september 1972/concert recordings in
berlin philharmonie

berliner philharmoniker/alexis weissenberg

bach brandenburg concerto no 1; stravinsky symphony in c;
rachmaninov piano concerto no 2
these recordings remain unpublished

467b/27 september 1972/concert recording in
berlin philharmonie

european youth orchestra/david oistrakh

mozart violin concerto no 5 K219
lp: melodiya C10 17501-17504

468/9-13 october 1972/decca sessions in berlin
jesus-christus-kirche

berliner philharmoniker/chor der deutschen oper/
mirella freni/elizabeth harwood/luciano pavarotti/
gianni maffeo/nicolai ghiaurov/michel senechal/
hans-dietrich pohl/hans dieter applet/*producers
ray minshull and john mallinson*

puccini la boheme
lp: SET 565-566/london (usa) OSA 1299
cd: 421 0492/473 9972/deutsche grammophon 479 4640

469/15 october 1972/concert recordings in belgrade
berliner philharmoniker
mozart symphony no 29; wagner tristan prelude and liebestod;
brahms symphony no 1
these variable quality recordings remain unpublished

470/4-6 november 1972 and 8 and 26 january 1973/
dg sessions in berlin jesus-christus-kirche
berliner philharmoniker/*producers hans hirsch*
and hans weber
strauss tod und verklärung
lp: 2530 368/2740 111/410 8391
cd: 423 2222/423 5552/429 1642/479 1671

471/7 november 1972/concert recording in berlin
philharmonie
berliner philharmoniker
mendelssohn symphony no 3 "scotch"
this recording remains unpublished

472/20-25 november 1972/emi sessions in berlin
jesus-christus-kirche
berliner philharmoniker/chor der deutschen oper/
gundula janowitz/werner hollweg/walter berry/
producer michel glotz
haydn die jahreszeiten
lp: SLS 969/1C195 02383-02385/2C167 02383-02385/
3C165 02383-02385/angel 3792
cd: 769 2242/511 9732/warner 2564 633628

473/7-8 december 1972 and 8 january 1973/
dg sessions in berlin jesus-christus-kirche
berliner philharmoniker/*producers hans hirsch
and hans weber*

strauss don juan; till eulenspiegels lustige streiche;
salome: dance of the seven veils
lp: 2530 349/2543 060 (don and till)/2740 111/2740 112 (don)/
410 8391 (don and till)/415 8531 (till and salome)
cd: 415 8532 (till and salome)/423 2222/423 5552/
429 7172 (don)/447 4412/463 4962 (salome)/479 1671

474/8-9 december 1972/dg sessions in berlin
jesus-christus-kirche
berliner philharmoniker/*producers hans hirsch and
hans weber*

berg three orchestral pieces op 6
lp: 2530 487/2711 014/413 8011
cd: 427 4242/457 7602/479 1671

475/January-may 1973/unitel film sessions in berlin
philharmonie
berliner philharmoniker/*film producer
herbert von karajan*

brahms the four symphonies: no 1 in c minor op 68; no 2
in d op 73; no 3 in f op 90; no 4 in e minor op 98
cd: private edition vienna
vhs: deutsche grammophon 072 1703 (nos 1 and 2)/
072 1713 (nos 3 and 4)
laserdisc: deutsche grammophon 072 1701 (nos 1 and 2)/
072 1711 (nos 3 and 4)
dvd: deutsche grammophon 073 4386

476/4 january 1973/concert recordings in london royal albert hall
berliner philharmoniker
beethoven symphony no 4; symphony no 5
these recordings remain unpublished

477/7 january 1973/concert recordings in berlin philharmonie
berliner philharmoniker/*thomas brandis
*vivaldi le 4 stagioni; strauss sinfonia domestica
these recordings remain unpublished

478/26 january and 6 march 1973/dg sessions in berlin jesus-christus-kirche
berliner philharmoniker/*producers hans hirsch and hans weber*
strauss also sprach zarathustra
lp: 2530 402/2543 061/2720 112/2740 111/
2740 261/415 8531
cd: 415 8532/447 4412/479 1671

479/13-16 february 1972/dg sessions in berlin jesus-christus-kirche
berliner philharmoniker/*gundula janowitz/*producers hans hirsch and hans weber*
*strauss vier letzte lieder
lp: 2530 368
cd: 423 8882/439 4672/447 4222/479 1671

mahler symphony no 5 in c sharp minor
lp: 2707 081
cd: 415 0962/439 4292/447 4502/479 1671

480/2-3 and 7-8 march 1973/dg sessions in berlin
jesus-christus-kirche
berliner philharmoniker/*norbert hauptmann/
producers hans hirsch and hans weber
webern six pieces op 6
lp: 2530 488/2711 014
cd: 423 2542/427 6242/479 1671

*strauss horn concerto no 2
lp: 2530 439/2543 059/2720 112
cd: 457 7252/479 0055

prussian and austrian marches: yorckscher; torgauer;
o du mein österreich; unter dem grillenbanner; des
grossen kurfürsten reiter; pariser einzug; unter dem
doppeladler; mir sein die kaiserjäger; florentiner;
finnländische reiterei; königgrätzer; regimentskinder;
wien bleibt wien; kreuzritter-fanfare; petersburger;
fehrbelliner reiter; pappenheimer; hoch- und
deutschmeister; vindobona; hohenfriedberger; erzherzog
albrecht; tiroler holzhackerbuab'n; preussens gloria;
coburger; kärntnerlieder; die bosniaken kommen;
fridericus-rex-grenadier; alte kameraden;
zigeunerbaron-einzug; nibelungen
lp: 2721 077
cd: 439 3462/479 1671

481/16 april 1973/concert recordings in salzburg
grosses festspielhaus
berliner philharmoniker
beethoven symphony no 4; symphony no 5
these recordings remain unpublished

482/17 april 1973/stage recording in salzburg
grosses festspielhaus
berliner philharmoniker/chor der wiener staatsoper/
helga dernesch/ruza baldani/jon vickers/jef vermeersch/
karl ridderbusch/bernd weikl/gerhard unger/
peter schreier
wagner tristan und isolde
this recording remains unpublished

483/april 1973/unitel film soundtrack recording
in salzburg grosses festspielhaus
berliner philharmoniker/thomas stewart/brigitte
fassbaender/birgit finnilä/Jeannine altmeyer/edda
moser/eva randova/lieselotte rebmann/hermin esser/
gerhard stolze/peter schreier/leif roar/zoltan kelemen/
karl ridderbusch/louis hendrikx/*film producer*
herbert von karajan
wagner das rheingold
cd: private edition vienna
laserdisc: deutsche grammophon 072 4121
dvd: deutsche grammophon 073 4390
film sessions for this recording were held in
november 1978 (session no 653)

484/30 april-2 may and 22-27 may 1973/emi and
unitel film sessions in berlin philharmonie and
ccc-film studios
berliner philharmonie/chor der deutschen oper/
mirella freni/stefania malagu/jon vickers/peter
glossop/aldo bottion/michel senechal/jose van dam/
hans helm/mario macchi/*film producer*
herbert von karajan
verdi otello
lp: SLS 975/EX 769 3081/1C195 02500-02/2C167 02500-02/
3C165 02500-02/angel 3809/eterna 826 891-826 893
cd: 769 3082/511 9732
vhs: deutsche grammophon 072 4013
laserdisc: deutsche grammophon 072 4011/072 5011
dvd: deutsche grammophon 073 0069
video recording was completed in november-december 1973

485/may 1973/unitel film sessions in berlin
philharmonie
berliner philharmoniker/*film producer*
herbert von karajan
tchaikovsky symphony no 5 in e minor op 64
vhs: deutsche grammophon 072 1403
laserdisc: deutsche grammophon 072 1401
dvd: deutsche grammophon 073 4384

486/10 june 1973/concert recordings in salzburg
grosses festspielhaus
berliner philharmoniker/christoph eschenbach/
justus frantz/herbert von karajan
mozart concerto for 3 pianos K242; bruckner
symphony no 4 in e flat "romantic"
these recordings remain unpublished

487/23-25 june 1973/emi sessions in paris
salle wagram
berliner philharmoniker/*producer michel glotz*
strauss sinfonia domestica
lp: ASD 2955/1C065 02445/2C069 02445/3C065 02445/
angel 36973
cd: 476 9032/769 5712/566 1072/512 0382/
warner 2564 633622

488/16-21 july 1973/dg-wdr sessions in cologne
leverkusen-wiesdorf
sinfonie-orchester des westdeutschen rundfunks/
chor des westdeutschen rundfunks/rias-kammerchor/
tölzer sängerknaben/christa ludwig/peter schreier/
josef greindl/colette lorand/jane marsh/kay griffel/
gwendolyn killebrew/kari lövaas/anna tomowa-sintov/
helga angervö/sylvia anderson/glenys loulis/erik geisen/
hans wegmann/hans helm/wolfgang anheisser/
siegfried rudolf frese/hermann patzalt/hannes jokel/
anton diakov/boris carmeli/hartmut porche/rolf
boysen (narrator)/*producers hans hirsch and
hans weber*
orff de temporum fine comoedia
lp: 2530 432
cd: 429 8592/479 1671

489/28 july 1973/stage recording in salzburg
grosses festspielhaus
wiener philharmoniker/chor der wiener staatsoper/
elizabeth harwood/teresa stratas/teresa berganza/
jane berbie/evelyn mandac/gunda spiluttini/tom
krause/walter berry/michel senechal/paolo
montarsolo/zoltan kelemen/willy caron
mozart le nozze di figaro
cd: private edition vienna

490/30 july 1973/concert recordings in salzburg
grosses festspielhaus
wiener philharmoniker/jean bernard pommier
bach piano concerto BWV1052;   bruckner symphony no 7
these recordings remain unpublished

491/27 august 1973/concert recordings in
salzburg grosses festspielhaus
berliner philharmoniker
bach brandenburg concerto no 6;   berg three
orchestral pieces op 6
cd: private edition vienna

brahms symphony no 1 in c minor op 68
this recording remains unpublished

492/28 august 1973/concert recording in
salzburg grosses festspielhaus
berliner philharmoniker
mahler symphony no 5 in c sharp minor
cd: private edition vienna

493/8 september 1973/concert recordings in berlin philharmonie

berliner philharmoniker

tchaikovsky symphony no 5 in e minor op 64
cd: private edition vienna

mozart symphony no 41 in c K551 "jupiter"
this recording remains unpublished

494/9 september, 20 and 22 november and 6 december 1973/dg sessions in berlin philharmonie/

berliner philharmoniker/*producers hans hirsch and hans weber*

berg lyric suite
lp: 2530 487/2711 014/413 8011
cd: 423 1322/427 4242/457 7602/479 1671

495/10-11 september 1973/unitel film sessions in berlin philarmonie

berliner philharmoniker/alexis weissenberg/

film producer herbert von karajan

rachmaninov piano concerto no 2 in c minor
vhs: deutsche grammophon 072 1043
laserdisc: deutsche grammophon 072 1041
dvd: deutsche grammophon 073 4399

496/23-28 september and 23 november 1973 and
3-5 january 1974/dg sessions in berlin philharmonie
berliner philharmoniker/wiener singverein/gundula
janowitz/christa ludwig/peter schreier/robert kerns/
karl ridderbusch/*producers hans weber and michel glotz*
bach mass in b minor BWV232
lp: 2709 049/2740 112/415 0221
cd: 413 6222/439 6962/479 1671

497/26 september 1973/concert recordings in
berlin philharmonie
berliner philharmoniker
beethoven symphony no 7; johann strauss der zigeunerbaron
overture; kaiserwalzer; tritsch-tratsch polka; fledermaus
overture
these recordings remain unpublished

497a/30 september 1973/concert recording in
berlin philharmonie
berliner philharmoniker/wiener singverein/
gundula janowitz/birgit finnilä/werner hollweg/
robert kerns/jose van dam
bach mass in b minor
this recording remains unpublished

498/25 october 1973/concert recordings in
tokyo nhk hall

berliner philharmoniker

beethoven symphony no 6; symphony no 5; japanese
and german national anthems
these recordings remain unpublished

499/26 october 1973/concert recordings in
tokyo nhk hall

berliner philharmoniker

bach brandenburg concerto no 1; bruckner symphony no 7
these recordings remain unpublished

500/27 october 1973/televised rehearsal performance
and interview in tokyo nhk hall

berliner philharmoniker

dvorak symphony no 8; wagner tristan prelude and liebestod;
tannhäuser overture
published as bonus dvd in the nhk karajan centenary
cd set NSDX 12264

501/28 october 1973/concert recordings in
tokyo nhk hall

berliner philharmoniker

mozart symphony no 41; tchaikovsky symphony no 4
these recordings remain unpublished

502/2 november 1973/concert recordings in osaka
symphony hall

berliner philharmoniker

beethoven symphony no 6; symphony no 5
these recordings remain unpublished

503/19-20 november and 6 december 1973/
dg sessions in berlin jesus-christus-kirche
berliner philharmoniker/producers hans hirsch
and hans weber
webern five movements op 5
lp: 2530 488/2711 014
cd: 423 2542/427 4242/479 1671

schoenberg verklärte nacht
lp: 2530 627/2543 510/2711 014
cd: 415 3262/427 4242/457 7212/479 1671

504/7 and 10 december 1973/dg sessions in berlin
philharmonie
berliner philharmoniker/christa ludwig/rene kollo/
producers hans hirsch and cord garben
mahler das lied von der erde
lp: 2707 082/2531 379/419 0581
cd: 419 0582/479 1671

505/8 december 1973/concert recordings in berlin
philharmonie
berliner philharmoniker/chor der deutschen oper/
anna tomova-sintow/helga angervö/rene kollo/
jose van dam
bach magnificat; bartok concerto for orchestra
these recordings remain unpublished

506/december 1973/unitel film sessions in berlin
philharmonie
berliner philharmoniker/*film producer*
herbert von karajan
tchaikovsky symphony no 4; symphony no 6 "pathetique"
vhs: deutsche grammophon 072 1401 (no 4)/072 1411 (no 6)
laserdisc: deutsche grammophon 072 1403 (no 4)/
072 1413 (no 6)
dvd: deutsche grammophon 073 4384

507/3-5 january and 11-18 february 1974/
dg sessions in berlin philharmonie
berliner philharmoniker/*producers hans hirsch*
and hans weber
schoenberg orchestral variations op 31
lp: 2530 627/2711 014
cd: 415 3262/427 4242/457 7602/479 1671

webern passacaglia op 1
lp: 2530 488/2711 014
cd: 423 2542/427 4242/457 6892/457 7602/479 1671

webern symphony op 21
lp: 2530 488/2711 014
cd: 423 2542/427 4242/457 6892/479 1671

508/24-26 january 1974/dg sessions in berlin
philharmonie
berliner philharmoniker/*producers hans hirsch*
and hans weber
schoenberg pelleas und melisande
lp: 2530 485/2711 014
cd: 423 1322/427 4242/457 7212/479 1671

509/28-31 january 1974/decca sessions in vienna sofiensäle

wiener philharmoniker/chor der wiener staatsoper/ mirella freni/christa ludwig/luciano pavarotti/ robert kerns/michel senechal/hans helm/marius rintzler/wolfgang schneider/giorgio stendoro/elke schary/siegfried rudolf frese/eva maria hurdes/ erna maria mühlberger/martha heigl/*producer christopher raeburn*

puccini madama butterfly
lp: SET 584-586/london (usa) OSA 1310
cd: 457 5772/473 9972/deutsche grammophon 479 4640
see also session no 530 below

509a/6 april 1974/concert recording in salzburg grosses festspielhaus

berliner philharmoniker/wiener singverein/ elizabeth harwood/christa ludwig/peter schreier/ robert kerns/karl ridderbusch

bach mass in b minor
this recording remains unpublished

510/8 april 1974/concert recordings in salzburg grosses festspielhaus

berliner philharmoniker/jean bernard pommier

beethoven piano concerto no 3; tchaikovsky symphony no 5
these recordings remain unpublished

511/9 april 1974/concert recordings in salzburg grosses festspielhaus

berliner philharmoniker

mozart divertimento no 15 K287; strauss sinfonia domestica
these recordings remain unpublished

512/3 may 1974/concert recordings in dortmund
berliner philharmoniker

beethoven symphony no 2; bartok concerto for orchestra
these recordings remain unpublished

513/8-9 may 1974/dg sessions in berlin philharmonie
berliner philharmoniker/christa ludwig/*producers*
hans hirsch and hans weber

mahler kindertotenlieder; rückert-lieder: ich bin der welt
abhanden gekommen; liebst du um schönheit; blicke mir
nicht in die lider; ich atmet einen linden duft; um mitternacht
lp: 2531 147/2707 081 (kindertotenlieder)/
2707 082 (rückert)/419 4761
cd: 415 0762 (kindertotenlieder)/415 0992 (rückert)/
439 6782/453 0402/457 7162/459 3352/479 1671

514/23-28 may 1974/emi sessions in berlin
philharmonie
berliner philharmoniker/*maurice andre/
producer michel glotz

bartok concerto for orchestra
lp: ASD 3046/1C065 02536/2C069 02536/3C065 02536
cd: 476 8972/763 3212/512 0382/warner 2564 633593

*telemann-grebe trumpet concerto in d; hummel-oubradous
trumpet concerto in e flat; leopold mozart-seiffert
trumpet concerto in d; vivaldi-thiede trumpet concerto
lp: ASD 3044/1C065 02544/2C069 02544/angel 37063
cd: 566 9092/749 2372/749 4742 (hummel and leopold
mozart)/769 9612/512 0382/warner 2564 633624

515/24 may and 6 september 1974/emi sessions in berlin philharmonie
berliner philharmoniker/*producer michel glotz*
strauss ein heldenleben
lp: ASD 3126/EG 29 08521/1C065 02577/2C069 02577/
3C065 02577/angel 37060
cd: 476 9032/566 1082/769 0272/512 0382/
warner 2564 633622

516/2 june 1974/concert recording in salzburg grosses festspielhaus
berliner philharmoniker/wiener singverein/
gundula janowitz/jose van dam
brahms ein deutsches requiem
this recording remains unpublished

517/17 june 1974/concert recordings in london royal festival hall
berliner philharmoniker
brahms symphony no 2; symphony no 4
these recordings remain unpublished

518/18 june 1974/concert recordings in london royal festival hall
berliner philharmoniker
brahms symphony no 3; symphony no 1
these recordings remain unpublished

519/26-27 june 1974/emi sessions in berlin
philharmonie
berliner philharmoniker/alexis weissenberg/
producer michel glotz
beethoven piano concerto no 5 in e flat op 73 "emperor"
lp: ASD 3043/SLS 5112/1C065 02535/2C069 02535/
3C065 02535/1C157 53060-53063/2C165 53060-53063/
angel 37062/3854
cd: 476 8852/252 1722/769 3362/566 0912/566 1122/
512 0382/deutsche grammophon 477 9830/
warner 2564 633624

520/26 july 1974/stage recording in salzburg
grosses festspielhaus
wiener philharmoniker/chor der wiener staatsoper/
tölzer knabenchor/edith mathis/edita gruberova/
reri grist/jane marsh/trudeliese schmidt/sylvia
anderson/rene kollo/hermann prey/jose van dam/
gerhard unger/peter meven/alf beinell/hans
christian/martin schomberg/martin egel
mozart die zauberflöte
cd: arkadia CDKAR 233

520a/31 july 1974/stage recording in salzburg
grosses festspielhaus
wiener philharmoniker/chor der wiener staatsoper/
elizabeth harwood/mirella freni/frederica von stade/
jose van dam/tom krause/jane berbie/michel senechal/
paolo montarsolo/elke schary
mozart le nozze di Figaro
lp: estro armonico EA 010

521/15 august 1974/concert recordings in salzburg
grosses festspielhaus
wiener philharmoniker/*maurizio pollini
*schumann piano concerto in a minor
cd: exclusive EX 92 T17/live classic best (japan) LCB 132/
private edition vienna

dvorak symphony no 8 in g op 88
cd: andante 2060

522/1 september 1974/concert recordings in
lucerne kunsthaus
berliner philharmoniker
berg three orchestral pieces op 6; bruckner symphony no 4
these recordings remain unpublished

523/22 september-1 october and 15-19 october 1974/
emi sessions in berlin philharmonie
berliner philharmoniker/*chor der deutschen oper/
producer michel glotz
wagner lohengrin prelude; tristan prelude and liebestod;
*tannhäuser overture and venusberg music
lp: ASD 3130/EG 29 04111/1C065 02603/2C069 02603/
3C065 02603/angel 37097
cd: 476 8962 (tristan and tannhäuser)/769 0192/764 3342/
763 4692/566 1062 (tristan and lohengrin)/512 0382/
warner 2564 633622

wagner fliegende holländer overture; meistersinger overture;
lohengrin act three prelude; parsifal preludes acts one and three
lp: ASD 3160/1C065 02604/2C069 02604/3C065 02604/
angel 37098
cd: 476 8962 (holländer, lohengrin and meistersinger)/
769 0192/764 3342/566 1072 (lohengrin)/566 1082 (holländer)/
512 0382/warner 2564 633622

524/23-28 september 1974/emi sessions in berlin
philharmonie
berliner philharmoniker/wiener singverein/
gundula janowitz/agnes baltsa/peter schreier/
jose van dam/*producer michel glotz*
beethoven missa solemnis op 123
lp: SLS 979/CFPD 4420-4421/CFP 41 44203/1C193 02581-2/
2C167 02581-2/3C165 02581-2/angel 3821
cd: 769 2462/769 2472/511 9732/warner 2564 633628

525/14-15 october 1974 and 21 february 1975/
dg sessions in berlin philharmonie
berliner philharmoniker/*producers hans hirsch
and hans weber*
berlioz symphonie fantastique
lp: 2530 597
cd: 415 3252/479 1671

526/9 november 1974/concert recordings in
new york carnegie hall
berliner philharmoniker
brahms symphony no 4; symphony no 2
these recordings remain unpublished

527/10 november 1974/concert recording in
new york carnegie hall
berliner philharmoniker
bruckner symphony no 8
this recording remains unpublished

528/11 november 1974/concert recordings in
new york carnegie hall
berliner philharmoniker
strauss ein heldenleben
these recordings remain unpublished

529/13 november 1974/concert recordings in
new york carnegie hall
berliner philharmoniker
brahms symphony no 3; symphony no 1
these recordings remain unpublished

530/november 1974/unitel film sessions in vienna
wiener philharmoniker/konzertvereinigung wiener
staatsoper/cast as for session 509 but with placido
domingo replacing luciano pavarotti as pinkerton/
film producer jean-pierre ponnelle
puccini madama butterfly
vhs: decca 071 4043
laserdisc: decca 071 4041
dvd: decca 071 4049
sessions not involving placid domingo probably use
the decca soundtrack recorded in session 509

531/8 december 1974/concert recordings in
berlin philharmonie
berliner philharmoniker
bartok music for strings percussion and celesta;
dvorak symphony no 9
these recordings remain unpublished

532/3-8 january 1975/emi and unitel film
sessions in berlin philharmonie
berliner philharmoniker/mstislav rostropovich/
ulrich koch/*film producer herbert von karajan*
strauss don quixote
lp: ASD 3118/1C065 02641/2C069 02641/3C065 02641/
EX 29 13311/1C137 54360-54363/angel 37057
cd: 476 9032/749 3082/566 1062/512 0382/
warner 2564 633624
vhs: deutsche grammophon 072 1043
laserdisc: deutsche grammophon 072 1041
dvd: deutsche grammophon 073 4381

533/4 january 1975/emi sessions in berlin
philharmonie
berliner philharmoniker/*producer michel glotz*
haydn symphony no 104 in d "london"
lp: ASD 3203/1C065 02643/2C069 02643/3C065 02643
cd: 476 8892/764 5632/769 9612/566 0972/512 0382/
warner 2564 633627

534/4 and 8 january 1975/emi sessions in berlin
philharmonie
berliner philharmoniker/*producer michel glotz*
johann strauss fledermaus overture; annen polka; an der
schönen blauen donau; zigeunerbaron overture; tritsch-tratsch
polka; kaiserwalzer
lp: ASD 3132/EG 29 06141/SXLP 30506 (zigeunerbaron)/
1C065 02642/2C069 02642/3C065 02642/angel 37144
cd: 769 0182/764 6292 (zigeunerbaron)/512 0382/
warner 2564 633622

schubert symphony no 8 in b minor D759 "unfinished"
lp: ASD 3203/SLS 5127/EG 29 05721/1C065 02643/2C069 02643/
3C065 02643/1C157 03285-03289/2C167 54312-54314/
3C165 03285-03289/angel 37058/3862
cd: 476 8952/769 0162/769 8842/764 4422/764 6282/
764 5632/566 1052/566 1142/512 0382/warner 2564 633627

535/5 january 1975/concert recordings in berlin
philharmonie
berliner philharmoniker/mstislav rostropovich/
ulrich koch
haydn symphony no 104; strauss don quixote
these recordings remain unpublished

536/20 january and 17-20 february 1975/dg sessions in berlin philharmonie

berliner philharmoniker/*producers hans hirsch, magdalena padberg and michel glotz*

mahler symphony no 6 in a minor

lp: 2707 106

cd: 415 0992/437 7162/457 7162/479 1671

recording was completed on 18-19 february and 9 march 1977

537/20-23 january and 22 april 1975/dg sessions in berlin philharmonie

berliner philharmoniker/*producers hans hirsch and michel glotz*

bruckner symphony no 8 in c minor

lp: 2707 085/2740 264

cd: 419 1962/429 6482/429 6772/439 9692/439 9702/ 477 8005/479 1671

538/21-22 january 1975/unitel film sessions in
berlin philharmonie
berliner philharmoniker/*film producer*
herbert von karajan
beethoven egmont overture; coriolan overture
vhs: deutsche grammophon 072 1313
laserdisc: deutsche grammophon 072 1311
dvd: deutsche grammophon 073 4399

rossini guillaume tell overture
laserdisc: japan VHM 68107
dvd: deutsche grammophon 073 4399

wagner tannhäuser overture; weber freischütz overture
vhs: deutsche grammophon 072 1833
laserdisc: deutsche grammophon 072 1831
dvd: deutsche grammophon 073 4399

wagner meistersinger overture
this video recording remains unpublished

539/23-24 january and 19-22 october 1976/
dg sessions in berlin philharmonie
berliner philharmoniker/*producers hans hirsch,*
magdalena padberg and michel glotz
beethoven symphony no 1 in c op 21;
symphony no 2 in d op 36
lp: 2531 101/2721 200/2740 172/419 0481 (no 1)/
419 0501 (no 2)
cd: 419 0482 (no 1)/419 0502 (no 2)/429 0892/429 6772/
477 8005/479 1671
recordings of these two symphonies were completed
on 29-31 january and 8-9 march 1977

540/20-21 february 1975/dg sessions in berlin
philharmonie
berliner philharmoniker/chor der deutschen oper/
*anna tomova-sintow/*agnes baltsa/*peter schreier/
*benjamin luxon/*producers hans hirsch, hans weber,
michel glotz and cord garben*
stravinsky symphonie de psaumes
lp: 2531 048
cd: 423 2522/479 1671

*bach magnificat BWV243
lp: 2531 048/2531 342
cd: 479 1671
*recording of bach magnificat was completed on
8 december 1977, 25-27 january 1978 and
19-21 february 1979*

541/2 march 1975/concert recordings in vienna
musikvereinssaal
wiener philharmoniker/alexis weissenberg
beethoven piano concerto no 5;   bruckner symphony no 7
these recordings remain unpublished

542/22 march 1975/stage recording in salzburg
grosses festspielhaus
berliner philharmoniker/chor der wiener staatsoper/
mirella freni/renate holm/luciano pavarotti/rolando
panerai/paolo washington/gianni maffeo/claudio
giombi/saverio porzano/franco calabrese/gerhard
eder/johann pipal/karl caslavsky
puccini la boheme
this recording remains unpublished

543/23 march 1975/stage recording in salzburg
grosses festspielhaus
berliner philharmoniker/chor der wiener staatsoper/
wiener singverein/kammerchor der salzburger
festspiele/gundula janowitz/kerstin meyer/rene
kollo/peter schreier/karl ridderbusch/peter lagger/
dieter ellenbeck/martin egel/jef vermeersch/willy
caron/manfred jung/martin vantin/hans christian/
hannes jokel/alois pernerstorfer/oskar hillebrandt/
gerhard stolze
wagner die meistersinger von nürnberg
cd: private edition vienna

544/24 march 1975/concert recording in salzburg
grosses festspielhaus
berliner philharmoniker
ravel bolero
this recording remains unpublished

545/25 march 1975/concert recording in salzburg
grosses festspielhaus
berliner philharmoniker/wiener singverein/gundula
janowitz/christa ludwig/peter schreier/karl ridderbusch
beethoven missa solemnis op 123
cd: private edition vienna

546/14-15 april 1975/dg sessions in berlin
philharmonie
berliner philharmoniker/*producers hans hirsch,
magdalena padberg and michel glotz*
bruckner symphony no 7 in e
lp: 2707 102/2740 264
cd: 419 1952/429 6482/429 6772/477 8005/479 1671

547/19 april 1975/concert recordings in berlin
philharmonie
berliner philharmoniker
berg lyric suite; bruckner symphony no 4
these recordings remain unpublished

548/21 april 1975/dg sessions in berlin philharmonie
berliner philharmoniker/*producers hans hirsch,
magdalena padberg and michel glotz*
bruckner symphony no 4 in e flat "romantic"
lp: 2530 674/2543 038/2720 111/2740 264
cd: 415 2772/429 6482/429 6542/429 6772/
439 5222/477 8005/479 1671

549/17 may 1975/concert recordings in salzburg
grosses festspielhaus

berliner philharmoniker/yuuko shiokawa
brahms violin concerto; symphony no 2
these recordings remain unpublished

550/18 may 1975/concert recording in salzburg
grosses festspielhaus (matinee concert)

bläser der berliner philharmoniker/

wiener singverein
bruckner mass no 2 in e minor
cd: private edition Vienna

550a/18 may 1975/concert recordings in salzburg
grosses festspielhaus (evening concert)

berliner philharmoniker
brahms symphony no 3; symphony no 4
these recordings remain unpublished

551/19 may 1975/concert recording in salzburg
grosses festspielhaus

berliner philharmoniker/maurizio pollini
brahms piano concerto no 2
cd: private edition vienna
brahms symphony no 1
this recording remains unpublished

552/30 july 1975/stage recording in salzburg
grosses festspielhaus

wiener philharmoniker/chor der wiener staatsoper/
elizabeth harwood/edith mathis/frederica von stade/
jane berbie/elke schary/gunda spiluttini/tom krause/
jose van dam/michel senechal/paolo montarsolo/
zoltan kelemen/willy caron
mozart le nozze di figaro
this recording remains unpublished

553/11 august 1975/stage recording in salzburg
grosses festspielhaus
wiener philharmoniker/chor der wiener staatsoper/
wiener singverein/mirella freni/christa ludwig/
gabriele fuchs/anna tomowa-sintow/placido
domingo/nicolai ghiaurov/piero cappuccilli/georghe
crasnaru/robert kerns/lee davis/istvan gati/hannes
jokel/richard jokel/richard lombardi/eberhard storz/
klaus walprecht
verdi don carlo
cd: private edition vienna

554/24 august 1975/concert recording in salzburg
grosses festspielhaus
wiener philharmoniker/wiener singverein/mirella
freni/fiorenza cossotto/placido domingo/
nicolai ghiaurov
verdi messa da requiem
cd: private edition vienna

555/27 august 1975/concert recordings in salzburg
grosses festspielhaus
berliner philharmoniker/mstislav rostropovich/
ulrich koch
beethoven symphony no 4; strauss don quixote
these recordings remain unpublished

556/28 august 1975/concert recording in salzburg grosses festspielhaus
berliner philharmoniker
bruckner symphony no 8 in c minor
this recording remains unpublished

557/1 september 1975/concert recordings in lucerne kunsthaus
berliner philharmoniker
debussy prelude a l'apres-midi d'un faune; ravel bolero
these recordings remain unpublished

558/6 september 1975/concert recordings in berlin philharmonie
berliner philharmoniker
schoenberg verklärte nacht; bruckner symphony no 7
these recordings remain unpublished

559/13-16 september 1975/dg sessions in berlin philharmonie
berliner philharmoniker/*producers hans hirsch, magdalena padberg and michel glotz*
bruckner symphony no 9 in d minor
lp: 2530 828/2740 264
cd: 419 0832/429 6482/429 6572/429 6772/
477 8005/479 1671

560/22-30 september 1975/dg sessions in berlin
philharmonie
berliner philharmoniker/wiener singverein/anna
tomova-sintow/agnes baltsa/werner krenn/peter
schreier (bruckner)/jose van dam/*producers hans
hirsch, magdalena padberg and michel glotz*
mozart requiem in d minor K626
lp: 2530 705
cd: 419 8672/429 8002/429 8212/459 4092/479 1671

mozart mass in c K317 "coronation"
lp: 2530 704/2531 342
cd: 423 9132/429 8002/429 8202/453 0162/479 1671

bruckner te deum
lp: 2530 704
cd: 423 9132/453 0912/479 1671
*recording of bruckner te deum was completed on
28 may 1976*

verdi overtures: nabucco; macbeth; il corsaro; luisa miller;
rigoletto; la traviata; vespri siciliani; un ballo in maschera;
la forza del destino; aida
lp: 2531 145/2707 090/415 5441
cd: 419 6222/453 0582/479 1671

verdi overtures: oberto; un giorno di regno; ernani;
giovanna d'arco; alzira; attila; i masnadieri;
la battaglia di legnano; aroldo
lp: 2707 090
cd: 453 0582/479 1671

561/25 september 1975/concert recordings in
berlin philharmonie
berliner philharmoniker
strauss metamorphosen; also sprach zarathustra
these recordings remain unpublished

562/20-22 october 1975/dg sessions in berlin
philharmonie
berliner philharmoniker/*producers hans hirsch,
magdalena padberg and michel glotz*
tchaikovsky symphony no 5 in e minor op 64
lp: 2530 699/2543 048/2720 104/2720 112/2740 219/419 0661
cd: 419 0662/423 5042/423 5072/429 6752/429 6772/
453 0882/477 8005/479 1671

liszt lamento e trionfo; hungarian rhapsodies
no 4 in d minor and no 5 in e minor
lp: 2530 698/2726 517/413 6281
cd: 415 9672/419 8622 (no 5)/429 1562 (no 5)/
453 1302/479 1671
*recordings of these liszt works were completed on
13 november 1975*

563/17-19 november 1975/dg sessions in berlin
philharmonie
berliner philharmoniker/lazar berman/*producers
hans hirsch, magdalena padberg and michel glotz*
tchaikovsky piano concerto no 1 in b flat minor op 23
lp: 2530 677/2543 050/2720 112/410 9781
cd: 423 2242/423 5552/429 1662/479 1671/480 7073

564/3-5 december 1975/dg sessions in berlin philharmonie
berliner philharmoniker/*producers hans hirsch, magdalena padberg and michel glotz*
mozart symphony no 39 in e flat K543
lp: 2531 137/2543 022/2720 104/2720 111/2740 189/419 4781
cd: 419 4782/429 6682/429 6772/429 8002/453 0462/
477 8005/479 1671

stravinsky le sacre du printemps
lp: 2530 884/2543 064/2720 112
cd: 415 9792/453 6152/479 1671
this recording was completed on 10 december 1976
and 30 january 1977

565/8-11 december 1975 and 3-8 march 1976/
emi sessions in berlin philharmonie
berliner philharmoniker/chor der deutschen oper/
anna tomova-sintow/dunja vezjovic/rene kollo/
siegmund nimsgern/karl ridderbusch/robert
kerns/klaus lang/peter maus/martin vantin/
josef becker/*producer michel glotz*
wagner lohengrin
lp: SLS 5237/EX 769 3141/1C165 43200-43204/
2C165 43200-43204/angel 3829
cd: 769 3142/511 9732
additional sessions to complete this recording took
place on 22-23 may 1981

566/6-7 march 1976/emi sessions in berlin philharmonie

berliner philharmoniker/gidon kremer/

producer michel glotz

brahms violin concerto in d op 77

lp: ASD 3261/EG 29 02741/1C065 02781/2C069 02781/ 3C065 02781

cd: 566 1012/569 3342/512 0382/warner 2564 633624

567/10 april 1976/stage recording in salzburg grosses festspielhaus

berliner philharmoniker/chor der wiener staatsoper/ tölzer sängerknaben/anna tomova-sintow/ursula schröder-feinen/rene kollo/karl ridderbusch/ siegmund nimsgern/robert kerns/toni krämer/ ewald aichberger/hans christian/nikos kepetas

wagner lohengrin

this recording remains unpublished

568/11 april 1976/concert recordings in salzburg grosses festspielhaus

berliner philharmoniker/alexis weissenberg

beethoven piano concerto no 5; schumann symphony no 4

these recordings remain unpublished

569/12 april 1976/concert recordings in salzburg grosses festspielhaus

berliner philharmoniker

mozart symphony no 39; strauss also sprach zarathustra

these recordings remain unpublished

570/13 april 1976/concert recording in salzburg
grosses festspielhaus
berliner philharmoniker/wiener singverein/
montserrat caballe/fiorenza cossotto/jose
carreras/jose van dam
verdi messa da requiem
cd: private edition vienna

571/5 and 7 may 1976/dg sessions in berlin
philharmonie
berliner philharmoniker/*producers hans hirsch,
magdalena padberg and michel glotz*
tchaikovsky symphony no 6 in b minor op 74 "pathetique"
lp: 2530 774/2543 049/2720 104/2720 112/
2740 219/419 4851
cd: 419 4852/423 5042/429 6752/429 6772/453 0882/
477 8005/479 1671

beethoven symphony no 3 in e flat op 55 "eroica"
lp: 2531 103/2543 027/2720 111/2721 200/
2740 172/419 0491
cd: 419 0492/429 0892/429 6772/477 8005/479 1671
*additional sessions for this recording were held on
30-31 january and 8 march 1977*

572/10 and 26 may 1976/dg sessions in berlin
philharmonie
berliner philharmoniker/*producers hans hirsch,*
magdalena padberg and michel glotz
mozart symphony no 41 in c K551 "jupiter"
lp: 2531 138/2543 023/2740 104/2720 111/2740 189
cd: 423 2102/423 5552/429 4322/429 6682/429 6772/
435 5022/453 0462/477 8005/479 1671

573/12 may 1976/concert recordings in london
royal festival hall
berliner philharmoniker
beethoven symphony no 8; strauss ein heldenleben
these recordings remain unpublished

574/25-26 may 1976/dg sessions in berlin
philharmonie
berliner philharmoniker/*producers hans hirsch,*
magdalena padberg and michel glotz
mozart symphony no 40 in g minor K550
lp: 2531 138/2543 023/2720 104/2720 111/2740 189
cd: 415 5922/429 6682/429 6772/453 0462/
477 8005/479 1671
this recording was completed on 17 february 1977

mozart symphony no 35 in d K385 "haffner"
lp: 2531 136/2720 104/2740 189
cd: 429 6682/429 6772/435 0702/453 0462/
477 8005/479 1671

575/5 june 1976/concert recordings in salzburg
grosses festspielhaus
berliner philharmoniker/alexis weissenberg
tchaikovsky piano concerto no 1; symphony no 5
these recordings remain unpublished

576/6 june 1976/concert recordings in salzburg
grosses festspielhaus
berliner philharmoniker
tchaikovsky romeo and juliet; symphony no 6
these recordings remain unpublished

577/7 june 1976/concert recordings in salzburg
grosses festspielhaus
berliner philharmoniker/philip hirschhorn
tchaikovsky violin concerto; symphony no 4
these recordings remain unpublished

578/25 july 1976/concert recordings in salzburg
grosses festspielhaus
wiener philharmoniker/gidon kremer
bach violin concerto BWV1042; bruckner symphony no 9
these recordings remain unpublished

579/26 july 1976/stage recording in salzburg
grosses festspielhaus
wiener philharmoniker/chor der wiener staatsoper/
wiener singverein/mirella freni/fiorenza cossotto/
jose carreras/nicolai ghiaurov/piero cappuccilli/
jules bastin/edita gruberova/anna tomova-sintow/
walburga wallner/giorgio stendoro
verdi don carlo
this recording remains unpublished

580/15 august 1976/concert recordings in salzburg
grosses festspielhaus
sächsische staatskapelle dresden/emil gilels
beethoven piano concerto no 3; shostakovich symphony no 10
these recordings remain unpublished

581/27 august 1976/concert recordings in salzburg
grosses festspielhaus
berliner philharmoniker
mozart symphony no 29; wimberger plays; debussy
prelude a l'apres-midi d'un faune; ravel bolero
these recordings remain unpublished

582/12 september 1976/emi sessions in berlin philharmonie
berliner philharmoniker/*alexis weissenberg/
producer michel glotz
*beethoven piano concerto no 4 in g op 58
lp: SLS 5112/1C157 53060-53063/2C165 53060-53063/
1C063 03853/2C069 03853/angel 3854
cd: 476 8862/769 3352/252 1722/566 0922/566 1122/
512 0382/deutsche grammophon 477 8005/
warner 2564 633624

sibelius finlandia
lp: ASD 3374/1C065 02878/2C069 02878/3C065 02878/
angel 37408
cd: 476 8472/769 0172/764 5312/512 0382/
disky 703 362/warner 2564 633627/2434 768462

583/20-21 september and 18 october 1976/
emi sessions in berlin philharmonie
berliner philharmoniker/*producer michel glotz*
sibelius symphony no 5 in e flat op 82
lp: ASD 3409/EG 29 06131/1C065 02948/2C069 02948/
3C065 02948/angel 37490
cd: 764 5632/769 2442/512 0382/warner 2564 633627

584/22-23 september and 6 december 1976
and 27-28 january 1977/dg sessions in berlin
philharmonie
berliner philharmoniker/wiener singverein/anna
tomova-sintow/agnes baltsa/peter schreier/jose
van dam/*producers hans hirsch, magdalena
padberg and michel glotz*
beethoven symphony no 9 in d minor op 125 "choral"
lp: 2707 109/2721 200/2740 172/413 8321
cd: 415 8322/429 0892/429 6772/477 8005/479 1671

beethoven symphony no 4 in b flat op 60
lp: 2531 104/2721 200/2740 172/419 0481
cd: 419 0482/429 0892/429 6772/477 8005/479 1671

585/25-28 september 1976/emi sessions in
berlin philharmonie
berliner philharmoniker/wiener singverein/
anna tomova-sintow/jose van dam/*producer
michel glotz*
brahms ein deutsches requiem
lp: SLS 996/CFP 41 44223/1C157 03580-03581/
2C167 03580-03581/3C165 03580-03581/angel 3838
cd: 565 8242/769 2292/511 9732/disky DCL 705 872/
warner 2564 633628

585a/26 september 1973/concert recording
in berlin philharmonie
international youth orchestra
wagner meistersinger overture
this recording remains unpublished

586/30 september and 17-18 october 1976/
emi sessions in berlin philharmonie
berliner philharmoniker/*producer michel glotz*
brahms haydn variations op 56a
lp: SLS 996/CFP 41 44223/1C157 02580-1/2C167 02580-1/
3C165 02580-1/angel 3838
cd: 566 0932/763 3212/512 0382/warner 2564 633632

587/16 october 1976/concert recordings in berlin
philharmonie
berliner philharmoniker
sibelius symphony no 5 in e flat op 82
cd: private edition vienna

mozart sinfonia concertante K297b; sibelius finlandia
these recordings remain unpublished

588/19-20 october 1976/dg sessions in berlin
philharmonie
berliner philharmoniker/*producers hans hirsch,
magdalena padberg and michel glotz*
beethoven symphony no 6 in f op 68 "pastoral"
lp: 2531 106/2543 029/2720 111/2721 200/
2740 172/415 8331
cd: 415 8332/429 0892/429 6772/477 8005/479 1671

beethoven symphony no 5 in c minor op 67
lp: 2531 105/2543 028/2720 111/2721 200/
2740 172/419 0511
cd: 419 0512/429 0892/429 6772/477 8005/479 1671
this recording was completed on 31 january and 8 march 1977

589/21-22 october 1976 and 27-28 january 1977/
dg sessions in berlin philharmonie
berliner philharmoniker/*producers hans hirsch,*
magalena padberg and michel glotz
beethoven symphony no 8 in f op 93
lp: 2707 109/2721 200/2740 172/419 0511
cd: 419 0512/429 0892/429 6772/477 8005/479 1671

beethoven symphony no 7 in a op 92
lp: 2531 107/2721 200/2740 172/419 0501
cd: 419 0502/429 0892/429 6772/477 8005/479 1671
this recording was completed on 9 march 1977

590/4 november 1976/concert recordings in
new york carnegie hall
berliner philharmoniker
schoenberg verklärte nacht; beethoven symphony no 3
these recordings remain unpublished

591/14 november 1976/concert recording in
new york carnegie hall
berliner philharmoniker/wiener singverein/anna
tomova-sintow/agnes baltsa/karl walter böhm/
jose van dam
beethoven symphony no 9 in d minor op 125 "choral"
this recording remains unpublished

592/15 november 1976/concert recordings in
new york carnegie hall
berliner philharmoniker/wiener singverein/anna
tomova-sintow/agnes baltsa/werner krenn/
jose van dam
mozart requiem; bruckner te deum
these recordings remain unpublished

593/16 november 1976/concert recording in
new york carnegie hall
berliner philharmoniker/wiener singverein/
mirella freni/fiorenza cossotto/luciano pavarotti/
jose van dam
verdi messa da requiem
this recording remains unpublished

594/28-29 november 1976/emi sessions in
berlin philharmonie
berliner philharmoniker/*producer michel glotz*
sibelius the swan of tuonela
lp: ASD 3374/1C063 02878/2C069 02878/
3C065 02878/angel 37408
cd: 476 8472/764 3312/769 4332/512 0382/
warner 2564 633627/2434 768462

594/28-29 november 1976/emi sessions in berlin
philharmonie/concluded
sibelius en saga; tapiola
lp: ASD 3374/ASD 3409 (en saga)/ASD 3485 (tapiola)/
1C063 02878/1C063 02948 (en saga)/1C063 02978 (tapiola)/
2C069 02878/2C069 02948 (en saga)/2C069 02978 (tapiola)/
3C065 02878/3C065 02948 (en saga)/3C065 02978 (tapiola)/
angel 37408/37490 (en saga)/37462 (tapiola)
cd: 476 8472/764 3312/769 0172/512 0382/
warner 2564 633627/2434 768462

595/6-11 december 1976/dg sessions in berlin
philharmonie
berliner philharmoniker/_producers hans hirsch,
magdalena padberg and michel glotz_
bruckner symphony no 5 in b flat
lp: 2707 101/2740 264
cd: 415 9852/429 6482/429 6492/429 6772/477 8005/479 1671

tchaikovsky symphony no 4 in f minor op 36
lp: 2530 883/2720 104/2740 219
cd: 419 8722/423 5042/429 6752/429 6772/453 0882/
477 8005/479 1671

596/27-28 december 1976/emi sessions in berlin
philharmonie
berliner philharmoniker/_producer michel glotz_
sibelius symphony no 4 in a minor
lp: ASD 3485/EG 29 06131/1C065 02978/2C069 02978/
3C065 02978/angel 37462
cd: 769 2442/512 0382/warner 2564 633627

597/31 december 1976/concert recording in berlin
philharmonie
berliner philharmoniker
mozart symphony no 41 "Jupiter"
this recording remains unpublished

598/2-7 january 1977/emi sessions in berlin
philharmonie
berliner philharmoniker/*producer michel glotz*
dvorak symphony no 9 in e minor op 95 "from the new world";
smetana the moldau
lp: ASD 3407/EG 29 10701 (symphony)/1C065 02920/
2C069 02920/3C065 02920/2C167 54312-4/angel 37437
cd: 476 8982 (symphony)/522 0492 (moldau)/769 0052/
764 3252 (symphony)/764 5632/512 0382/
warner 2564 633593

debussy la mer; prelude a l'apres-midi d'un faune;
ravel bolero
lp: ASD 3431/EG 29 08561/1C065 02953/2C069 02953/
1C137 54360-54363/2C167 54312-54314/angel 37455
cd: 569 4582 (bolero)/749 8952 (bolero)/763 5272 (bolero)/
764 3572/764 5632/769 0072/512 0382/warner 2564 633593

599/24 january 1977/concert recordings in
berlin philharmonie
berliner philharmoniker
gerhard wimberger plays; berlioz symphonie fantastique
these recordings remain unpublished

600/18-21 february 1977/dg sessions in berlin philharmonie

berliner philharmoniker/*producers hans hirsch, magdalena padberg, michel glotz and cord garben*

wagner siegfried idyll

lp: 2707 102/2543 510

cd: 419 1962/439 9692/449 7252/479 1671

this recording was completed on 9 march 1977

mozart symphony no 38 in d K504 "prague"

lp: 2531 137/2543 022/2720 104/2720 111/2740 189/ 410 8401/419 4781

cd: 419 4782/429 6682/429 6772/429 8002/429 8022/ 453 2462/477 8005/479 1671

this recording was completed on 17-18 october 1977

601/3 april 1977/concert recording in salzburg grosses festspielhaus

berliner philharmoniker

mahler symphony no 6 in a minor

this recording remains unpublished

602/4 april 1977/concert recording in salzburg grosses festspielhaus

berliner philharmoniker

bruckner symphony no 5 in b flat

this recording remains unpublished

602a/5 april 1977/concert recording in salzburg grosses festspielhaus

berliner philharmoniker/wiener singverein/ tölzer sängerknaben/anna tomova-sintow/ruza baldani/werner krenn/peter schreier/jose van dam/ robert kerns/gerd nienstedt

bach matthäus-passion

this recording remains unpublished

603/6 april 1977/stage recording in salzburg
grosses festspielhaus
berliner philharmoniker/chor der wiener staatsoper/
leontyne price/fiorenza cossotto/franco bonisolli/
piero cappuccilli/jose van dam/maria venuti/heinz
zednik/martin egel/ewald aichberger
verdi il trovatore
cd: private edition vienna

603a/8 may 1977/stage recording in vienna staatsoper
orchester und chor der wiener staasoper/leontyne
price/christa ludwig/luciano pavarotti/piero
cappuccilli/jose van dam/maria venuti/heinz zednik/
karl caslavsky/ewald aichberger
verdi il trovatore
cd: artists' live recordings FED 002-003

604/9-18 may 1977/decca sessions for emi in
vienna sofiendäle
wiener philharmoniker/hildegard behrens/agnes
baltsa/helga angervö/karl walter böhm/jose van dam/
heinz zednik/david knutson/martin vantin/gerhard
unger/erich kunz/jules bastin/dieter ellenbeck/gerd
nienstedt/kurt rydl/helge bömches/horst nitsche/
producer michel glotz
strauss salome
lp: SLS 5139/1C165 02908-02909/2C167 02908-02909/angel 3848
cd: 749 3582/567 0802/511 9732

605/10 may 1977/stage recording in vienna staatsoper
orchester und chor der wiener staatsoper/anna
tomova-sintow/ileana cotrubas/frederica von stade/
jane berbie/janet perry/tom krause/jose van dam/
jules bastin/heinz zednik/kurt equiluz/zoltan kelemen
mozart le nozze di figaro
cd: private edition vienna/orfeo C856 123D

606/13 may 1977/stage recording in vienna staatsoper
orchester und chor der wiener staatsoper/mirella
freni/renate holm/jose carreras/rolando panerai/
paolo washington/gianni maffeo/claudio giombi/
franco calabrese/saverio porzano/nikolaus simkowsky/
friedrich strack/willem reyso
puccini la boheme
cd: private edition vienna

607/15 may 1977/stage recording in vienna staatsoper
orchester und chor der wiener staatsoper/leontyne
price/christa ludwig/luciano pavarotti/piero cappuccilli/
jose van dam/heinz zednik/karl caslavsky/ewald
aichberger
verdi il trovatore
cd: private edition vienna

608/28 may 1977/concert recordings in salzburg
grosses festspielhaus
berliner philharmoniker
strauss also sprach zarathustra
cd: live classic best (japan) LCB 129

mozart symphony no 39 in e flat K543
this recording remains unpublished

609/29 may 1977/concert recordings in salzburg grosses festspielhaus

berliner philharmoniker/*anne-sophie mutter

strauss don juan; till eulenspiegels lustige streiche
cd: live classic best (japan) LCB 129

*mozart violin concerto no 3 in g K216
this recording remains unpublished

610/30 may 1977/concert recordings in salzburg grosses festspielhaus

berliner philharmoniker

mozart symphony no 41; strauss ein heldenleben
these recordings remain unpublished

611/10-12 june 1977/emi sessions in berlin philharmonie

berliner philharmoniker/*producer michel glotz*

schubert symphony no 9 in c D944 "great"
lp: SLS 5127/EG 29 06121/1C065 03289/2C069 03289/
1C157 03285-03289/3C165 03285-03289/angel 3682
cd: 476 8952/566 1052/566 1142/763 5292/764 6282/
512 0382/warner 2564 633627

612/16 june 1977/concert recordings in paris theatre des champs-elysees

berliner philharmoniker

beethoven symphony no 6; symphony no 5
these recordings remain unpublished

613/26 july 1977/stage recording in salzburg
grosses festspielhaus
wiener philharmoniker/hildegard behrens/agnes
baltsa/helga angervö/karl walter böhm/jose van dam/
wieslaw ochman/michel senechal/david knutson/
martin vantin/gerhard unger/erich kunz/jules bastin/
dieter ellenbeck/gerd nienstedt/kurt rydl/helge
bömches/horst nitsche
strauss salome
cd: private edition vienna

614/15 august 1977/concert recording in salzburg
grosses festspielhaus
wiener philharmoniker/konzertvereinigung wiener
staatsopernchor/edith mathis/peter schreier/
jose van dam
haydn die schöpfung
cd: private edition vienna

615/28 august 1977/concert recording in salzburg
grosses festspielhaus
berliner philharmoniker
beethoven symphony no 3 in e flat op 55 "eroica"
this recording remains unpublished

616/31 august 1977/concert recordings in
lucerne kunsthaus
berliner philharmoniker
beethoven symphony no 2; sibelius symphony no 5
these recordings remain unpublished

617/20-22 and 26-27 september 1977/emi sessions in berlin philharmonie
berliner philharmoniker/chor der deutschen oper/ leontyne price/elena obraztzowa/maria venuti/ franco bonisolli/piero cappuccilli/ruggiero raimondi/ horst nitsche/martin egel/*producer michel glotz*
verdi il trovatore
lp: SLS 5111/EX 29 09533/1C165 02981-83/2C167 02981-83/ 3C165 02981-83/angel 3855/melodiya C10 11315-11320
cd: 769 3112/511 9732

618/25 september 1977/concert recordings in berlin philharmonie
berliner philharmoniker/kammerchor ernst senff/ walton grönroos/werner thärichen/oswald vogler
werner thärichen paukenkrieg; stravinsky sacre du printemps
these recordings remain unpublished

619/27-28 september 1977/emi sessions in berlin philharmonie
berliner philharmonie/*alexis weissenberg/ *producer michel glotz*
*beethoven piano concerti: no 1 in c op 15; no 2 in b flat op 19; no 3 in c minor op 37
lp: SLS 5112/1C157 53060-63/2C165 53060-63/angel 3854
cd: 476 8852 (no 3)/769 3342/252 1722/566 0902 (nos 1 & 2)/ 566 0912 (no 3)/566 1122/512 0382/warner 2564 633624/ deutsche grammophon 477 9830

620/29-30 september and 31 december 1977 and
2-6 january 1978/emi sessions in berlin philharmonie
berliner philharmoniker/_producer michel glotz_
schubert symphonies: no 1 in d D82; no 2 in b flat D125;
no 3 in d D200; no 4 in c minor D417 "tragic"; no 5
in b flat D485; no 6 in c D589; rosamunde overture D644;
rosamunde ballet music nos 1 and 2 D797
lp: SLS 5127/EG 29 05721 (no 5)/1C157 03285-03289/
3C165 03285-03289/angel 3862
cd: 566 1032 (rosamunde)/566 1042/566 1142/512 0382/
warner 2564 633627

621/17-18 october 1977/dg sessions in berlin
philharmonie
berliner philharmoniker/_producers hans hirsch,_
magdalena padberg and michel glotz
mozart symphonies: no 32 in g K318; no 36 in c K425 "linz"
lp: 2531 136/2720 104/2740 189/410 8401 (no 36)
cd: 429 6682/429 6772/429 8042/435 0702/439 8002/
453 0462 (no 36)/477 8005/479 1671

622/19-20 october and 7 december1977,
23-27 january and 19 february 1978/dg sessions
in berlin philharmonie
berliner philharmoniker/_producers hans hirsch,_
magdalena padberg, michel glotz and cord garben
brahms symphonies: no 1 in c minor op 68; no 2 in d op 73;
symphony no 4 in e minor op 98
lp: 2531 131 (no 1)/2531 132 (no 2)/2531 134 (no 4)/2740 193
cd: 427 2532 (no 1)/429 6442/429 6772/431 0672 (no 2)/
453 0972/477 8005/479 1671

623/21 october 1977/concert recordings in berlin philharmonie

berliner philharmoniker/thomas brandis/
ottomar borwitzky

brahms double concerto; symphony no 2
these recordings remain unpublished

624/9 november 1977/concert recording in osaka symphony hall

berliner philharmoniker

brahms symphony no 1
this recording remains unpublished

625/10 november 1977/televised concert in tokyo nhk hall

berliner philharmoniker/alexis weissenberg

beethoven piano concerto no 4
this video recording remains unpublished

626/13 november 1977/concert recordings in tokyo nhk hall

berliner philharmoniker

beethoven symphony no 1; symphony no 3
these recordings remain unpublished

627/14 november 1977/concert recordings in tokyo nhk hall

berliner philharmoniker/alexis weissenberg

beethoven piano concerto no 3; symphony no 2
these recordings remain unpublished

628/15 november 1977/concert recordings in
berliner philharmoniker
beethoven symphony no 4; symphony no 7
these recordings remain unpublished

629/16 november 1977/concert recordings in
tokyo nhk hall
berliner philharmoniker
beethoven symphony no 6; symphony no 5
these recordings remain unpublished

630/17 november 1977/concert recordings in
tokyo nhk hall
berliner philharmoniker/alexis weissenberg
beethoven symphony no 8; piano concerto no 5
these recordings remain unpublished

631/18 november 1977/concert recording in
tokyo nhk hall
berliner philharmoniker/nhk chorus/barbara
hendricks/helga angervö/hermann winkler/
hans sotin
beethoven symphony no 9 "choral"
this recording remains unpublished

632/5-6 december 1977, 6 january and 13 and 29
february 1978/dg sessions in berlin philharmonie
berliner philharmoniker/*producers hans hirsch,
magdalena padberg, cord garben and michel glotz*
respighi fontane di roma; pini di roma
lp: 2531 055
cd: 413 8222/449 7242/479 1671

633/9-12 december 1977/dg sessions in berlin
philharmonie
berliner philharmoniker/*producers hans hirsch
and cord garben*
tchaikovsky symphonies: no 1 "winter dreams" ; no 3 "polish"
lp: 2531 284 (no 1)/2531 286 (no 3)/2720 104/
2740 219/415 0241
cd: 419 1762 (no 1)/419 1782 (no 3)/423 5042 (no 3)/
429 6752/429 6772/431 6052 (no 3)/431 6062 (no 1)/
477 8005/479 1671
*these recordings were completed in january and february 1978
and january and february 1979*

634/13 december 1977/concert recordings in
aachen stadttheater
berliner philharmoniker
beethoven symphony no 6; brahms symphony no 1
these recordings remain unpublished

635/31 december 1977/televised concert in berlin
philharmonie
berliner philharmoniker/chor der deutschen oper/
anna tomova-sintow/agnes baltsa/rene kollo/jose
van dam/*film producer humphrey burton*
beethoven symphony no 9 in d minor op 125 "choral"
vhs: deutsche grammophon 072 1333
laserdisc: deutsche grammophon 072 1331
dvd: euroarts 207 2724

636/4 january 1978/concert recording in berlin
philharmonie
berliner philharmoniker/agnes baltsa/hermann winkler
mahler das lied von der erde
this recording remains unpublished

637/21 january 1978/dg sessions in berlin
philharmonie
berliner philharmoniker/*producers hans hirsch,
magdalena padberg, cord garben and michel glotz*
brahms symphony no 3 in f op 90
lp: 2531 133/2740 193
cd: 429 6442/429 6772/437 6452/453 0972/477 8005/479 1671

638/28 january 1978/concert recordings in berlin
philharmonie
berliner philharmoniker
sibelius symphony no 4; beethoven symphony no 7
these recordings remain unpublished

639/13-19 february 1978/dg sessions in berlin
philharmonie
berliner philharmoniker/anne-sophie mutter/
producers hans hirsch, magdalena padberg
and michel glotz
mozart violin concerti: no 3 K216 and no 5 K219
lp: 2531 049/2543 024 (no 5)/2720 111 (no 5)/410 9821
cd: 415 3272/415 5652/423 2112 (no 5)/423 5552 (no 5)/
429 8002/429 8142/437 7462 (no 5)/447 0702 (no 3)/
457 7462/459 0422 (no 5)/459 0702 (no 5)/479 1671

640/14-15 february 1978/unitel film sessions in
berlin philharmonie
berliner philharmoniker/*film producer*
herbert von karajan
debussy la mer; prelude a l'apres-midi d;un faune;
ravel daphnis et chloe: second suite
vhs: deutsche grammophon 072 1383
laserdisc: deutsche grammophon 072 1381
dvd: deutsche grammophon 073 4399

641/19 march 1978/stage recording in salzburg
grosses festspielhaus
berliner philharmoniker/chor der wiener staatsoper/
hildegard behrens/edith mathis/hermann winkler/
heinz zednik/paul plishka/siegmund nimsgern/
jose van dam/horst nitsche/kurt rydl
beethoven fidelio
this recording remains unpublished

642/20 march 1978/concert recording in salzburg
grosses festspielhaus
berliner philharmoniker/radu lupu
beethoven piano concerto no 3 in c minor
cd: private edition Vienna

beethoven symphony no 3 in e flat "eroica"
this recording remains unpublished

643/22 march 1978/televised concert in salzburg
grosses festspielhaus
berliner philharmoniker/wiener singverein/
gundula janowitz/jose van dam
brahms ein deutsches requiem
vhs: deutsche grammophon 072 1353
laserdisc: deutsche grammophon 972 1351

644/17-30 april 1978/decca sessions in vienna
sofiensäle
wiener philharmoniker/chor der wiener staatsoper/
anna tomova-sintow/lleana cotrubas/frederica
von stade/christine barbaux/jane berbie/tom
krause/jose van dam/jules bastin/heinz zednik/
kurt equiluz/zoltan kelemen/marjon lambriks/
producer christopher raeburn
mozart le nozze di figaro
lp: D132 D4/london (usa) OSA 1443
cd: 421 1252/455 0592/deutsche grammophon 479 4640

644a/1 may 1978/televised performance in vienna staatsoper

orchester und chor der wiener staatsoper/raina kabaiwanska/fiorenza cossotto/placido domingo/ piero cappuccilli/jose van dam/maria venuti/heinz zednik/karl caslavsky/ewald aichberger

verdi il trovatore
cd: rca/bmg 74321 619512/74321 619532
dvd: tdk DV-CLOPIT

645/7 may 1978/televised concert in vienna musikvereinssaal

wiener philharmoniker/wiener singverein/anna tomova-sintow/agnes baltsa/david rendall/ jose van dam

bruckner symphony no 9 in d minor; te deum
cd: private edition vienna (te deum)/live classic best (japan) LCB 141 (symphony)
vhs: deutsche grammophon 072 1373
laserdisc: deutsche gramophone 072 1375
dvd: deutsche grammophon 073 4395

646/13 may 1978/concert recording in salzburg grosses festspielhaus

berliner philharmoniker

mahler symphony no 6 in a minor
this recording remains unpublished

647/15 may 1978/concert recording in salzburg grosses festspielhaus

berliner philharmoniker

mahler symphony no 5 in c sharp minor
this recording remains unpublished

648/24 june 1978/televised french feature programme
with music and interviews in paris ortf studios
berliner philharmoniker/alexis weissenberg/mstislav
rostropovich/anne-sophie mutter/mirella freni/raina
kabaiwanska/herbert von karajan/jacques chancel
(presenter)
verdi la forza del destino overture; mozart piano concerto K467
(weissenberg is soloist in first and second movements, karajan
himself in the second movement); wagner der fliegende
holländer overture; offenbach les contes d'hoffmann: barcarolle;
josef strauss delirienwalzer; leoncavallo pagliacci: stridono lassu
(kabaiwanska); puccini la boheme: si mi chiamano mimi (freni);
massenet thais: meditation; strauss don quixote: epilogue;
sibelius valse triste; mussorgsky-ravel pictures at an exhibition:
great gate of kiev
these recordings remain unpublished; surviving sound recording
omits certain items, and it is also understood that the actual
programme included additional items not conducted by karajan

649/1-3 july 1978 and 28-29 january 1979/dg sessions
in berlin philharmonie
berliner philharmoniker/*producers hans hirsch*
and michel glotz
bach the six brandenburg concerti BWV1046-BWV1051
lp: 2531 332 (nos 1-3)/2531 333 (nos 4-6)/2707 112
cd: 415 3752/474 2872 (nos 3 and 5)/479 1671

650/15 august 1978/concert recording in salzburg
grosses festspielhaus
wiener philharmoniker
bruckner symphony no 8 in c minor
this recording remains unpublished

651/27 august 1978/concert recordings in salzburg
grosses festspielhaus
berliner philharmoniker/*anne-sophie mutter/
*yo yo ma/*mark zeltser
*beethoven triple concerto
cd: private edition vienna

stravinsky le sacre du printemps
this recording remains unpublished

652/28 august 1978/concert recording in salzburg
grosses festspielhaus
berliner philharmoniker/wiener singverein/mirella
freni/agnes baltsa/jose carreras/nicolai ghiaurov
verdi messa da requiem
this recording remains unpublished

653/31 august 1978/concert recordings in lucerne
kunsthaus
berliner philharmoniker/anne-sophie mutter/
yo yo ma/mark zeltser
beethoven triple concerto; stravinsky le sacre du printemps
these recordings remain unpublished

654/15-20 september 1978/emi sessions in berlin philharmonie

berliner philharmoniker/chor der deutschen oper/ mirella freni/agnes baltsa/edita gruberova/barbara hendricks/jose carreras/nicolai ghiaurov/piero cappuccilli/ruggiero raimondi/jose van dam/horst nitsche/roberto banuelas/Josef becker/walton grönroos/klaus lang/manfred röhrl/ivan sardi/ *producer michel glotz*
verdi don carlo
lp: SLS 5154/EX 769 3041/1C157 03450-53/2C167 03450-53/ 3C165 03450-53/angel 3875
cd: 769 3042/769 3052/511 9732

656/22 october 1978/dg session in berlin philharmonie
berliner philharmoniker/*producers hans hirsch, magdalena padberg, michel glotz and cord garben*
brahms tragic overture op 81
lp: 2531 133/2543 042/2720 112/2740 193
cd: 423 2052/423 5552/439 4782/445 0092/445 6272/479 1671

656/1-19 november 1978/unitel film sessions in munich bavaria-atelier/*film producer herbert von karajan*
wagner das rheingold
soundtrack recording to accompany the film was made in april 1973 (see session 483 for cast and issue details); martha mödl appears in the film as erda, vladimir de kanel as donner and gerd nienstedt as fasolt

657/18-21 december 1978/emi sessions in berlin philharmonie

berliner philharmoniker/chor der deutschen oper/ frederica von stade/nadine denize/christine barbaux/ richard stilwell/jose van dam/ruggiero raimondi/ *producer michel glotz*

debussy pelleas et melisande
lp: SLS 5172/EX 749 3501/1C165 03650-52/2C167 03650-52/ angel 3885
cd: 749 3502/567 0572/511 9732

658/29 december 1978-3 january 1979/emi sessions in berlin philharmonie

berliner philharmoniker/*producer michel glotz*
berlioz la damnation de faust: marche hongroise; bizet l'arlesienne: second suite; chabrier espana; gounod faust: ballet music
lp: ASD 3761/EG 29 10681/1C065 03626/2C069 03626/ angel 37687
cd: 522 0492 (berlioz)/569 4582/749 8952/763 5272/ 512 0382/warner 2564 633593

dvorak symphony no 8 in g op 88; slavonic dance op 46 no 8
lp: ASD 3775/EG 29 10701/SXLP 30506 (slavonic dance)/ 1C047 02381 (slavonic dance)/1C065 03627/2C069 03627/ angel 37686
cd: 476 8982 (symphony)/763 3212 (symphony)/764 3252 (symphony)/512 0382/warner 2564 633593

659/31 december 1978/televised concert in berlin philharmonie

berliner philharmoniker

verdi la forza del destino overture; bizet l'arlesienne: movements from the second suite; liszt hungarian rhapsody no 2; berlioz la damnation de faust: marche hongroise; mascagni amico fritz intermezzo; suppe leichte kavallerie overture

vhs: deutsche grammophon 072 1833

laserdisc: deutsche grammophon 072 1831

660/4 january 1979/concert recordings in berlin philharmonie

berliner philharmoniker

bach brandenburg concerto no 3; berg three pieces op 6; dvorak symphony no 8

these recordings remain unpublished

661/22-26 january 1979/dg sessions in berlin philharmonie

berliner philharmoniker/*edith mathis/*producers hans hirsch, magdalena padberg and michel glotz*

*mahler symphony no 4 in g

lp: 2531 205/2543 057/2720 112

cd: 415 3232/419 8632/479 1671

tchaikovsky symphony no 2 in c minor "little russian"

lp: 2531 285/2720 104/2740 219/415 0241

cd: 419 1772/423 5042/423 5052/429 6752/429 6772/ 477 8005/479 1671

this recording was completed on 28 february 1979

662/27 january 1979/concert recordings in berlin
philharmonie
berliner philharmoniker/mark zeltser
webern five pieces; schumann symphony no 4;
tchaikovsky piano concerto no 1
these recordings remain unpublished

663/7 april 1979/televised concert in salzburg
grosses festspielhaus
berliner philharmoniker/wiener singverein/anna
tomova-sintow/ruza baldani/eric tappy/jose van dam
beethoven missa solemnis op 123
vhs: deutsche grammophon 072 1343
laserdisc: deutsche grammophon 072 1341

664/9 april 1979/concert recording in salzburg
grosses festspielhaus
berliner philharmoniker
bruckner symphony no 7 in e
this recording remains unpublished

665/16 april 1979/concert recordings in salzburg
grosses festspielhaus
berliner philharmoniker
dvorak symphony no 8; mussorgsky-ravel
pictures from an exhibition
these recordings remain unpublished

666/6 may 1979/stage recording in vienna staatsoper
orchester und chor der wiener staatsoper/mirella
freni/agnes baltsa/edita gruberova/marjon lambricks/
jose carreras/ruggiero raimondi/piero cappuccilli/
matti salminen/luigi roni/ewald aichberger
verdi don carlo
cd: orfeo C816 133D

667/7-14 may 1979/emi sessions in vienna
musikvereinssaal
wiener philharmoniker/chor der wiener staatsoper/
mirella freni/agnes baltsa/katia ricciarelli/jose carreras/
piero cappuccilli/ruggiero raimondi/jose van dam/
thomas moser/*producer michel glotz*
verdi aida
lp: SLS 5205/EX 29 08083/1C165 03574-76/2C167 03574-76/
angel 3888
cd: 769 3002/511 9732

668/2 june 1979/concert recordings in salzburg
grosses festspielhaus
berliner philharmoniker
bach brandenburg concerto no 4
cd: private edition vienna

bruckner symphony no 4 "romantic"
cd: live classic best (japan) LCB 141

669/3 june 1979/concert recordings in salzburg
grosses festspielhaus
berliner philharmoniker
debussy la mer
cd: private edition vienna

debussy prelude a l'apres-midi d'un faune; ravel bolero
these recordings remain unpublished

670/4 june 1979/televised concert in sankt florian
stiftskirche
wiener philharmoniker
bruckner symphony no 8 in c minor
vhs: deutsche grammophon 072 1363
laserdisc: deutsche grammophon 072 1361
dvd: deutsche grammophon 073 4395

671/18 june 1979/concert recordings in london
royal festival hall
berliner philharmoniker/anne-sophie mutter/
yo yo ma/mark zeltser
beethoven triple concerto; strauss also sprach zarathustra
these recordings remain unpublished

672/19 june 1979/concert recording in london
royal festival hall
berliner philharmoniker
bruckner symphony no 8 in c minor
this recording remains unpublished

673/26 july 1979/stage recording in salzburg
grosses festspielhaus
wiener philharmoniker/chor der wiener staatsoper/
sofia opera chorus/mirella freni/marilyn horne/
marjon lambricks/jose carreras/piero cappuccilli/
nicolai ghiaurov/ruggero raimondi/thomas moser
verdi aida
cd: private edition vienna

674/29 july 1979/concert recordings in salzburg
grosses festspielhaus
wiener philharmoniker
haydn symphony no 104 in d "london"
cd: andante 2060

dvorak symphony no 9 in e minor "from the new world"
this recording remains unpublished

675/27 august 1979/concert recordings in salzburg
grosses festspielhaus
berliner philharmoniker
strauss also sprach zarathustra
cd: private edition vienna

mozart divertimento no 15 K287
this recording remains unpublished

676/28 august 1979/concert recordings in salzburg
grosses festspielhaus
berliner philharmoniker
stravinsky apollon musagete
cd: private edition vienna

tchaikovsky symphony no 6 "pathetique"
this recording remains unpublished

285

677/10-21 september 1979/dg sessions in berlin philharmonie
berliner philharmoniker/chor der deutschen oper/ schöneberger sängerknaben/katia ricciarelli/jose carreras/ruggiero raimondi/gottfried hornik/heinz zednik/fernando corena/victor von halem/ wolfgang bünten/*producer michel glotz*
puccini tosca
lp: 2707 121
cd: 413 8152/479 4640
this recording was completed on 25 november 1979

678/24-29 september 1979/dg sessions in berlin philharmonie
berliner philharmoniker/*anne-sophie mutter/ *producers günther breest and michel glotz*
*beethoven violin concerto in d op 61
lp: 2531 250/2543 032/2720 111/2740 282
cd: 413 8182/415 5652/453 7072/477 9830/479 1671
this recording was completed on 18 december 1979

bruckner symphony no 6 in a
lp: 2531 295/2740 264
cd: 419 1942/429 6482/429 6552/429 6772/ 447 5232/477 8005/479 1671

679/18 october 1979/concert recordings in tokyo nhk hall
berliner philharmoniker
schubert symphony no 8; tchaikovsky symphony no 5
cd: nhk karajan centenary set NSDX 12264

680/19 october 1979/concert recordings in
tokyo nhk hall
berliner philharmoniker
dvorak symphony no 8; mussorgsky-ravel
pictures from an exhibition
cd: nhk karajan centenary set NSDX 12264

681/21 october 1979/concert recording in
tokyo nhk hall
berliner philharmoniker/wiener singverein/anna
tomova-sintow/ruza baldani/peter schreier/
jose van dam
beethoven symphony no 9 in d minor op 125 "choral"
cd: deutsche grammophon (japan) UCCG 9396

682/24-26 october 1979/concert recording in
tokyo nhk hall
berliner philharmoniker/wiener singverein/
mirella freni/agnes baltsa/luis lima/nicolai ghiaurov
verdi messa da requiem
cd: nhk karajan centenary set NSDX 12264

683/22-23 november 1979/dg sessions in berlin
philharmonie
berliner philarmoniker/*producers günther breest,
michel glotz and cord garben*
mahler symphony no 9
lp: 2707 125
cd: 439 6782/453 0402/479 1671

684/25 november 1979/concert recordings in
berlin philharmonie
berliner philharmoniker
bach brandenburg concerto no 1; beethoven symphony no 3
these recordings remain unpublished

685/4-29 december 1979 and 2-4 january 1980/
dg sessions in berlin philharmonie
berliner philharmoniker/chor der deutschen oper/
dunja vejzovic/peter hofmann/kurt moll/siegmund
nimsgern/jose van dam/victor von halem/claes
ahnsjö/kurt rydl/marjon lambricks/anne gjevang/
heiner hopfner/georg tichy/barbara hendricks/
janet perry/doris soffel/inga nielsen/audrey
michael/rohangiz yachmi/hanna schwarz/
producers günther breest and michel glotz
wagner parsifal
lp: 2741 002
cd: 413 3472/479 4640
this recording was completed on 15 april and 1 july 1980

686/18 december 1979/dg sessions in berlin
philharmonie
berliner philharmoniker/anne-sophie mutter/
yo yo ma/mark zeltser/*producers günther breest
and cord garben*
beethoven triple concerto
lp: 2531 262/2740 262
cd: 415 2762/435 0962/447 9072/453 7002/
453 7072/477 9830/479 1671

687/20-28 january and 14 april 1980/dg sessions in berlin philharmonie
berliner philharmoniker/chor der deutschen oper/ tölzer sängerknaben/edith mathis/janet perry/ karin ott/anna tomova-sintow/agnes baltsa/hanna schwarz/francisco araiza/gottfried hornik/jose van dam/claudio nicolai/heiner hopfner/leopold valente/heinz kruse/volker horn/victor von halem/ *producer michel glotz*
mozart die zauberflöte
lp: 2741 001
cd: 410 9672/479 4640

688/15 february 1980/concert recordings in berlin philharmonie
berliner philharmoniker/anne-sophie mutter
beethoven violin concerto; prokofiev symphony no 5
these recordings remain unpublished

689/30 march 1980/stage recording in salzburg
grosses festspielhaus
berliner philharmoniker/chor der wiener staatsoper/
wiener singverein/tölzer sängerknaben/salzburger
kammerchor/dunja vejzovic/peter hofmann/kurt
moll/jose van dam/victor von halem/gottfried
hornik/claes ahnsjö/kurt rydl/heiner hopfner/georg
tichy/barbara hendricks/janet perry/doris soffel/
marjon lambricks/inga nielsen/audrey michael/
rohangiz yachmi/hanna schwarz
wagner parsifal
this recording remains unpublished

690/31 march 1980/concert recordings in salzburg
grosses festspielhaus
berliner philharmoniker/*anne-sophie mutter
*beethoven violin concerto in d
this recording remains unpublished

tchaikovsky symphony no 4 in f minor op 36
cd: private edition vienna

691/1 april 1980/concert recordings in salzburg
grosses festspielhaus
berliner philharmoniker/wiener singverein/anna
tomova-sintow/agnes baltsa/francisco araiza/
victor von halem
verdi te deum; mozart requiem K626
these recordings remain unpublished

692/2 april 1980/concert recordings in salzburg
grosses festspielhaus
berliner philharmoniker/edith mathis
bach brandenburg concerto no 1; mahler symphony no 4
this recording remains unpublished

693/17 may 1980/concert recordings in vienna
musikvereinssaal
berliner philharmoniker/edith mathis
mahler symphony no 4 in g
cd: private edition vienna

stravinsky apollon musagete
this recording remains unpublished

694/23 may 1980/concert recordings in salzburg
grosses festspielhaus
berliner philharmoniker
mozart divertimento no 17 K334; berlioz symphonie fantastique
these recordings remain unpublished

695/25 may 1980/concert recordings in salzburg
grosses festspielhaus
berliner philharmoniker/*kristian zimerman
*chopin piano concerto no 2 in f minor
this recording remains unpublished

schumann symphony no 4 in d minor
cd: private edition vienna

696/27-31 may 1980/philips sessions in vienna
musikvereinssaal
wiener philharmoniker/chor der wiener staatsoper/
giuseppe taddei/rolando panerai/francisco araiza/
raina kabaiwanska/janet perry/christa ludwig/
trudeliese schmidt/piero de palma/heinz zednik/
federico davia/*producer michel glotz*
verdi falstaff
lp: 6769 060
cd: 412 2632/deutsche grammophon 447 6862/479 4640

697/10-15 june and 29-30 september 1980/
dg sessions in berlin philharmonie
berliner philharmoniker/*producers günther breest
and michel glotz*
offenbach orphee aux enfers overture; les contes
d'hoffmann: barcarolle
lp: 2532 006/419 4691
cd: 400 0442/415 3402/431 1602/445 2862/479 3839

offenbach overtures: barbe-bleue; la grande duchesse
de gerolstein; la belle helene; vert-vert
lp: 2532 006
cd: 400 0442/479 3839

johann strauss an der schönen blauen donau; elyen a magyar;
accelerationen; persischer marsch; fledermaus overture;
leichtes blut; künstlerleben; unter donner und blitz
lp: 2532 025/2741 003
cd: 410 0272/419 7352/445 5702/479 3839
these recordings were completed on 4 december 1980

697/10-15 june and 29-30 september 1980/
dg sessions in berlin philharmonie/concluded
johann strauss kaiserwalzer; tritsch-tratsch polka; rosen
aus dem süden; zigeunerbaron overture; annen polka;
wein weib und gesang; auf der jagd
lp: 2532 026/2741 003
cd: 410 0272/419 7352/445 5702/479 3839

johann strauss g'schichten aus dem wienerwald;
fledermaus-quadrille; perpetuum mobile; wiener
blut: napoleon-marsch; josef strauss sphärenklänge;
delirienwalzer; johann strauss father radetzky-marsch
lp: 2532 027/2741 003
cd: 410 0272/419 7352/445 5702/479 3839
these recordings were completed on 4 december 1980

698/15 and 29 june, 1 july and 30 september 1980/
dg sessions in berlin philharmonie
berliner philharmoniker/*producers günther breest,
michel glotz and werner mayer*
haydn paris symphonies: no 82 "bear"; no 83 "hen";
no 84; no 85 "la reine"; no 86; no 87
lp: 2532 037 (82 and 87)/2532 038 (84 and 85)/
2532 039 (83 and 86)/2543 028 (82 and 85)/
2720 111 (82 and 85)/2741 005/2741 008 (82 and 83)
cd: 419 7412/445 5322/477 8005/479 3839

699/30 july 1980/stage recording in salzburg
grosses festspielhaus
wiener philharmoniker/chor der wiener staatsoper/
sofia opera chorus/salzburger kammerchor/mirella
freni/ruza baldani/marjon lambricks/jose carreras/
ruggiero raimondi/piero cappuccilli/thomas moser/
agosto ferrin
verdi aida
this recording remains unpublished

700/12 august 1980/televised rehearsal and
performance in salzburg grosses festspielhaus
european youth orchestra/*anne-sophie mutter
*beethoven violin concerto in d op 61
laserdisc: toshiba TOLW 3533

mozart symphony no 41 in c K551 "jupiter"
this video recording remains unpublished

701/15 august 1980/concert recording in salzburg
grosses festspielhaus
wiener philharmoniker
bruckner symphony no 7 in e
this recording remains unpublished

702/1 september 1980/concert recordings in
lucerne kunsthaus
berliner philharmoniker/kristian zimerman
chopin piano concerto no 2; prokofiev symphony no 5
cd: private edition vienna/exclusive EX92 T41 (chopin)

703/20-25 september 1980/dg sessions in berlin
philharmonie

berliner philharmoniker/_producers günther breest
and michel glotz_

bruckner symphony no 3 in d minor
lp: 2532 007/2740 264
cd: 413 3622/429 6482/429 6512/429 6772/477 8005/479 3839

tchaikovsky serenade for strings op 48; dvorak serenade
for strings op 22
lp: 2532 012
cd: 400 0382/431 6052 (tchaikovsky)/479 3839

strauss metamorphosen
lp: 2532 074
cd: 410 8922/445 6002/447 4222/479 3839

704/26-28 september 1980/dg sessions in berlin
philharmonie

berliner philharmoniker/anne-sophie mutter/
producers günther breest and michel glotz

mendelssohn violin concerto in e minor
lp: 2532 016/2543 024/2720 111/2740 282/2741 008
cd: 400 0312/415 5652/423 2112/423 5552/445 5152/479 3839

bruch violin concerto no 1 in g
lp: 2532 016/2740 282/2741 008
cd: 400 0312/415 5652/459 0422/459 0702/479 3839

705/16-20 november 1980/emi sessions in berlin philharmonie
berliner philharmoniker/*anne-sophie mutter/
producer michel glotz
sibelius symphony no 2 in d op 43
lp: ASD 4060/1C065 43040/2C069 43040/3C065 43040/
angel 37816
cd: 769 2432/512 0382/warner 2564 633619

sibelius symphony no 6 in d op 106
lp: EL 27 04071
cd: 763 3212/763 8962/512 0382/warner 2564 633619

sibelius karelia suite
lp: ASD 4097/EL 27 04071/1C063 43050/2C069 43050/
3C065 43050
cd: 476 8492/764 3312/769 0282/512 0382/
warner 2564 633619/2434 768462

sibelius valse triste
lp: EL 27 04071
cd: 476 8492/569 4582/763 3212/764 5632/512 0382/
warner 2564 633619/2434 768462

*massenet thais: meditation
lp: ASD 4072/EG 29 10581/103 9731/1C065 03973/
2C069 03973/angel 37810
cd: 522 0492/512 0382/764 6292/769 0202/
warner 2564 633624

705/16-20 november 1980/emi sessions in berlin
philharmonie/concluded
operatic overtures and intermezzi: cherubini anacreon;
schmidt notre dame; puccini suor angelica; manon lescaut
mascagni amico fritz; humperdinck hänsel und gretel;
weber der freischütz
lp: ASD 4072/EG 29 10581/103 9731/1C065 03973/
2C069 03973/angel 37810
cd: 764 6292/769 0202/512 0382warner 2564 633593
(except freischütz)/2564 633627 (freischütz)

706/22 november 1980/concert recording in
berlin philharmonie
berliner philharmoniker
bruckner symphony no 5 in b flat
this recording remains unpublished

707/1-4 december 1980/dg sessions in berlin
philharmonie
berliner philharmoniker/*producers günther breest
and michel glotz*
strauss eine alpensinfonie
lp: 2532 015
cd: 400 0392/439 0172/479 3839

bruckner symphony no 2 in c minor
lp: 2532 063/2740 264
cd: 415 9882/429 6482/429 6772/477 8005/479 3839
this recording was completed on 22-27 january 1981

708/27 december 1980/concert recordings in berlin philharmonie
berliner philharmoniker/*maurizio pollini
*beethoven piano concerto no 3 in c minor op 37
cd: exclusive EX92 T41

tchaikovsky symphony no 6 in b minor "pathetique"
this recording remains unpublished

709/31 december 1980/concert recordings in berlin philharmonie
berliner philharmoniker/anna tomova-sintow/
mstislav rostropovich
strauss vier letzte lieder; don quixote
these recordings remain unpublished

710/1 january 1981/concert recordings in berlin philharmonie
berliner philharmoniker/anne-sophie mutter
bruch violin concerto no 1; tchaikovsky symphony no 6
cd: private edition vienna

711/2 january 1981/emi sessions in berlin philharmonie
berliner philharmoniker/*producer michel glotz*
sibelius symphony no 1 in e minor
lp: ASD 4097/1C063 43050/2C069 43050/3C065 43050
cd: 763 8962/769 0282/512 0382/warner 2564 633619

712/26-31 january and 20-26 february 1981/
dg sessions in berlin philharmonie
berliner philharmoniker/*rias-kammerchor/
producers günther breest and michel glotz
bruckner symphony no 1 in c minor
lp: 2532 062/2740 264
cd: 415 9852/429 6482/429 6772/477 8005/479 3839

*holst the planets
lp: 2532 019
cd: 400 0282/435 2892/439 0112/479 3839
this recording was completed on 20 march 1981

mozart serenade no 13 K525 "eine kleine nachtmusik"
lp: 2532 031
cd: 400 0342/423 6102/431 2722/431 2922/479 3839

grieg holberg suite
lp: 2532 031/419 4741
cd: 400 0342/419 4742/427 8082/439 0102/479 3839

prokofiev symphony no 1 "classical"
lp: 2532 031
cd: 400 0342/423 2162/423 5552/437 2532/479 3839

713/20-27 february 1981/dg sessions in berlin
philharmonie
berliner philharmoniker/wiener singverein/barbara
hendricks/janet perry/peter schreier/benjamin luxon/
producers günther breest, michel glotz and
werner meyer
mozart mass in c minor K427 "great"
lp: 2532 028
cd: 400 0672/431 2872/431 2922/439 0122/479 3839

shostakovich symphony no 10 in e minor
lp: 2532 030
cd: 413 3612/459 0362/479 3839

nielsen symphony no 4 "inextinguishable"
lp: 2532 029
cd: 413 3132/445 5182/479 3839

714/11 april 1981/stage recording in salzburg
grosses festspielhaus
berliner philharmoniker/chor der wiener staatsoper/
wiener singverein/salzburger kammerchor/tölzer
sängerknaben/dunja vejzovic/peter hofmann/kurt
moll/jose van dam/gottfried hornik/victor von halem/
volker horn/erich knodt/heiner hopfner/georg tichy/
marjon lambricks/anne gjevang/barbara vogel/janet
perry/hanna schwarz/inga nielsen/audrey michael/
rohangiz yachmi
wagner parsifal
cd: private edition vienna

300

715/12 april 1981/concert recording in salzburg
grosses festspielhaus
berliner philharmoniker/wiener singverein/
edith mathis/francisco araiza/jose van dam
haydn die schöpfung
this recording remains unpublished

716/13 april 1981/concert recordings in salzburg
grosses festspielhaus
berliner philharmoniker
schönberg verklärte nacht; beethoven symphony no 7
these recordings remain unpublished

717/10 may 1981/concert recording in vienna
musikvereinssaal
wiener philharmoniker
bruckner symphony no 5 in b flat
cd: private edition vienna

718/11-18 may 1981/dg sessions in vienna
musikvereinssaal
wiener philharmoniker/chor der wiener staatsoper/
tölzer sängerknaben/katia ricciarelli/barbara
hendricks/placido domingo/francisco araiza/
ruggiero raimondi/piero de palma/gottfried hornik/
heinz zednik/siegmund nimsgern/
producer michel glotz
puccini turandot
lp: 2741 013
cd: 410 0962/423 8552/479 4640

719/27 may 1981/concert recording in london
royal festival hall
berliner philharmoniker
bruckner symphony no 5 in b flat
cd: private edition vienna

720/28 may 1981/concert recording in oxford
sheldonian theatre
berliner philharmoniker/anne-sophie mutter
bach brandenburg concerto no 2; mozart violin concerto no 3;
strauss metamorphosen
these recordings remain unpublished

721/6 june 1981/concert recording in salzburg
grosses festspielhaus
berliner philharmoniker/yo yo ma/wolfram christ
strauss don quixote
cd: private edition vienna

722/7 june 1981/concert recordings in salzburg
grosses festspielhaus
berliner philharmoniker
haydn symphony no 104; brahms symphony no 1
these recordings remain unpublished

723/26 july 1981/stage recording in salzburg
grosses festspielhaus
wiener philharmoniker/chor der wiener staatsoper/
giuseppe taddei/rolando panerai/francisco araiza/
raina kabaiwanska/janet perry/christa ludwig/
trudeliese schmidt/piero de palma/heinz zednik/
federico davia
verdi falstaff
cd: private edition vienna

724/16 august 1981/concert recordings in salzburg
grosses festspielhaus
wiener philharmoniker/anne-sophie mutter
mozart maurerische trauermusik; brahms violin concerto;
dvorak symphony no 8
these recordings remain unpublished

725/27 august 1981/concert recordings in salzburg
grosses festspielhaus
berliner philharmoniker/konzertvereinigung
wiener staatsopernchor
bach brandenburg concerto no 3; stravinsky
symphonie de psaumes
cd: private edition vienna

strauss metamorphosen
this recording remains unpublished

726/28 august 1981/concert recordings in salzburg
grosses festspielhaus
berliner philharmoniker/francois-rene duchable
bartok piano concerto no 3; tchaikovsky symphony no 6
these recordings remain unpublished

727/20-22 september 1981/dg sessions in berlin philharmonie
berliner philharmoniker/anne-sophie mutter/
pierre cochereau/*producers günther breest
and michel glotz*
brahms violin concerto in d op 77
lp: 2532 032/2740 282
cd: 400 0642/415 5652/439 0072/445 5152/
449 6972/479 3839

saint-saens symphony no 3 in c minor "organ symphony"
lp: 2532 045
cd: 400 0632/439 0142/479 3839

728/21-25 september 1981, 2-4 and 25-28 january
and 16 february 1982/dg sessions in berlin
philharmonie
berliner philharmoniker/*producers günther breest,
michel glotz and werner meyer*
haydn symphonies: no 93 in d; no 94 in g "surprise"
lp: 2741 015/410 6491
cd: 410 8692 (no 94)/427 8092/429 6582/429 6772/
463 0832 (no 94)/477 8005/479 3839

haydn symphonies: no 95 in c minor; no 96 in d "miracle"
lp: 2741 015/410 8671
cd: 410 9752 (no 96)/429 6582/429 6772/
463 0832 (no 96)/477 8005/479 3839

haydn symphonies: no 97 in c; no 98 in b flat
lp: 2741 015/410 9571
cd: 429 6582/429 6772/477 8005/479 3839

728/21-25 september 1981, 2-4 and 25-28 january
and 26 february 1982/dg sessions in berlin
philharmonie/concluded
haydn symphonies: no 99 in e flat; no 100 in g "military"
lp: 2741 015/410 9581
cd: 410 9752 (no 100)/429 8092 (no 100)/429 6582/
429 6772/477 8005/479 3839

haydn symphonies: no 101 in d "clock"; no 102 in b flat
lp: 2741 015/410 8681
cd: 410 8692 (no 101)/429 6582/429 6772/
477 8005/479 3839

haydn symphonies: no 103 in e flat "drum roll";
no 104 in d "london"
lp: 2741 015/410 5171
cd: 410 5172/423 2102 (no 104)/423 5552 (no 104)/
429 6582/429 6772/463 0832 (no 104)/477 8005/479 3839

729/27-28 september 1981 and 3 january 1982/
dg sessions in berlin philharmonie
berliner philharmoniker/kristian zimerman/
producers günther breest and michel glotz
grieg piano concerto in a minor; schumann
piano concerto in a minor
lp: 2532 043
cd: 410 0212/439 0152/479 3839

730/28 october 1981/televised concert in tokyo
nhk hall

berliner philharmoniker

beethoven symphony no 1; symphony no 3 "eroica"
these video recordings remain unpublished

731/29 october 1981/televised concert in tokyo
nhk hall

berliner philharmoniker/anne-sophie mutter

beethoven violin concerto; symphony no 5
these video recordings reain unpublished

732/30 october 1981/televised concert in tokyo
nhk hall

berliner philharmoniker

brahms symphony no 3; symphony no 1
these video recordings remain unpublished

733/31 october 1981/concert recordings in
tokyo nhk hall

berliner philharmoniker

brahms symphony no 2; symphony no 4
these recordings remain unpublished

734/2 november 1981/concert recordings in
tokyo nhk hall

berliner philharmoniker

debussy la mer; prelude a l'apres-midi d'un faune;
ravel bolero; rapsodie espagnole
these recordings remain unpublished

734a/5 november 1981/concert recordings in tokyo nhk hall

berliner philharmoniker/anne-sophie mutter

beethoven violin concerto; symphony no 5

these recordings remain unpublished

735/8 november 1981/concert recordings in tokyo nhk hall

berliner philharmoniker

beethoven symphony no 6; tchaikovsky symphony no 6

these recordings remain unpublished

736/23 november 1981/concert recording in berlin philharmonie

berliner philharmoniker

bruckner symphony no 9 in d minor

cd: private edition vienna

737/2-9 december 1981/emi sessions in berlin philharmonie

berliner philharmoniker/konzertvereinigung wiener staatsopernchor/dunja vejzovic/kaja borris/ peter hofmann/thomas moser/jose van dam/ kurt moll/*producer michel glotz*

wagner der fliegende holländer

lp: EX 27 00133

cd: 747 0548/764 6502/511 9732

this recording was completed in salzburg grosses
festspielhaus on 28 march 1982 and in berlin
philharmonie on 19 september 1983

738/31 december 1981/concert recordings in berlin philharmonie
berliner philharmoniker/anne-sophie mutter
bruch violin concerto no 1; strauss eine alpensinfonie
these recordings remain unpublished

739/24 january 1982/concert recording in berlin philharmonie
berliner philharmoniker/francois-rene duchable
bartok piano concerto no 3
this recording remains unpublished

740/26-28 january 1982/dg sessions in berlin philharmonie
berliner philharmoniker/*producers günther breest and michel glotz*
strauss tod und verklärung
lp: 2532 074
cd: 410 8922/447 4222/479 3839

grieg peer gynt: first and second suites
lp: 2532 068
cd: 410 0262/439 0102/479 3839

sibelius pelleas and melisande suite
lp: 2532 068
cd: 410 0262/445 5502/479 3839
recordings of the grieg and sibelius items were completed on 17-18 february 1982

741/22 february 1982/concert recording in
berlin philharmonie
berliner philharmoniker/chor der deutschen
oper/katia ricciarelli/jose carreras/ruggiero
raimondi/heinz zednik/gottfried hornik/
victor von halem/fernando corena/ein tölzer
sängerknabe
puccini tosca
this recording remains unpublished

742/3 april 1982/stage recording in salzburg
grosses festspielhaus
berliner philharmoniker/konzertvereinigung
wiener staatsopernchor/catarina ligendza/kaja
borris/jose van dam/kurt moll/reiner goldberg/
thomas moser
wagner der fliegende holländer
this recording remains unpublished

743/6 april 1982/concert recordings in salzburg
grosses festspielhaus
berliner philharmoniker/anna tomova-sintow
strauss vier letzte lieder; eine alpensinfonie
cd: private edition vienna/live classic best (japan)
LCB 143 (alpensinfonie)

744/30 april 1982/televised concert in berlin philharmonie
berliner philharmoniker
mozart symphony no 41 in c K551 "jupiter"
this recording remains unpublished

beethoven symphony no 3 in e flat op 55 "eroica"
vhs: sony SHV 48434
laserdisc: sony SLV 48434

745/1 may 1982/concert recording in berlin philharmonie
berliner philharmoniker
mahler symphony no 9
this recording remains unpublished

746/4 may 1982/concert recording in vienna musikvereinssaal
berliner philharmoniker/wiener singverein/anna tomova-sintowa/agnes baltsa/reiner goldberg/ kurt moll
beethoven symphony no 9 in d minor op 125 "choral"
this recording remains unpublished

747/4-8 may 1982/telemondial film and dg
sound sessions in vienna musikvereinssaal
wiener philharmoniker/wiener singverein/
barbara hendricks/jose van dam/*film producer*
herbert von karajan/sound producers günther
breest and michel glotz
brahms ein deutsches requiem
lp: 410 5211
cd: 410 5212/431 6512/479 3839
the video recording remains unpublished

748/28 may 1982/concert recordings in salzburg
grosses festspielhaus
berliner philharmoniker/anne-sophie mutter
bruch violin concerto no 1 in g minor
cd: live classic best (japan) LCB 125

brahms symphony no 2 in d
this recording remains unpublished

749/29 may 1982/concert recording in salzburg
grosses festspielhaus
berliner philharmoniker
bruckner symphony no 8 in c minor
this recording remains unpublished

750/30 may 1982/concert recordings in salzburg
grosses festspielhaus
berliner philharmoniker
mozart symphony no 29 in a K201
cd: live classic best (japan) LCB 102

shostakovich symphony no 10 in e minor
this recording remains unpublished

750a/30 july 1982/televised performance in
salzburg grosses festspielhaus
wiener philharmoniker/konzertvereinigung
wiener staatsopernchor/raina kabaiwanska/
janet perry/christa ludwig/trudeliese schmidt/
francisco araiza/giuseppe taddei/rolando panerai/
heinz zednik/piero de palma/federico davia
verdi falstaff
vhs: sony SHV 48422
laserdisc: sony S2LV 48422
dvd: sony SVD 48422

751/16-18 august 1982/rehearsal and concert
recording in salzburg grosses festspielhaus
wiener philharmoniker/wiener singverein/edith
mathis/ann murray/franciso araiza/jose van dam
haydn die schöpfung
lp: deutsche grammophon 2741 017
cd: deutsche grammophon 410 7182/479 3839

752/27 august 1982/concert recording in salzburg
grosses festspielhaus
berliner philharmoniker
mahler symphony no 9
this recording remains unpublished

753/28 august 1982/concert recordings in salzburg
grosses festspielhaus
berliner philharmoniker
stravinsky apollon musagete; strauss eine alpensinfonie
these recordings remain unpublished

754/1 september 1982/concert recordings in
lucerne kunsthaus
berliner philharmoniker
stravinsky apollon musagete; bruckner symphony no 7
these recordings remain unpublished

755/19-26 september 1982/dg sessions in berlin
philharmonie
berliner philharmoniker/choeurs de l'opera de paris/
schöneberger sängerknaben/agnes baltsa/karia
ricciarelli/jose carreras/jose van dam/christine
barbaux/jane berbie/alexander malta/gino quilico/
heinz zednik/michel marinpouille/anne-marie tostain/
alain picard/*producer michel glotz*
bizet carmen
lp: 2741 029
cd: 410 0882/479 4640
this recording was completed on 16 february and on
8-10 april 1983; dialogues were recorded separately
with a cast of french-speaking actors

756/21-22 and 27 september 1982/dg sessions in
berlin philharmonie
berliner philharmoniker/*producers günther breest*
and michel glotz
tchaikovsky romeo and Juliet fantasy overture;
casse-noisette: standard ballet suite
lp: 2532 096/2561 408
cd: 410 8732/439 0212/479 3839

757/30 september 1982/concert recording in
berlin philharmonie
berliner philharmoniker
mahler symphony no 9
cd: 410 7262/439 0242/479 3839

313

758/18-21 november 1982/telemondial film
and dg sound sessions in berlin philharmonie
berliner philharmoniker/*film producer herbert
von karajan/sound producers günther breest
and michel glotz*
beethoven symphony no 5 in c minor op 67
lp: 410 9321/415 0661
cd: 410 9322/415 0662/439 0042/439 2002/
477 9830/479 3839
vhs: sony SHV 46366/SHV 48365
laserdisc: sony SLV 46366
dvd: sony SVD 46366/88697 196439

beethoven symphony no 6 in f op 68 "pastoral"
lp: 410 9361/415 0661
cd: 410 9362/415 0662/439 0042/439 2002/
477 9830/479 3839
vhs: sony SHV 46367/SHV 48365
laserdisc: sony SLV 46367
dvd: sony SVD 46367/88697 196439

759/20 november 1982/concert recordings in
berlin philharmonie
berliner philharmoniker
beethoven symphony no 6 "pastoral"; symphony no 5
these recordings remain unpublished

760/22 november-4 december 1982/dg sessions in
vienna musikvereinssaal
wiener philharmoniker/konzertvereinigung wiener
staatsopernchor/anna tomova-sintow/agnes baltsa/
janet perry/kurt moll/gottfried hornik/vinson cole/
wilma lipp/helga müller-molinari/brigitte poschner/
waltraud winsauer/margaretha hintermeier/gabriele
sima/heinz zednik/victor von halem/kurt equiluz/
karl terkal/franz kasemann/carlos feller/horst nitsche/
adolf tomaschek/johann reinprecht/wolfgang scheider/
gerhard panzenböck/ingo koblitz/wolfgang holzherr/
walter zeh/hannes lichtenberger/johann reautschnigg/
producers michel glotz and werner meyer
strauss der rosenkavalier
lp: 413 1631
cd: 413 1632/423 8502/479 4640
this recording was completed on 9-10 may 1983 and
on 8-10 january 1984

761/31 january 1983/concert recordings in berlin
phiharmonie
berliner philharmoniker
beethoven symphony no 4; symphony no 7
these recordings remain unpublished

762/16-19 february 1983/dg sessions in berlin
philharmonie
berliner philharmoniker/anne-sophie mutter/
antonio meneses/*producers günther breest,
michel glotz and werner meyer*
brahms double concerto in a minor op 102
lp: 410 6031
cd: 410 6032/439 0072/449 6072/479 3839

brahms tragic overture op 81
lp: 2531 133/419 6031
cd: 410 6032/427 4962/427 6022/449 6012/479 3839

brahms haydn variations op 56a
cd: 423 1422/427 6022/449 6012/479 3839

strauss don juan
lp: 410 9591
cd: 410 9592/439 0162/479 3839
this recording was completed on 16 november 1983

763/19 february 1983/concert recordings in
berlin philharmonie
berliner philharmoniker/anne-sophie mutter/
antonio meneses
brahms double concerto; symphony no 1
these recordings remain unpublished

764/26 march 1983/stage recording in salzburg
grosses festspielhaus
berliner philharmoniker/chor der wiener staatsoper/
catarina ligendza/kaja borris/jose van dam/kurt moll/
reiner goldberg/gösta winbergh
wagner der fliegende holländer
this recording remains unpublished

765/15 august 1983/concert recording in salzburg
grosses festspielhaus
wiener philharmoniker/wiener singverein/
barbara hendricks/jose van dam
brahms ein deutsches requiem
this recording remains unpublished

766/27 august 1983/concert recordings in salzburg
grosses festspielhaus
berliner philharmoniker
brahms symphony no 4 in e minor op 98
cd: live classic best (japan) LCB 123

brahms symphony no 2 in d op 73
this recording remains unpublished

767/28 august 1983/concert recordings in salzburg
grosses festspielhaus
berliner philharmoniker
brahms symphony no 3; symphony no 1
these recordings remain unpublished

317

768/1 september 1983/concert recording in lucerne kunsthaus

berliner philharmoniker

bruckner symphony no 8 in c minor
this recording remains unpublished

769/20-27 september 1983/telemondial film and dg sound sessions in berlin philharmonie

berliner philharmoniker/wiener singverein/janet perry/agnes baltsa/vinson cole/jose van dam/ *film producer herbert von karajan/sound producers günther breest and michel glotz*

beethoven symphony no 9 in d minor op 125 "choral"
lp: 413 9331/415 0661
cd: 410 9872/415 0662/439 0062/439 2002/
477 9830/479 3839
the video version of this recording remains unpublished: the later (1986) video recording of the work (session 835a) is incorrectly dated 1983, but clearly has the vocal soloists from the later year

770/28 september 1983/dg sessions in berlin philharmonie

berliner philharmoniker/*producers günther breest and michel glotz*

bizet l'arlesienne: first and second suites
lp: 415 1061
cd: 415 1062/479 3839
415 1061 and 415 1062 also contained carmen suite drawn from the complete opera recording (session no 755)

771/28-30 september 1983/dg sessions in berlin philharmonie

berliner philharmoniker/*producers günther breest, michel glotz and werner meyer*

strauss also sprach zarathustra
lp: 410 9591
cd: 410 9592/439 0162/479 3839
albinoni-giazotto adagio in g minor; vivaldi concerto RV439;
bach air from third orchestral suite; pachelbel-seiffert
canon and gigue in d; gluck orfeo ed euridice: reigen
seliger geister; mozart serenata notturna K239
lp: 413 3091
cd: 413 3092/431 2722/445 2822/449 7242/
463 2912/479 3839
not all re-issues contain all the items listed

771a/19-20 november 1983/televised concerts in berlin philharmonie
berliner philharmoniker
strauss eine alpensinfonie
vhs: sony SHV 46400/laserdisc: sony SLV 46400/
dvd: sony SVD 46400/88697 195469

772/29 november-6 december 1983/telemondial film and dg sound sessions in berlin philharmonie
berliner philharmoniker/*film producer herbert von karajan/sound producers günther breest and michel glotz*
beethoven symphony no 4 in b flat op 60;
symphony no 7 in a op 92
lp: 415 1211/415 0661
cd: 415 1212/415 0662/439 0032/439 2002/477 9830/479 3839
vhs: sony SHV 46366 (no 4)/SHV 46367 (no 7)/SHV 48365
laserdisc: sony SLV 46366 (no 4)/SLV 46367 (no 7)
dvd: sony SVD 46366 (no 4)/SVD 46367 (no 7)/88697 196439

773/3 december 1983/concert recordings in
berlin philharmonie
berliner philharmoniker
beethoven symphony no 4; symphony no 7
these recordings remain unpublished

774/28-31 december 1983/dg sessions in berlin
philharmonie
berliner philharmoniker/*producers günther breest
and michel glotz*
smetana the moldau; liszt les preludes; hungarian
rhapsody no 5 in e minor; weber-berlioz aufforderung
zum tanz; rossini guilleaume tell overture
lp: 415 5871
cd: 415 5872/445 3402 (rossini)/445 5502
(moldau and preludes)/479 3839
*these recordings were completed on 24 and 30 january
and 24 february 1984*

775/31 december 1983/concert recording in berlin
philharmonie (first half of concert)
berliner philharmoniker
schubert symphony no 8 in b minor D759 "unfinished"
this recording remains unpublished

776/31 december 1983/televised concert in berlin philharmonie (second half of concert)

berliner philharmoniker

rossini guilleaume tell overture; sibelius valse triste;
smetana the moldau; josef strauss delirienwalzer;
johann strauss zigeunerbaron overture
vhs: sony SHV 46401
laserdisc: sony SLV 46401
dvd: sony SVD 46401

777/10-16 january 1984/telemondial film and dg sound sessions in vienna musikvereinssaal

wiener philharmoniker/konzertvereinigung wiener staatsopernchor/sofia opera chorus/anna tomova-sintow/agnes baltsa/jose carreras/ jose van dam/*film producer herbert von karajan/ sound producers uli märkle and michel glotz*

verdi messa da requiem
lp: 415 0911
cd: 415 0912/439 0332/479 3839
laserdisc: sony SLV 53481
main film sessions for verdi requiem were held on 5-13 june 1984

tchaikovsky symphony no 6 in b minor op 74 "pathetique"
lp: 415 0951
cd: 415 0952/435 3562/439 0202/479 3839
vhs: sony SHV 48311
laserdisc: sony SLV 48311
dvd: sony SVD 48311/88697 198439

778/25-31 january 1984/telemondial film and
dg sound sessions in berlin philharmonie
berliner philharmoniker/*film producer herbert
von karajan/sound producers günther breest
and michel glotz*
beethoven symphony no 3 in e flat op 55 "eroica";
symphony no 8 in f op 93
lp: 415 5061 (no 3)/415 5071 (no 8)/415 0661
cd: 415 5062 (no 3)/415 5072 (no 8)/415 0662/
439 0022 (no 3)/439 0052 (no 8)/439 2002/
477 9830/479 3839
vhs: sony SHV 46363 (no 8)/SHV 46365 (no 3)/SHV 48365
laserdisc: sony SLV 46363 (no 8)/SLV 46365 (no 3)
dvd: sony SVD 46363 (no 8)/SVD 46365 (no 3)/
88697 196439
*recording of symphony no 8 was completed on
18-24 february 1984*

779/18-24 february 1984/telemondial film
sessions in berlin philharmonie
berliner philharmoniker/anne-sophie mutter/
film producer herbert von karajan
beethoven violin concerto in d op 61
vhs: sony SHV 46385/SHV 48365
lasedisc: sony SLV 46385
dvd: sony SVD 46385

780/18-24 february 1984/dg sessions in berlin philharmonie

berliner philharmoniker/*producers günther breest and michel glotz*

wagner tannhäuser overture and venusberg; meistersinger act three prelude; tristan prelude and liebestod
lp: 413 7541
cd: 415 7542/439 0222/479 3839

sibelius finlandia; swan of tuonela; valse triste; tapiola
lp: 413 7551
cd: 413 7552/415 3402 (finalandia)/439 0102 (swan)/
445 2822 (valse)/445 5182 (tapiola)/445 5502 (finlandia)/
449 5152 (tapiola)/457 7482 (swan)/459 0102 (finlandia
and valse)/463 2912 (valse)/479 3839

781/18-24 february 1984/telemondial film and dg sound sessions in berlin philharmonie

berliner philharmoniker/*film producer herbert von karajan/sound producers günther breest and michel glotz*

beethoven symphony no 1 in c op 21;
symphony no 2 in d op 36
lp: 415 5051/415 0661
cd: 415 5052/415 0662/439 0012/439 2002/
477 9830/479 3839
vhs: sony SHV 46363 (no 1)/SHV 46365 (no 2)/SHV 48365
laserdisc: sony SLV 46363 (no 1)/SLV 46365 (no 2)
dvd: sony SVD 46363 (no 1)/SVD 46365 (no 2)/
88697 196439

782/25 february 1984/concert recordings in berlin philharmonie
berliner philharmoniker
beethoven symphony no 8; symphony no 2
these recordings remain unpublished

782a/13-22 march 1984/telemondial film and dg sound sessions in vienna musikvereinssaal/*film producer herbert von karajan/sound producers uli märkle and michel glotz*
tchaikovsky symphony no 5 in e minor op 64
lp: 410 0941
cd: 410 0942/435 3562/439 0192/479 3839
vhs: sony SHV 48310
laserdisc: sony SLV 48310
dvd: sony SVD 48310/88697 198449

783/14 april 1984/stage recording in salzburg grosses festspielhaus
berliner philharmoniker/konzertvereinigung wiener staatsopernchor/tölzer sängerknaben/ anna tomova-sintow/dunja vezjovic/peter hofmann/kurt moll/siegmund nimsgern/franz grundheber/volker horn/imre remenyi/james johnson/alfred muff
wagner lohengrin
cd: private edition vienna

784/16 april 1984/concert recordings in salzburg grosses festspielhaus
berliner philharmoniker/anne-sophie mutter/ antonio meneses
brahms double concerto; strauss also sprach zarathustra
these recordings remain unpublished

785/17 april 1984/concert recording in salzburg
grosses festspielhaus
berliner philharmoniker/wiener singverein/janet
perry/helga müller-molinari/eberhard büchner/
jose van dam
beethoven symphony no 9 in d minor op 125 "choral"
this recording remains unpublished

786/june 1984/emi sessions in vienna
zeremoniensaal der hofburg
wiener philharmoniker/anne-sophie mutter/
producer peter alward
vivaldi le 4 stagioni: concerti RV269, RV315, RV 293 and RV297
lp: EL 27 01021
cd: 747 0432/512 0382/warner 2564 633624

787/31 july 1984/televised performance in salzburg
grosses festspielhaus
wiener philharmoniker/konzertvereinigung wiener
staatsopernchor/anna tomova-sintow/agnes baltsa/
janet perry/kurt moll/gottfried hornik/vinson cole/
wilma lipp/helga müller-molinari/heinz zednik/
john van kesteren/franz kasemann/kurt rydl/
alfred sramek/karl terkal
strauss der rosenkavalier
cd: private edition vienna
vhs: sony S2HV 48313
laserdisc: sony S2LV 48313
dvd: sony SVD 48313

788/27 august 1984/concert recordings in salzburg
grosses festspielhaus
wiener philharmoniker/anne-sophie mutter
vivaldi le 4 stagioni; tchaikovsky symphony no 6
these recordings remain unpublished

789/28 august 1984/concert recordings in salzburg
grosses festspielhaus
wiener philharmoniker/kristian zimerman
schumann piano concerto; brahms symphony no 1
these recordings remain unpublished

790/31 august 1984/concert recordings in lucerne
kunsthaus
wiener philharmoniker/kristian zimerman
schumann piano concerto; brahms symphony no 1
these recordings remain unpublished

791/september 1984/telemondial film and dg sound
sessions in vienna musikvereinssaal
wiener philharmoniker/*film producer herbert von
karajan/sound producers uli märkle and michel glotz*
tchaikovsky symphony no 4 in f minor op 36
lp: 415 3481
cd: 415 3482/433 3562/439 0182/479 3839
vhs: sony SHV 48309
laserdisc: sony SLV 48309
dvd: sony SVD 48309/88697 198439

792/28 september 1984/dg sessions in vienna
musikvereinssaal
wiener philharmoniker/wiener singverein/janet
perry/helga müller-molinari/gösta winbergh/
alexander malta/*producers günther breest and
michel glotz*
bruckner te deum
lp: 410 5211
cd: 410 5212/429 9802/479 3839

793/18 october 1984/televised concert in osaka
symphony hall
berliner philharmoniker
mozart divertimento no 15 K287; strauss don juan
laserdisc: sony SLV 53484

respighi pini di roma
cd: private edition vienna
laserdisc: sony SLV 53484

794/19 october 1984/concert recordings in osaka
symphony hall
berliner philharmoniker
debussy la mer; prelude a l'apres-midi d'un faune;
ravel daphnis et chloe: second suite
these in-house recordings remain unpublished

795/22 october 1984/concert recordings in tokyo
nhk hall

berliner philharmoniker

beethoven symphony no 6; symphony no 5
these in-house recordings remain unpublished

796/23 october 1984/concert recordings in tokyo
nhk hall

berliner philharmoniker

brahms symphony no 3; symphony no 1
these in-house recordings remain unpublished

797/24 october 1984/concert recordings in tokyo
nhk hall

berliner philharmoniker

debussy la mer; prelude a l'apres-midi d'un faune;
ravel daphnis et chloe: second suite
these in-house recordings remain unpublished

798/24-25 november 1984/concert recording in
berlin philharmonie (first half of concert)

berliner philharmoniker

brahms symphony no 4 in e minor op 98
this recording remains unpublished

799/24-25 november 1984/televised concert in
berlin philharmonie (second half of concert)
berliner philharmoniker
strauss metamorphosen; tod und verklärung
laserdisc: sony SLV 48984
dvd: sony 88697 195469

800/12 december 1984/concert recordings in
berlin philharmonie
berliner philharmoniker
honegger symphony no 3; brahms symphony no 1
cd: private edition vienna

801/15 december 1984/concert recording in
vienna musikvereinssaal
wiener philharmoniker
tchaikovsky romeo and juliet fantasy overture
cd: private edition vienna

802/31 december 1984/televised concert in
berlin philharmonie
berliner philharmoniker/rias-kammerchor/
anne-sophie mutter/judith blegen/helga
müller-molinari/francisco araiza/robert holl
bach violin concerto BWV1042; magnificat BWV243
vhs: sony SHV 45983
laserdisc: sony SLV 45983
dvd: sony SVD 45983

803/13 january-10 february 1985/telemondial film and dg sound sessions in vienna musikvereinssaal
wiener philharmoniker/*film producer herbert von karajan/sound producers uli märkle and michel glotz*
dvorak symphony no 8 in g op 88
lp: 415 9711
cd: 415 9712/431 0952/479 3839
vhs: sony SHV 48420
laserdisc: sony SLV 48420
dvd: sony SVD 48420/88697 202409

dvorak symphony no 9 in e minor op 95 "from the new world"
lp: 415 5091
cd: 415 5092/439 0092/479 3839
vhs: sony SHV 48421
laserdisc: sony SLV 48421
dvd: sony SVD 48421/88697 202409
88697 202409 incorrectly describes orchestra as berliner philharmoniker

804/21-28 january 1985/dg sessions in berlin philharmonie
berliner philharmoniker/chor der deutschen oper/ samuel ramey/anna tomova-sintow/agnes baltsa/ kathleen battle/gösta winbergh/ferruccio furlanetto/ alexander malta/paata burchuladze/*producers michel glotz and werner meyer*
mozart don giovanni
lp: 419 1791
cd: 419 1792/419 8102/479 4640

805/26 january 1985/concert recordings in berlin philharmonie

berliner philharmoniker/pierre amoyal

berg violin concerto; brahms symphony no 2

cd: private edition vienna

806/18-20 february 1985/telemondial film and dg sound sessions in berlin philharmonie

berliner philharmoniker/*film producer herbert von karajan/sound producers uli märkle and michel glotz*

strauss ein heldenleben

lp: 415 5081

cd: 415 5082/439 0392/479 3839

laserdisc: sony SLV 46390

dvd: sony 88697 195469

807/23 february 1985/concert recordings in berlin philharmonie

berliner philharmoniker

brahms symphony no 3; strauss ein heldenleben

these recordings remain unpublished

808/25 april 1985/concert recordings in brussels palais des beaux arts

berliner philharmoniker

beethoven symphony no 4; symphony no 7

these recordings remain unpublished

809/27 april 1985/concert recordings in london
royal festival hall
berliner philharmoniker
beethoven symphony no 4; strauss ein heldenleben
cd: private edition vienna (strauss)/testament SBT 1430

810/may 1985/dg session in vienna musikvereinssaal
wiener philharmoniker/*producers günther breest
and michel glotz*
smetana ma vlast: the moldau
lp: 415 5091
cd: 415 5092/439 0092/479 3839

811/21-26 may 1985/telemondial film sessions in
vienna musikvereinsssaal
wiener philharmoniker/wiener singverein/
kathleen battle/jose van dam/*film producer
herbert von karajan*
brahms ein deutsches requiem
cd: private edition vienna
laserdisc: sony SLV 53485
additional session for this recording was held in june 1987

812/29 june 1985/televised performance in the framework of solemn high mass conducted by the pope in rome basilica san pietro

wiener philharmoniker/wiener singverein/ kathleen battle/trudeliese schmidt/gösta winbergh/ferruccio furlanetto

mozart mass in c K317 "coronation mass"

lp: 419 0961

cd: 419 0962/429 9802/445 5432/479 3839

vhs: sony SHV 46382

laserdisc: sony SLV 46382

dvd: sony SVD 46382/88697 195479

429 9802 and 445 5432 contain the musical performance only

813/26 july 1985/stage recording in salzburg grosses festspielhaus

wiener philharmoniker/konzertvereinigung wiener staatsopernchor/agnes baltsa/janet perry/ jose carreras/jose van dam/graciela de gyldenfeldt/ jane berbie/alexander malta/michel senechal/ heinz zednik/albert medina

bizet carmen

cd: private edition vienna

brief rehearsal extract recorded but unpublished

814/15 august 1985/concert recordings in salzburg grosses festspielhaus

wiener philharmoniker/anne-sophie mutter

tchaikovsky violin concerto; symphony no 4

these recordings remain unpublished

815/27 august 1985/concert recording in salzburg grosses festspielhaus
berliner philharmoniker/wiener singverein/kathleen battle/agnes baltsa/gösta winbergh/jose van dam
bach mass in b minor BWV232
cd: private edition vienna

816/28 august 1985/concert recordings in salzburg grosses festspielhaus
berliner philharmoniker
debussy la mer; prelude a l'apres-midi d'un faune; ravel bolero
these recordings remain unpublished

817/31 august 1985/concert recording in lucerne kunsthaus
berliner philharmoniker
bruckner symphony no 9
this recording remains unpublished

818/25-29 september 1985/telemondial film and dg sound sessions in berlin philharmonie
berliner philharmoniker/wiener singverein/lella cuberli/trudeliese schmidt/vinson cole/jose van dam/ *film producer herbert von karajan/sound producers uli märkle and michel glotz*
beethoven missa solemnis op 123
lp: 419 1661
cd: 419 1662/445 5432/479 3839
laserdisc: sony SVD 53483

819/18-20 november 1985/dg sessions in berlin
philharmonie
berliner philharmoniker/anna tomova-sintow/
producers günther breest and michel glotz
strauss vier letzte lieder; die heiligen drei könige;
capriccio: mondscheinmusik and closing scene
(morgen mittag um elf)
lp: 419 1881
cd: 419 1882/445 0662/479 3839
although these recordings are described as a co-production
with telemondial, no video version has been published

820/24 november 1985/televised concert in
berlin philharmonie
berliner philharmoniker
bruckner symphony no 9 in d minor
vhs: sony SHV 46381
laserdisc: sony SLV 46381
dvd: sony SVD 46381/88697 202399

821/28 november-8 december 1985/telemondial
film and dg sound sessions in berlin philharmonie
berliner philharmoniker/*film producer herbert
von karajan/sound producers uli märkle and
michel glotz*
debussy la mer; prelude a l'apres-midi d'un faune; ravel
daphnis et chloe: second suite; pavane pour une infant defunte
lp: 413 5891
cd: 419 5892/439 0082/439 5152 (pavane)/
463 2912 (pavane)/479 3839
vhs: sony SHV 53479 (all except pavane)
laserdisc: sony SLV 53479 (all except pavane)
dvd: sony SVD 53479 (all except pavane)

beethoven overtures: egmont; coriolan; leonore no 3; fidelio
lp: 415 5061 (egmont)/415 5071 (all except egmont)/415 0661
cd: 415 5062 (egmont)/415 5072 (all except egmont)/
439 0022/439 2002/479 3839
laserdisc: sony SLV 48314
dvd: sony SVD 48314

822/7 december 1985/concert recordings in berlin
philharmonie
berliner philharmoniker
debussy la mer; prelude a l'apres-midi d'in faune;
ravel daphnis et chloe: second suite
these recordings remain unpublished

823/29 december 1985/dg session in berlin
philharmonie
berliner philharmoniker/*producers günther*
breest and michel glotz
ravel bolero
lp: 413 5881
cd: 413 5882/423 8032/439 0132/479 3839

824/31 december 1985/televised concert in
berlin philharmonie
berliner philharmoniker
weber freischütz overture; leoncavallo pagliacci intermezzo;
puccini manon lescaut intermezzo; liszt hungarian
rhapsody no 5; ravel bolero; Josef strauss sphärenklänge
vhs: sony SHV 46402 (all except sphärenklänge)
laserdisc: sony SLV 46402 (all except sphärenklänge)
dvd: sony SVD 46402 (all except sphärenklänge)

825/22-25 january 1986/telemondial film and
dg sound sessions in berlin philharmonie
berliner philharmoniker/antonio meneses/wolfram
christ/*film producer herbert von karajan/sound
producers uli märkle and michel glotz*
strauss don quixote
lp: 419 5991
cd: 419 5992/439 0272/479 3839
vhs: sony SHV 46389
laserdisc: sony SLV 46389
dvd: sony SVD 46389/88697 195469

strauss till eulenspiegels lustige streiche
lp: 419 5991
cd: 419 5992/439 0272/479 3839
*this recording was completed on 18 june 1986;
video version remains unpublished*

826/25 january 1986/concert recordings in
berlin philharmonie
berliner philharmoniker/antonio meneses/
wolfram christ
schubert symphony no 8; strauss don quixote
these recordings remain unpublished

338

827/17-22 february 1986/telemondial film and dg sound sessions in berlin philharmonie

berliner philharmoniker/*film producer herbert von karajan/sound producers uli märkle and michel glotz*

mussorgsky-ravel pictures from an exhibition

lp: 413 5881

cd: 413 5882/439 0132/479 3839

laserdisc: sony SLV 53480

dvd: sony 88697 195479

828/22 february 1986/concert recordings in berlin philharmonie

berliner philharmoniker

haydn symphony no 104; ravel pavane pour une infante defunte; mussorgsky-ravel pictures from an exhibition

these recordings remain unpublished

829/24 march 1986/concert recordings in salzburg grosses festspielhaus

berliner philharmoniker/anne-sophie mutter

bach violin concerto BWV1042; bruckner symphony no 9

these recordings remain unpublished

829a/31 march 1986/televised performance in salzburg grosses festspielhaus

berliner philharmoniker/konzertvereinigung wiener staatsopernchor/chor der nationaloper sofia/ salzburger konzertchor/fiamma izzo d'amico/agnes baltsa/jose carreras/ferruccio furlanetto/piero cappuccilli/matti salminen/franco de grandis/ antonella bandelli/katharina schuchter/horst nitsche/volker horn

verdi don carlo

vhs: sony SHV 48312/laserdisc: SLV 48312/dvd: SVD 48312

830/26 may-2 june 1986/telemondial film and dg
sound sessions in vienna musikvereinssaal
wiener philharmoniker/wiener singverein/anna
tomova-sintow/helga müller-molinari/vinson cole/
paata burchuladze/*film producer herbert von karajan/*
sound producers uli märkle and michel glotz
mozart requiem mass K626
lp: 419 6101
cd: 419 6102/431 2882/431 2922/439 0232/479 3839
vhs: sony SHV 46384
laserdisc: sony SLV 46384
dvd: sony SVD 46384

831/15-19 june 1986/telemondial film and dg
sound sessions in berlin philharmonie
berliner philharmoniker/*film producer herbert*
von karajan/sound producers günther breest
and michel glotz
brahms symphony no 2 in d op 73
lp: 423 1421
cd: 423 1422/427 6022/449 6012/479 3839
laserdisc: sony SLV 53477
dvd: sony 88697 202419

brahms tragic overture
laserdisc: sony SLV 48314
dvd: sony SVD 48314

832/26 july 1986/stage recordings in salzburg
grosses festspielhaus
wiener philharmoniker/konzertvereinigung wiener
staatsopernchor/tölzer sängerknaben/helga
müller-molinari/fiamma izzo d'amico/graciela de
gyldenfeldt/jane berbie/jose carreras/jose van dam/
alexander malta/michel senechal/heinz zednik/
albert medina
bizet carmen
cd: private edition vienna

833/17 august 1986/concert recording in salzburg
grosses festspielhaus
wiener philharmoniker
bruckner symphony no 8 in c minor
cd: private edition vienna

834/27 august 1986/concert recording in salzburg
grosses festspielhaus
berliner philharmoniker/wiener singverein/lella
cuberli/trudeliese schmidt/vinson cole/jose van dam
beethoven missa solemnis op 123
this recording remains unpublished

835/31 august 1986/concert recordings in lucerne
kunsthaus
berliner philharmoniker
mozart divertimento no 15 K287; brahms symphony no 2
these recordings remain unpublished

341

835a/19-29 september 1986/telemondial film sessions in berlin philharmonie/*film producer herbert von karajan*

berliner philharmoniker/wiener singverein/lella cuberli/helga müller-molinari/vinson cole/franz grundheber

beethoven symphony no 9 in d minor op 125 "choral"

cd: private edition freunde der salzburger festspiele

vhs: sony SHV 48366/S5HV 48365

laserdisc: sony SLV 48364

all editions are incorrectly dated 1983

836/1 january 1987/televised concert in vienna musikvereinssaal

wiener philharmoniker

zigeunerbaron overture; sphärenklänge; annen polka; delirienwalzer; fledermaus overture; beliebte annen polka; vergnügungszug; kaiserwalzer; pizzicato polka; perpetuum mobile; unter donner und blitz; frühlingsstimmen; ohne sorgen; an der schönen blauen donau; radetzky-marsch

lp: 419 6161

cd: 419 6162/457 6892/477 6336/479 3839

vhs: sony SHV 45985

laserdisc: sony SLV 45985

dvd: sony SVD 45985

original lp and cd editions omitted certain items

837/26-28 january 1987/telemondial film and dg sound sessions in berlin philharmonie

berliner philharmoniker/*film producer herbert von karajan/sound producers günther breest and michel glotz*

brahms symphony no 1 in c minor op 68

lp: 423 1411

cd: 423 1412/427 6022/449 6012/479 3839

laserdisc: sony SLV 53477/dvd: sony 88697 202419

838/1 february 1987/concert recordings in berlin philharmonie

berliner philharmoniker

brahms haydn variations; symphony no 1

these recordings remain unpublished

839/23-24 and 28 february 1987/dg sessions in berlin philharmonie

berliner philharmoniker/*producers günther breest and michel glotz*

ravel rapsodie espagnole

lp: 415 5881

cd: 415 5882/439 0132/479 3839

a possible video version of this recording remains unpublished

mozart symphony no 29 in a K201

lp: 423 3741

cd: 423 3742/431 2682/431 2922/477 8005/479 3839

840/1 march 1987/concert recordings in berlin philharmonie

berliner philharmoniker

mozart symphony no 29; berlioz symphonie fantastique

cd: private edition Vienna

841/12 april 1987/rehearsal recording in salzburg #grosses festspielhaus

berliner philharmoniker/antonio meneses/ wolfram christ

strauss don quixote

this recording remains unpublished

842/13 april 1987/concert recordings in salzburg grosses festspielhaus

berliner philharmoniker

beethoven symphony no 6 in f op 68 "pastoral"; mussorgsky-ravel pictures from an exhibition

these recordings remains unpublished

343

843/14 april 1987/concert recordings in salzburg grosses festspielhaus
berliner philharmoniker/antonio meneses/ wolfram christ
schubert symphony no 8; strauss don quixote
these recordings remain unpublished

844/19 april 1987/concert recordings in salzburg grosses festspielhaus
berliner philharmoniker/antonio meneses/ wolfram christ
schubert symphony no 8; strauss don quixote
these recordings remain unpublished

845/30 april 1987/concert recording in berlin philharmonie
berliner philharmoniker
mozart divertimento no 17 in d K334
lp: 423 3751
cd: 423 3752/479 3839

846/1 may 1987/televised concert in berlin philharmonie
berliner philharmoniker
mozart divertimento no 17 in d K334; strauss also sprach zarathustra
vhs: sony SHV 46388
laserdisc: sony SLV 46388
dvd: sony SVD 46388/88697 296099 (mozart)/ 88697 195469 (strauss)

847/24 may 1987/concert recordings in vienna musikvereinssaal

wiener philharmoniker

mozart symphony no 41 in c K551 "jupiter"
this recording remains unpublished

schumann symphony no 4 in d minor op 120
cd: 431 0952/477 8005/479 3839

848/10 june 1987/concert recordings in london royal festival hall

berliner philharmoniker

brahms symphony no 4; symphony no 2
these recordings remain unpublished

849/13 june 1987/concert recordings in paris

berliner philharmoniker

mozart divertimento no 15; berlioz symphonie fantastique
these recordings remain unpublished

850/14 june 1987/concert recordings in paris

berliner philharmoniker

brahms symphony no 4; symphony no 2
these recordings remain unpublished

345

851/26 july 1987/televised performance in salzburg grosses festspielhaus

wiener philharmoniker/konzertvereinigung wiener staatsopernchor/anna tomova-sintow/julia varady/ kathleen battle/samuel ramey/gösta winbergh/ ferruccio furlanetto/alexander malta/paata burchuladze

mozart don giovanni
vhs: sony SHV 46383
laserdisc: sony SLV 46383
dvd: sony SVD 46383/88697 296049
rehearsal extracts were also published by deutsche grammophon on vhs 072 1143 and lasersisc 072 1141; sony states that the filming took place between 18-31 july 1987

852/15 august 1987/concert recordings in salzburg grosses festspielhaus

wiener philharmoniker/jessye norman

wagner tannhäuser overture; siegfried idyll; tristan prelude and liebestod
lp: 423 6131
cd: 423 6132/479 3839
video recording of rehearsal performance of tannhäuser overture remains unpublished; rehearsal and performance of tristan liebestod were published by deutsche grammophon on vhs 072 1143 and laserdisc 072 1141

853/27 august 1987/concert recordings in salzburg
grosses festspielhaus

berliner philharmoniker

schubert symphony no 8; berlioz symphonie fantastique
these recordings remain unpublished

854/28 august 1987/concert recordings in salzburg
grosses festspielhaus

berliner philharmoniker

beethoven symphony no 4; mussorgsky-ravel
pictures from an exhibition
these recordings remain unpublished

855/31 august 1987/concert recording in lucerne
kunsthaus

berliner philharmoniker

mozart divertimento no 17 in d K334
this recording remains unpublished

856/21-22 september 1987/dg sessions in berlin
philharmonie

berliner philharmoniker/producers günther breest
and michel glotz

mozart divertimento no 15 in b flat K287
lp: 423 6101
cd: 423 6102/431 2722/431 2922/479 3839

mozart symphony no 39 in e flat K543
lp: 423 3741
cd: 423 3742/431 2682/431 2922/479 3839

857/26 september 1987/concert recording in berlin philharmonie

berliner philharmoniker/wiener singverein/lella cuberli/franz grundheber

brahms ein deutsches requiem

this recording remains unpublished

858/28 october 1987/televised concert in berlin kammermusiksaal der philharmonie

berliner philharmoniker/anne-sophie mutter

vivaldi le 4 stagioni

vhs: sony SHV 46380

laserdisc: sony SLV 46380

dvd: sony SVD 46380

859/1 november 1987/concert recordings in berlin philharmonie

berliner philharminoker

mozart symphony no 39; strauss eine alpensinfonie

these recordings remain unpublished

860/5 november 1987/concert recordings in cologne philharmonie

berliner philharmoniker

beethoven symphony no 6; mussorgsky-ravel pictures from an exhibition

these in-house recordings remain unpublished

861/6 november 1987/concert recordings in
frankfurt-am-main alte oper
berliner philharmoniker
schubert symphony no 8; berlioz symphonie fantastique
these in-house recordings remain unpublished

862/31 december 1987/concert recordings in
berlin philharmonie
berliner philharmoniker/*jessye norman
wagner siegfried idyll; *tristan prelude and liebestod
these recordings remain unpublished

wagner tannhäuser overture
cd: live classic best (japan) LCB 130

863/26 march 1988/stage recording in salzburg
grosses festspielhaus
berliner philharmoniker/konzertvereinigung
wiener staatsopernchor/zürcher sängerknaben/
fiamma izzo d'amico/luis lima/franz grundheber/
franco de grandis/alfredo mariotti/piero de palma/
wolfgang scheider/walter zeh/tammy hensrud
puccini tosca
this in-house recording remains unpublished

864/28 march 1988/concert recordings in salzburg grosses festspielhaus

berliner philharmoniker

mozart symphony no 39 in e flat K543
this recording remains unpublished

strauss eine alpensinfonie
cd: private edition vienna

865/29 april 1988/concert recordings in osaka symphony hall

berliner philharmoniker

mozart symphony no 29; tchaikovsky symphony no 6
these in-house recordings remain unpublished

866/30 april 1988/concert recordings in osaka symphony hall

berliner philharmoniker

beethoven symphony no 4; mussorgsky-ravel pictures from an exhibition
these in-house recordings remain unpublished

867/2 may 1988/concert recordings in tokyo suntory hall

berliner philharmoniker

mozart symphony no 29; tchaikovsky symphony no 6
cd: universal music (japan) UCCG 1402

868/4 may 1988/concert recordings in tokyo
suntory hall
berliner philharmoniker
beethoven symphony no 4; mussorgsky-ravel
pictures from an exhibition
cd: universal music (japan) UCCG 1401

869/5 may 1988/concert recordings in tokyo
suntory hall
berliner philharmoniker
mozart symphony no 39; brahms symphony no 1
cd: universal music (japan) UCCG 1400

870/6 august 1988/stage recording in salzburg
grosses festspielhaus
wiener philharmoniker/konzertvereinigung wiener
staatsopernchor/anna tomova-sintow/julia varady/
kathleen battle/samuel ramey/john aler/alexander
malta/ferruccio furlanetto/paata burchuladze
mozart don giovanni
this recording remains unpublished

871/15 august 1988/concert recordings in salzburg
grosses festspielhaus
wiener philharmoniker/*anne-sophie mutter
*tchaikovsky violin concerto in d op 35
lp: 429 2411
cd: 429 2412/479 3839

schumann symphony no 4 in d minor op 120
cd: private edition vienna

872/28 august 1988/concert recording in salzburg
grosses festspielhaus
berliner philharmoniker/wiener singverein/
sarah reese/franz grundheber
brahms ein deutsches requiem
this recording remains unpublished

873/31 august 1988/concert recordings in lucerne
kunsthaus
berliner philharmoniker
schoenberg verklärte nacht; brahms symphony no 1
theses recordings remain unpublished

874/30 september 1988/concert recording in
berlin philharmonie
berliner philharmoniker/wiener singverein/julia
varady/florence quivar/vinson cole/john tomlinson
verdi messa da requiem
this recording remains unpublished

875/6 october 1988/concert recordings in london
royal festival hall
berliner philharmoniker
schoenberg verklärte nacht; brahms symphony no 1
cd: testament SBT 1431

876/21-23 october 1988/telemondial film and dg
sound sessions in berlin philharmonie
berliner philharmoniker/*film producer herbert
von karajan/sound producers uli märkle and
michel glotz*
brahms symphony no 3 in f op 90;
symphony no 4 in e minor op 98
lp: 427 4961 (no 3)/427 4971 (no 4)
cd: 427 4962 (no 3)/427 4972 (no 4)/429 6022/
449 6012/479 3839
*video versions of these recording remain unpublished
and presumably incomplete*

877/22 october 1988/concert recordings in berlin
philharmonie
berliner philharmoniker
brahms symphony no 3; symphony no 4
these recordings remain unpublished

878/november 1988/telemondial film and dg
sound sessions in vienna musikvereinssaal
wiener philharmoniker/*film producer herbert
von karajan/sound producers uli märkle and
michel glotz*
bruckner symphony no 8 in c minor
cd: 427 6112
vhs: sony SHV 46403
laserdisc: sony SLV 46403
dvd: SVD 46403/88697 202399

879/3 december 1988/concert recordings in berlin philharmonie

berliner philharmoniker

prokofiev symphony no 1; beethoven symphony no 5
these recordings remain unpublished

880/4 december 1988/concert recordings in berlin philharmonie

berliner philharmoniker

prokofiev symphony no 1; beethoven symphony no 5
these in-house recordings, including an encore of the prokofiev fourth movement, remain unpublished

881/31 december 1988/televised concert in berlin philharmonie

berliner philharmoniker/evgeny kissin

prokofiev symphony no 1 in d "classical"; tchaikovsky piano concerto no 1 in b flat op 23
lp: 427 4851
cd: 427 4852/479 3839
vhs: sony SHV 45986
laserdisc: sony SLV 45986
dvd: sony SVD 45986
concert also includes scriabin piano solos played by kissin

354

882/January-february 1989/dg sessions in vienna
musikvereinssaal
wiener philharmoniker/konzertvereinigung wiener
staatsopernchor/josephine barstow/florence quivar/
sumi jo/placido domingo/leo nucci/jean-luc
chaignaud/kurt rydl/wolfgang witte/adolf
tomaschek/*producer michel glotz*
verdi un ballo in maschera
lp: 427 6351
cd: 427 6352/449 5882/479 4640

883/26 february 1989/concert recording in
new york carnegie hall
wiener philharmoniker
bruckner symphony no 8 in c minor
cd: private edition vienna

884/28 february 1989/concert recordings in
new york carnegie hall
wiener philharmoniker
schubert symphony no 8 "unfinished"; johann strauss
zigeunerbaron overture; sphärenklänge; annen polka;
perpetuum mobile; kaiserwalzer; josef strauss
delirienwalzer; johann and josef radetzky-marsch
these recordings remain unpublished

355

885/24 march 1989/stage recording in salzburg
grosses festspielhaus
berliner philharmoniker/konzertvereinigung
wiener staatsopernchor/zürcher sängerknaben/
josephine barstow/luciano pavarotti//alain
fondary/alfred hemm/italo tajo/piero de palma/
wolfgang scheider/walter zeh/tammy hensrud
puccini tosca
this in-house recording remains unpublished

886/26 march 1989/concert recordings in salzburg
grosses festspielhaus
berliner philharmoniker/evgeny kissin
prokofiev symphony no 1; tchaikovsky piano concerto no 1
these in-house recordings remain unpublished

887/27 march 1989/concert recording in salzburg
grosses festspielhaus
berliner philharmoniker/wiener singverein/anna
tomova-sintow/agnes baltsa/vinson cole/
paata burchuladze
verdi messa da requiem
this in-house recording remains unpublished

888/20-23 april 1989/dg sessions in vienna
musikvereinssaal
wiener philharmoniker/*producers cord garben
and michel glotz*
bruckner symphony no 7 in e
lp: 429 2261
cd: 429 2262/439 0372/479 3839

889/23 april 1989/concert recording in vienna
musikvereinssaal
wiener philharmoniker
bruckner symphony no 7 in e
cd: private edition vienna

CORRECTION

801/the date of this vienna concert was 14-15
january 1984 and not 15 december 1984

HERBERT VON KARAJAN DISCOGRAPHY:
COMPOSER LISTING

numbers are those of the session numbers in the main
chronological discography; numbers in brackets
indicate unpublished recordings

ADOLPHE ADAM (1803-1856)
giselle, standard abridged version of the ballet
(1 version)
239/vienna 1961

TOMASO ALBINONI (1671-1751)
adagio, arranged by giazotto (2 versions)
393/sankt moritz 1969   771/berlin 1983

JOHANN SEBASTIAN BACH (1685-1750)
matthäus-passion BWV 244 (5 versions)
(039)/vienna 1948   050/vienna 1950
445/berlin 1971-1972   457/salzburg 1972
602a/salzburg 1977

mass in b minor BWV232 (7 versions)
052/vienna 1950
074 and 076/vienna 1952 and london 1953
238/salzburg 1961   496/berlin 1973-1974
(497a)/berlin 1973   (509a)/salzburg 1974
815/salzburg 1985

mass in b minor BWV232: excerpts (1 version)
051/vienna 1950

bach/**magnificat BWV243** (5 versions)

107/rome 1953	(359)/edinburgh 1967
(505)/berlin 1973	540/berlin 1977
802/berlin 1984	

die kunst der fuge BWV1080 (1 version)

(015)/salzburg 1944

brandenburg concerto no 1 in f BWV1046 (9 versions)

290/sankt moritz 1964	346/salzburg 1967
374/salzburg 1968	388/moscow 1969
(467a)/berlin 1972	(499)/tokyo 1973
649/berlin 1978-1979	(684)/berlin 1979
692/salzburg 1980	

brandenburg concerto no 2 in f BWV1047 (4 versions)

290/sankt moritz 1964	374/salzburg 1968
649/berlin 1978-1979	(720)/oxford 1981

brandenburg concerto no 3 in g BWV1048 (8 versions)

290/sankt moritz 1969	346/salzburg 1967
342/berlin1967	351/florence 1967
374/salzburg 1968	649/berlin 1978-1979
(660)/berlin 1979	725/salzburg 1981

brandenburg concerto no 4 in g BWV1049 (5 versions)

290/sankt moritz 1964	374/salzburg 1968
418/berlin 1976	649/berlin 1978-1979
668/salzburg 1979	

bach/**brandenburg concerto no 5 in d BWV1050**
(4 versions)

290/sankt moritz 1964	(361)/berlin 1967
374/salzburg 1968	649/berlin 1978-1979

brandenburg concerto no 6 in b flat BWV1051
(5 versions)

300/berlin 1965	(330)/hiroshima 1966
374/salzburg 1968	491/salzburg 1973
649/berlin 1978-1979	

orchestral suite no 2 in b minor BWV1067 (4 versions)

(238a)/edinburgh 1961	290/sankt moritz 1964
(342)/berlin 1967	(346)/salzburg 1967

orchestral suite no 3 in d BWV1068 (1 version)
290/sankt moritz 1964

air from orchestral suite no 3 (2 versions)

179/tokyo 1957	771/berlin 1983

piano concerto BWV1052 (1 version)
(490)/salzburg 1973

piano concerto BWV1053 (1 version)
(395)/sankt moritz 1969

concerto for 4 pianos BWV1065 (1 version)
(437)/salzburg 1971

bach/**violin concerto BWV1041** (1 version)
336/sankt moritz 1966

violin concerto BWV1042 (5 versions)

336/sankt moritz 1966	346/salzburg 1967
(578)/salzburg 1976	802/berlin 1984
(829)/salzburg 1986	

concerto for 2 violins BWV1043 (1 version)
336/sankt moritz 1966

MILY BALAKIREV (1837-1910)
symphony no 1 (1 version)
048/london 1949

BELA BARTOK (1881-1945)
concerto for orchestra Sz116 (7 versions)

077/london 1952-1953	(084)/torino 1953
310/berlin 1965	(505)/berlin 1973
(512)/dortmund 1974	514/berlin 1974
(531)/berlin 1974	

music for strings, percussion and celesta Sz106
(4 versions)

048/london 1949	227/berlin 1960
398/berlin 1969	(531)/berlin 1974

bartok/**piano concerto no 3 Sz119** (4 versions)

111/torino 1954	461a/salzburg 1972
(726)/salzburg 1981	(739)/berlin 1982

cantata profana Sz94 (1 version)
130/rome 1954

LUDWIG VAN BEETHOVEN (1770-1827)

symphony no 1 in c op 21 (12 versions)

102/london 1953	(112)/rome 1954
194/new york 1958	243/berlin 1961
(322)/tokyo 1966	337/salzburg 1966
406/vienna 1970	446/berlin 1971
539/berlin 1975-1977	(626)/tokyo 1977
(730)/tokyo 1981	781/berlin 1984

symphony no 2 in d op 36 (13 versions)

(084)/torino 1953	100/london 1953
(156)/london 1956	243/berlin 1961-1962
(323)/tokyo 1966	408/vienna 1970
443/berlin 1971	(512)/dortmund 1974
539/berlin 1977	(616)/lucerne 1977
(627)/tokyo 1977	781/berlin 1984
(782)/berlin 1984	

beethoven/**symphony no 3 in e flat op 55 "eroica"**
(16 versions)

016/berlin 1944	075/london 1952
096/berlin 1953	181/tokyo 1957
261/berlin 1962	(322)/tokyo 1966
406/vienna 1970	442/berlin 1971
571/berlin 1975-1977	(590)/new york 1976
(615)/salzburg 1977	(626)/tokyo 1977
(642)/salzburg 1978	(730)/tokyo 1981
744/berlin 1982	778/berlin 1984

symphony no 4 in b flat op 60 (22 versions)

(080)/rome 1952	099/london 1953
105/rome 1953	249/berlin 1962
(321)/tokyo 1966	351/florence 1967
407/vienna 1970	446/berlin 1972-1973
(476)/london 1973	(481)/salzburg 1973
(528)/new york 1974	(555)/salzburg 1975
584/berlin 1976	(628)/tokyo 1977
(761)/berlin 1983	772/berlin 1983
(773)/berlin 1983	(808)/brussels 1985
809/london 1985	(854)/salzburg 1987
(866)/osaka 1988	868/tokyo 1988

beethoven/symphony no 5 in c minor op 67 (28 versions)

(032)/torino 1948	034/vienna 1948
(095)/london 1953	(105)/rome 1953
124/london 1954	179/tokyo 1957
208/tokyo 1959	248/berlin 1962
316/berlin 1966	(320)/tokyo 1966
(351)/florence 1967	387/moscow 1969
407/vienna 1970	453/berlin 1972
(476)/london 1973	(481)/salzburg 1973
(498)/tokyo 1973	(502)/osaka 1973
588/berlin 1976	(612)/paris 1977
(629)/tokyo 1977	(731)/tokyo 1981
(734a)/tokyo 1981	758/berlin 1982
(759)/berlin 1982	(795)/tokyo 1984
(879)/berlin 1988	(880)/berlin 1988

symphony no 6 in f op 68 "pastoral" (21 versions)

091/london 1953	(111)/torino 1954
247/berlin 1962	(320)/tokyo 1966
362/berlin 1967	387/moscow 1969
405/vienna 1970	459/london 1972
(498)/tokyo 1973	(502)/osaka 1973
588/berlin 1976	(612)/paris 1977
(615)/salzburg 1977	(629)/tokyo 1977
(634)/aachen 1977	(735)/tokyo 1981
758/berlin 1982	(759)/berlin 1982
(795)/tokyo 1984	(842)/salzburg 1987
(860)/cologne 1987	

beethoven/**symphony no 7 in a op 92** (21 versions)

008/berlin 1941	065/london 1951
(080)/rome 1952	149/lucerne 1955
163/vienna 1957	198/vienna 1959
248/berlin 1962	(303)/paris 1965
(321)/tokyo 1966	368/salzburg 1968
405/vienna 1970	442/berlin 1971
(497)/berlin 1973	589/berlin 1976-1977
(628)/tokyo 1977	(638)/berlin 1978
(716)/salzburg 1981	(761)/berlin 1983
772/berlin 1983	(773)/berlin 1983
(808)/brussels 1985	

symphony no 8 in f op 93 (13 versions)

017/vienna 1946	(099)/london 1953
139/london 1955	234/london 1961
245/berlin 1962	(323)/tokyo 1966
408/vienna 1970	443/berlin 1971
(573)/london 1976	589/berlin 1976-1977
(630)/tokyo 1977	778/berlin 1984
(782)/berlin 1984	

beethoven/**symphony no 9 in d minor op 125 "choral"**
(22 versions)

022/vienna 1947	(114a)/tokyo 1954
128/rome 1954	143/vienna 1955
147/vienna 1955	166/berlin 1957
194/new york 1958	259/berlin 1962
269/salzburg 1963	272/berlin 1963
(324)/tokyo 1966	365/berlin 1968
409/vienna 1970	584/berlin 1975-1977
(591)/new york 1976	(631)/tokyo 1977
635/berlin 1977	681/tokyo 1979
(746)/vienna 1982	769/berlin 1983
(785)/salzburg 1984	835a/berlin 1986

violin concerto in d op 61 (9 versions)

149/lucerne 1955	344/berlin 1967
678/berlin 1979	(688)/berlin 1980
(690)/salzburg 1980	700/salzburg 1980
(731)/tokyo 1981	(734a)/tokyo 1981
779/berlin 1984	

triple concerto in c op 56 (5 versions)

397/berlin 1969	651/salzburg 1978
(653)/lucerne 1978	(671)/london 1979
686/berlin 1979	

beethoven/**piano concerto no 1 in c op 15** (2 versions)

340/berlin 1966   619/berlin 1977

piano concerto no 2 in b flat op 19 (1 version)

619/berlin 1977

piano concerto no 3 in c minor op 37 (7 versions)

170/berlin 1957   (510)/salzburg 1974

(580)/salzburg 1976   619/berlin 1976

(627)/tokyo 1977   642/salzburg 1978

708/berlin 1980

piano concerto no 4 in g op 58 (5 versions)

057/london 1951   073/vienna 1952

(434)/salzburg 1971   582/berlin 1974

(625)/osaka 1977

piano concerto no 5 in e flat op 73 "emperor"

(5 versions)

057/london 1951   519/berlin 1974

(541)/vienna 1975   (568)/salzburg 1976

(630)/tokyo 1977

missa solemnis in d op 123 (10 versions)

(064)/rome 1951   192/vienna 1958

204/salzburg 1959   317/berlin 1966

318/berlin 1966   524/berlin 1974

545/salzburg 1975   663/salzburg 1979

818/berlin 1985   (834)/salzburg 1986

beethoven/**ah perfido!, concert aria op 65** (1 version)
119/london 1954

coriolan overture op 62 (10 versions)

088/london 1953	149/lucerne 1955
310/berlin 1965	(320)/tokyo 1966
326/osaka 1966	368/salzburg 1968
387/moscow 1969	405/vienna 1970
538/berlin 1975	821/berlin 1985

egmont, complete incidental music op 84 (1 version)
380/berlin 1969

egmont overture op 84 (4 versions)

088/london 1953	(112)/torino 1954
538/berlin 1975	821/berlin 1985

fidelio op 72 (9 versions)

086/vienna 1953	171/salzburg 1957
228/vienna 1960	230/milan 1960
251/vienna 1962	277/munich 1963
419/berlin 1970	(433)/salzburg 1971
(641)/salzburg 1977	

fidelio op 72: abscheulicher wo eilst du hin?
(1 version)
119/london 1954

beethoven/**fidelio overture op 72b** (2 versions)

310/berlin 1965   821/berlin 1985

die geschöpfe des prometheus overture op 43
(1 version)
380/berlin 1969

grosse fuge in b flat op 133, arranged by weingartner
(1 version)
394/sankt moritz 1969

könig stephan overture op 117 (1 version)
380/berlin 1969

leonore no 1 overture op 138 (1 version)
380/berlin 1969

leonore no 2 overture op 72 (1 version)
380/berlin 1969

leonore no 3 overture op 72a (7 versions)

012/amsterdam 1943   088/london 1953
271/berlin 1963   310/berlin 1965
(323)/tokyo 1966   403/vienna 1970
821/berlin 1985

namensfeier overture op 115 (1 version)
380/berlin 1969

beethoven/**die ruinen von athen overture op 113**
(1 version)
380/berlin 1969

die weihe des hauses overture op 124 (2 versions)
(118)/london 1954   380/berlin 1969

wellingtons sieg oder die schlacht bei vittoria op 91
(1 version)
380/berlin 1969

ALBAN BERG (1885-1935)
violin concerto (1 version)
805/berlin 1985

three pieces from the lyric suite, orchestral version
(2 versions)
494/berlin 1972-1974   (547)/berlin 1975

three orchestral pieces op 6 (4 versions)
474/berlin 1972   491/salzburg 1973
(522)/lucerne 1974   (660)/berlin 1979

THEODOR BERGER (1905-1992)
sinfonia parabolica (1 version)
175/salzburg 1957

legende vom prinzen eugen (1 version)
209/tokyo 1959

HECTOR BERLIOZ (1803-1869)

symphonie fantastique (10 versions)

116/london 1954	299a/berlin 1964
410/paris 1971	525/berlin 1974
(599)/berlin 1977	(694)/salzburg 1980
(840)/berlin 1987	(849)/paris 1987
(853)/salzburg 1987	(861)/frankfurt 1987

le carnaval romain overture (1 version)
183/london 1958

la damnation de faust: marche hongroise (3 versions)

185/london 1958	658/berlin 1978-1979
659/berlin 1978	

**la damnation de faust: ballet des sylphes et
menuet des folleta** (1 version)
440/berlin 1971

les troyens: royal hunt and storm (1 version)
196/london 1959

GEORGES BIZET (1838-1875)

carmen (10 versions)

121/vienna 1954	135/milan 1955
242/vienna 1961	276/vienna 1963
334/salzburg 1966	354/salzburg 1967
353 and 355/vienna and munich 1967	
755/berlin 1982	813/salzburg 1985
832/salzburg 1986	

bizet/**carmen: suite from the opera** (2 versions)
185/london 1958 424/berlin 1970

carmen: preludes to acts 2 and 3 (1 version)
(118)/london 1954

carmen: prelude to act 4 (1 version)
118/london 1954

l'arlesienne: first suite from the incidental music
(4 versions)
185/london 1958 424/berlin 1970
(447)/berlin 1972 770/berlin 1983

l'arlesienne: second suite from the incidental music
(5 versions)
185/london 1958 424/berlin 1970
658/berlin 1978-1979 659/berlin 1978
770/berlin 1983

LUIGI BOCCHERINI (1743-1805)
quintettino "la ritrata di madrid" (1 version)
393/sankt moritz 1969

ALEXANDER BORODIN (1833-1887)
**prince igor: dance of the polovtsian maidens and
polovtsian dances** (3 versions)
122/london 1954 224/london 1960
425/berlin 1970-1971

JOHANNES BRAHMS (1833-1897)

symphony no 1 in c minor op 68 (29 versions)

012/amsterdam 1943

069/london 1952

137/washington 1955

200/vienna 1959

207/tokyo 1959

270/berlin 1963

(327)/osaka 1966

(359)/edinburgh 1967

(469)/belgrade 1972

475/berlin 1973

(491)/salzburg 1973

(518)/london 1974

(529)/new york 1974

(551)/salzburg 1975

622/berlin 1977-1978

(624)/osaka 1977

(634)/aachen 1977

(722)/salzburg 1981

(732)/tokyo 1981

(763)/berlin 1983

(767)/salzburg 1983

(789)/salzburg 1984

(790)/lucerne 1984

(796)/tokyo 1984

800/berlin 1984

837/berlin 1987

(838)/berlin 1987

869/tokyo 1988

875/london 1988

brahms/**symphony no 2 in d op 73** (22 versions)

044/vienna 1949

(078)/rome 1952

083/rome 1953

141/london 1955

180/tokyo 1957

270/berlin 1963

(325)/sapporo 1966

(455)/salzburg 1972

475/berlin 1973

(517)/london 1974

(526)/new york 1974

(549)/salzburg 1975

622/berlin 1977

(623)/berlin 1977

(733)/tokyo 1981

(748)/salzburg 1982

(766)/salzburg 1983

805/berlin 1985

831/berlin 1986

(835)/lucerne 1986

(848)/london 1987

(850)/paris 1987

symphony no 3 in f op 90 (13 versions)

226/vienna 1960

295/berlin 1964

475/berlin 1973

(518)/london 1974

(529)/new york 1974

(550a)/salzburg 1975

637/berlin 1978

(732)/tokyo 1981

(767)/salzburg 1983

(796)/tokyo 1984

(807)/berlin 1985

876/berlin 1988

(877)/berlin 1988

brahms/**symphony no 4 in e minor op 98** (16 versions)

141/london 1955	(156)/london 1956
209/tokyo 1959	270/berlin 1963
475/berlin 1973	(517)/london 1974
(526)/new york 1974	(550a)/salzburg 1975
622/berlin 1977	(733)/tokyo 1981
766/salzburg 1983	(798)/berlin 1984
(848)/london 1987	(850)/paris 1987
876/berlin 1988	(877)/berlin 1988

violin concerto in d op 77 (6 versions)

176/lucerne 1957	282/berlin 1964
(549)/salzburg 1975	566/berlin 1976
(724)/salzburg 1981	727/berlin 1981

double concerto in a minor op 102 (4 versions)

(623)/berlin 1977	762/berlin 1983
(763)/berlin 1983	(784)/salzburg 1984

piano concerto no 2 in b flat op 83 (5 versions)

130/rome 1954	195/berlin 1958
284/vienna 1964	360/berlin 1967
551/salzburg 1975	

brahms/ein deutsches requiem op 45 (12 versions)

021/vienna 1947	177/salzburg 1957
283/vienna 1964	(369)/salzburg 1968
(516)/salzburg 1974	585/berlin 1976
643/salzburg 1978	747/vienna 1983
(765)/salzburg 1983	811/vienna 1985-1987
(857)/berlin 1987	(872)/salzburg 1988

haydn variations op 56a (7 versions)

139/london 1955	279/berlin 1964
(330)/hiroshima 1966	351/florence 1967
586/berlin 1976	762/berlin 1983
(838)/berlin 1987	

tragic overture op 81 (5 versions)

239/vienna 1961	417/berlin 1970
656/berlin 1977-1978	762/berlin 1983
831/berlin 1986	

hungarian dances nos 1, 3, 5, 6, 17, 18, 19 and 20
(1 version)
206/berlin 1959

BENJAMIN BRITTEN (1913-1976)
frank bridge variations (2 versions)

(085)/torino 1953	103/london 1953

MAX BRUCH (1838-1920)

violin concerto no 1 in g minor (4 versions)

704/berlin 1980	710/berlin 1981
(738)/berlin 1981	748/salzburg 1982

ANTON BRUCKNER (1824-1896)

symphony no 1 in c minor (1 version)

712/berlin 1981

symphony no 2 in c minor (1 version)

707/berlin 1980-1981

symphony no 3 in d minor (1 version)

703/berlin 1980

symphony no 4 in e flat "romantic" (6 versions)

417/berlin 1970	(486)/salzburg 1973
(522)/lucerne 1974	(547)/berlin 1975
548/berlin 1975	668/salzburg 1979

symphony no 5 in b flat (7 versions)

120/vienna 1954	396/salzburg 1969
595/berlin 1976	(602)/salzburg 1977
(706)/berlin 1980	717/vienna 1981
719/london 1981	

symphony no 6 in a (1 version)

678/berlin 1979

bruckner/**symphony no 7 in e** (15 versions)

250/london 1962	(287)/amsterdam 1964
337/salzburg 1966	(385)/salzburg 1969
391/london 1969	420/berlin 1970
(490)/salzburg 1973	(499)/tokyo 1973
(541)/vienna 1975	546/berlin 1975
(664)/salzburg 1979	(701)/salzburg 1980
(754)/lucerne 1982	888/vienna 1989
889/vienna 1989	

symphony no 8 in c minor (19 versions)

013-014/berlin 1944	(165)/vienna 1957
169/berlin 1957	172/salzburg 1957
302/london 1965	(331)/tokyo 1966
(333)/amsterdam 1966	347/salzburg 1967
(527)/new york 1974	538/berlin 1975
(556)/salzburg 1975	(650)/salzburg 1978
670/sankt florian 1979	(672)/london 1979
749/salzburg 1982	(768)/lucerne 1983
833/salzburg 1986	878/vienna 1988
883/new york 1989	

bruckner/**symphony no 9 in d minor** (10 versions)

(253)/vienna 1962	319/berlin 1966
401/berlin 1970	559/berlin 1975
578/salzburg 1976	645/vienna 1978
736/berlin 1981	(817)/lucerne 1985
820/berlin 1985	(829)/salzburg 1986

mass no 2 in e minor (1 version)
550/salzburg 1975

te deum (8 versions)

072/perugia 1952	221/salzburg 1960
(253)/vienna 1962	461/salzburg 1972
560/berlin 1975	(592)/new york 1976
645/vienna 1978	792/vienna 1984

EMMANUEL CHABRIER (1841-1894)

espana (4 versions)

030/vienna 1947	092/london 1953
225/london 1960	658/berlin 1978-1979

marche joyeuse (2 versions)

145/london 1955	224/london 1960

LUIGI CHERUBINI (1760-1842)

anacreon overture (2 versions)

003/berlin 1939	705/berlin 1980

FREDERIC CHOPIN (1810-1849)
piano concerto no 2 in f minor (2 versions)
(695)/salzburg 1980   702/lucerne 1980

les sylphides: ballet suite arranged by douglas
(1 version)
235/berlin 1961

FRANCESCO CILEA (1866-1950)
adriana lecouvreur: intermezzo (1 version)
360/berlin 1967

ARCANGELO CORELLI (1653-1713)
concerto grosso op 6 no 8 "christmas concerto"
(1 version)
414/sankt moritz 1970

CLAUDE DEBUSSY (1862-1918)
pelleas et melisande (3 versions)
132/rome 1954   244/vienna 1962
657/berlin 1978

la mer (12 versions)
093/london 1953   281/berlin 1964
(328)/yokohama 1966   598/berlin 1977
640/berlin 1978   669/salzburg 1979
(734)/tokyo 1981   (794)/osaka 1984
(797)/tokyo 1984   (816)/salzburg 1985
821/berlin 1985-1986   (822)/berlin 1985

debussy/**prelude a l'apres-midi d'un faune** (14 versions)

281/berlin 1964	(328)/yokohama 1966
(456)/salzburg 1972	(557)/lucerne 1975
(581)/salzburg 1976	598/berlin 1977
640/berlin 1978	(669)/salzburg 1979
(734)/tokyo 1981	(794)/osaka 1984
(797)/tokyo 1984	(816)/salzburg 1985
821/berlin 1985-1986	(822)/berlin 1985

LEO DELIBES (1836-1891)

coppelia: suite from the ballet (1 version)

235/berlin 1961

GAETONO DONIZETTI (1797-1848)

lucia di lammermoor (2 versions)

108/milan 1954	150/berlin 1955

ANTONIN DVORAK (1841-1904)

symphony no 8 in g op 88 (10 versions)

240/vienna 1961	(328)/yokohama 1966
500/tokyo 1973	521/salzburg 1974
(531)/berlin 1974	658/berlin 1979
(665)/salzburg 1979	680/tokyo 1979
(724)/salzburg 1981	803/vienna 1985

dvorak/**symphony no 9 in e minor op 95**
"from the new world" (11 versions)

005/berlin 1940	(182)/berlin 1957-1958
189/berlin 1958	280/berlin 1964
316/berlin 1966	(329)/fukuoka 1966
437/salzburg 1971	(531)/berlin 1974
598/berlin 1977	(674)/salzburg 1979
803/vienna 1985	

cello concerto in b minor op 104 (1 version)
377/berlin 1968

scherzo capriccioso op 66 (1 version)
440/berlin 1971

serenade for strings op 22 (1 version)
703/berlin 1980

**slavonic dances: op 46 nos 1, 3 and 7; op 72
nos 10 and 16** (1 version)
206/berlin 1959

slavonic dance op 46 no 8 (1 version)
658/berlin 1977

GOTTFRIED VON EINEM (1918-1996)
piano concerto (1 version)
175/salzburg 1957

CESAR FRANCK (1822-1900)
symphony in d minor (1 version)
400/paris 1969

variations symphoniques pour piano et orchestra
(2 versions)
057/london 1951   467/berlin 1972

GIORGIO GHEDINI (1892-1965)
musica da camera per viola ed archi (1 version)
104/rome 1953

UMBERTO GIORDANO (1867-1948)
fedora: intermezzo (1 version)
360/berlin 1967

CHRISTOPH WILLIBALD GLUCK (1714-1787)
orfeo ed euridice (1 version)
203/salzburg 1959

orfeo ed euridice: dance of the blessed spirits
(1 version)
771/berlin 1983

orfeo ed euridice: fragment from the ballet music
(1 version)
(032a)/salzburg 1948

CHARLES GOUNOD (1818-1893)
faust: ballet music from the opera (4 versions)
185/london 1958   430/berlin 1971
(447)/berlin 1972   658/berlin 1978-1979

faust: waltz (1 version)
430/berlin 1971

faust: vous qui faites l'endormie (1 version)
049/london 1949

ENRIQUE GRANADOS (1867-1916)
goyescas: intermezzo (2 versions)
118/london 1954   196/london 1959

EDVARD GRIEG (1843-1907)
piano concerto in minor (2 versions)
057/london 1951   729/berlin 1981

peer gynt: first and second suites from the
incidental music (3 versions)
239/vienna 1961   440/berlin 1971
740/berlin 1982

holberg suite (1 version)
712/berlin 1981

sigurd jorsalfar: suite from the incidental music
(1 version)
440/berlin 1971

GEORGE FRIDERIC HANDEL (1685-1759)

water music: suite arranged by harty (3 versions)
(065)/london 1951   071/london 1952
210/berlin 1959

concerto grosso op 6 no 1 in g (1 version)
336/sankt moritz 1966

concerto grosso op 6 no 2 in f (1 version)
357/sankt moritz 1967

concerto grosso op 6 no 3 in e minor (1 version)
357/sankt moritz 1967

concerto grosso op 6 no 4 in a minor (1 version)
357/sankt moritz 1967

concerto grosso op 6 no 5 in d (1 version)
336/sankt moritz 1966

concerto grosso op 6 no 6 in g minor (1 version)
357/sankt moritz 1967

concerto grosso op 6 no 7 in b (1 version)
357/sankt moritz 1967

concerto grosso op 6 no 8 in c minor (1 version)
336/sankt moritz 1966

handel/**concerto grosso op 6 no 9 in f** (1 version)
357/sankt moritz 1967

concerto grosso op 6 no 10 in d minor (1 version)
336/sankt moritz 1966

concerto grosso op 6 no 11 in a (1 version)
336/sankt moritz 1966

concerto grosso op 6 no 12 in b minor (4 versions)
(113)/torino 1954   126/vienna 1954
(133)/torino 1955   336/sankt moritz 1966

giulio cesare: v'adoro pupille (1 version)
(223a)/berlin 1960

FRANZ JOSEF HAYDN (1732-1809)
symphony no 82 in c "l'ours" (1 version)
698/berlin 1980

symphony no 83 in g minor "la poule" (2 versions)
438/sankt moritz 1971   698/berlin 1980

symphony no 84 in e flat (1 version)
698/berlin 1980

symphony no 85 in b flat "la reine" (1 version)
698/berlin 1980

haydn/**symphony no 86 in d** (1 version)
698/berlin 1980

symphony no 87 in a (1 version)
698/berlin 1980

symphony no 93 in d (1 version)
728/berlin 1981-1982

symphony no 94 in g "surprise" (1 version)
728/berlin 1981-1982

symphony no 95 in c minor (1 version)
728/berlin 1981-1982

symphony no 96 in d "miracle" (1 version)
728/berlin 1981-1982

symphony no 97 in c (1 version)
728/berlin 1981-1982

symphony no 98 in b flat (1 version)
728/berlin 1981-1982

symphony no 99 in e flat (1 version)
728/berlin 1981-1982

symphony no 100 in g "military" (1 version)
728/berlin 1981-1982

haydn/**symphony no 101 in d "clock"** (2 versions)

438/sankt moritz 1971   728/berlin 1981-1982

symphony no 102 in b flat (1 version)

728/berlin 1981-1982

symphony no 103 in e flat "drum roll" (2 versions)

264/vienna 1963   728/berlin 1981-1982

symphony no 104 in d "london" (7 versions)

200/vienna 1959   533/berlin 1975

(535)/berlin 1975   674/salzburg 1979

(722//salzburg 1981   728/berlin 1981-1982

(828)/berlin 1986

die jahreszeiten (1 version)

472/berlin 1972

die schöpfung (5 versions)

308/salzburg 1965   317/berlin 1966

614/salzburg 1977   (715)/salzburg 1981

751/salzburg 1982

HANS WERNER HENZE (1926-2012)
antifone per orchestra (1 version)

(265)/munich 1963

PAUL HINDEMITH (1895-1963)
mathis der maler: symphony (2 versions)

163/vienna 1957   178/berlin 1957

GUSTAV HOLST (1874-1934)

the planets (2 versions)

239/vienna 1961   712/berlin 1981

ARTHUR HONEGGER (1892-1955)

symphony no 2 (2 versions)

(082)/torino 1954   394/sankt moritz 1969

symphony no 3 "liturgique" (5 versions)

126/vienna 1954   (131)/rome 1954

175/salzburg 1957   398/berlin 1969

800/berlin 1984

JOHANN NEPOMUK HUMMEL (1778-1837)

trumpet concerto in e flat, arranged by oubrados
(1 version)

514/berlin 1974

ENGELBERT HUMPERDINCK (1854-1921)

hänsel und gretel (2 versions)

089/london 1953   110/milan 1954

hänsel und gretel overture (1 version)

705/berlin 1980

CHARLES IVES (1874-1954)

the unanswered question (1 version)

202/los angeles 1959

ZOLTAN KODALY (1882-1967)
hary janos: intermezzo (2 versions)
118/london 1954   (196)/london 1959

psalmus hungaricus (1 version)
133/torino 1953

FRANZ LEHAR (1870-1948)
die lustige witwe (1 version)
451/berlin 1972

KURT LEIMER (1922-1974)
piano concerto in c minor (1 version)
125/london 1954

piano concerto for the left hand (2 versions)
085/torino 1953   125/london 1954

RUGGIERO LEONCAVALLO (1858-1919)
i pagliacci (2 versions)
312/milan 1965   372/milan 1968

I pagliacci: stridono lassu (1 version)
(648)/paris 1978

I pagliacci: intermezzo (4 versions)
118/london 1954   196/london 1959
360/berlin 1967   824/berlin 1985

FRANZ LISZT (1811-1886)

tasso, lamento e trionfo S96 (1 version)
562/berlin 1975

mazeppa S100 (1 version)
232/berlin 1961

mephisto waltz S110 (1 version)
440/berlin 1971

les preludes S97 (3 versions)
185/london 1958   350/berlin 1967
774/berlin 1983-1984

hungarian fantasy for piano and orchestra S123
(1 version)
229/berlin 1960

hungarian rhapsody no 2 in d minor (3 versions)
183/london 1958   350/berlin 1967
659/berlin 1978

hungarian rhapsody no 4 in d minor (2 versions)
232/berlin 1961   562/berlin 1975

hungarian rhapsody no 5 in e minor (4 versions)
229/berlin 1960   562/berlin 1975
774/berlin 1983-1984   824/berlin 1985

PIETRO LOCATELLI (1695-1764)
concerto grosso op 1 no 8 in f minor
"christmas concerto" (1 version)
414/sankt moritz 1970

GUSTAV MAHLER (1860-1911)
symphony no 4 in g (3 versions)
661/berlin 1979   (692)/salzburg 1980
693/vienna 1980

symphony no 5 in c sharp minor (3 versions)
479/berlin 1973   492/salzburg 1973
(647)/salzburg 1978

symphony no 6 in a minor (3 versions)
536/berlin 1975   (601)/salzburg 1977
(646)/salzburg 1978

symphony no 9 in d (4 versions)
683/berlin 1979   (745)/berlin 1982
(752)/salzburg 1982   757/berlin 1982

das lied von der erde (4 versions)
423/berlin 1970   (464)/berlin 1972
504/berlin 1973   (636)/berlin 1978

kindertotenlieder (1 version)
514/berlin 1974

mahler/**5 rückert-lieder: ich bin der welt abhanden gekommen; liebst du um schönheit; blicke mir nicht in die lieder; ich atmet einen linden duft; um mitternacht** (1 version)
514/berlin 1974

FRANCESCO MANFREDINI (1684-1762)
concerto grosso op 3 no 12 in c
"christmas concerto" (1 version)
414/sankt moritz 1970

FRANK MARTIN (1890-1974)
etudes for string orchestra (1 version)
(189)/berlin 1958

PIETRO MASCAGNI (1863-1945)
cavalleria rusticana (3 versions)
311/milan 1965 370/milan 1968
371/milan 1968

cavalleria rusticana: intermezzo (4 versions)
041/vienna 1949 118/london 1954
(196)/london 1959 360/berlin 1967

l'amico fritz: intermezzo (6 versions)
118/london 1954 196/london 1959
360/berlin 1967 (447)/berlin 1972
659/berlin 1978 705/berlin 1980

JULES MASSENET (1842-1912)
meditation pour violon et orchestre (5 versions)
118/london 1954   360/berlin 1967
(447)/berlin 1972   (648)/paris 1978
705/berlin 1980

FELIX MENDELSSOHN-BARTHOLDY (1809-1847)
symphony no 1 in c minor op 11 (1 version)
466/berlin 1972

symphony no 2 in b flat op 52 "lobgesang" (1 version)
466/berlin 1972

symphony no 3 in a minor op 56 "scotch" (2 versions)
429/berlin 1971   (471)/berlin 1972

symphony no 4 in a op 90 "Italian" (1 version)
448/berlin 1971

symphony no 5 in d op 107 "reformation" (1 version)
451/berlin 1972

violin concerto in e minor op 64 (1 version)
704/berlin 1980

he rides overture op 26 (2 versions)
223/berlin 1960   429/berlin 1971

CLAUDIO MONTEVERDI (1567-1643)
l'incoronazione di poppea (1 version)
263/vienna 1963

LEOPOLD MOZART (1719-1787)
cassation in g "kindersinfonie" (1 version)
168/london 1957

trumpet concerto in d, arranged by seiffert
(1 version)
514/berlin 1974

WOLFGANG AMADEUS MOZART (1756-1791)
symphony no 29 in a K201 (10 versions)

212/berlin 1960	(302)/london 1965
307/sankt moritz 1965	(469)/belgrade 1972
(581)/salzburg 1976	750/salzburg 1982
839/berlin 1987	(840)/berlin 1987
(865)/osaka 1988	867/tokyo 1988

symphony no 32 in g K318 (1 version)
621/berlin 1977

symphony no 33 in b flat K319 (2 versions)

018/vienna 1946	307/sankt moritz 1965

symphony no 35 in d K385 "haffner" (8 versions)

010/torino 1942	075/london 1952
122/london 1954	137/washington 1955
173/salzburg 1957	202/los angeles 1959
416/berlin 1970	574/berlin 1975-1977

symphony no 36 in c K425 "linz" (2 versions)

416/berlin 1970	621/berlin 1977

mozart/**symphony no 38 in d K504 "prague"**
(3 versions)

192/vienna 1958	416/berlin 1970
600/berlin 1975-1977	

symphony no 39 in e flat K543 (14 versions)

044/vienna 1949	(131)/rome 1954
(146)/london 1955	151/london 1955
154/salzburg 1956	416/berlin 1970
(465)/lucerne 1972	564/berlin 1975-1977
(569)/salzburg 1976	(608)/salzburg 1977
856/berlin 1987	(859)/berlin 1987
(864)/salzburg 1988	869/tokyo 1988

symphony no 40 in g minor K550 (5 versions)

010/torino 1942	200/vienna 1959
207/tokyo 1959	416/berlin 1970
574/berlin 1975-1977	

symphony no 41 in c K551 "jupiter" (19 versions)

010/torino 1942	(032)/rome 1948
(085)/torino 1953	(095)/london 1953
113/torino 1954	153/berlin 1956
173/salzburg 1957	193/new york 1958
250/london 1962	260/vienna 1962
416/berlin 1970	(493)/berlin 1973
(501)/tokyo 1973	572/berlin 1975-1977
(597)/berlin 1976	(610)/salzburg 1977
(700)/salzburg 1980	(744)/berlin 1982
(847)/vienna 1987	

mozart/**piano concerto no 20 in d minor K466**
(2 versions)

153/berlin 1956   154/salzburg 1956

piano concerto no 21 in c K467 (3 versions)
054/lucerne 1950   173/salzburg 1957
(648)/paris 1978

piano concerto no 23 in a K488 (2 versions)
057/london 1951   (078)/rome 1952

piano concerto no 24 in c minor K491 (1 version)
094/london 1953

concerto for three pianos K242 (4 versions)
356/salzburg 1967   390/london 1969
(441a)/paris 1971   (486)/salzburg 1973

violin concerto no 3 in g K216 (3 versions)
(609)/salzburg 1977   639/berlin 1978
(720)/oxford 1981

violin concerto no 5 in a K219 (3 versions)
315/vienna 1966   467b/berlin 1972
639/berlin 1978

bassoon concerto in b flat K191 (1 version)
438/berlin 1971

mozart/**clarinet concerto in a K622** (3 versions)

047/vienna 1949   146/london 1955

438/sankt moritz 1971

flute concerto no i in g K313 (1 version)

438/sankt moritz 1971

flute and harp concerto in c K299 (1 version)

438/sankt moritz 1971

**horn concerti: no 1 in d K412, no 2 in e flat K417
and no 3 in e flat K447** (2 versions)

098/london 1953   375/sankt moritz 1968

horn concerto no 4 in e flat K495 (2 versions)

104/london 1953   375/sankt moritz 1968

oboe concerto in c K314 (1 version)

438/sankt moritz 1971

sinfonia concertante for wind in e flat K297b

(4 versions)

101/london 1953   413/salzburg 1970

438/sankt moritz 1971   (587)/berlin 1976

**string divertimenti: in d K136, in b K137 and
in f K138** (1 version)

375/sankt moritz 1968

divertimenti nos 10 in f K247 and 11 in d K251

(1 version)

307/sankt moritz 1965

mozart/**divertimento no 15 in b flat K287** (14 versions)

(068)/london 1952	140a/london 1955
154/salzburg 1956	307/sankt moritz 1965
(332)/tokyo 1966	(358)/edinburgh 1967
458/london 1972	(511)/salzburg 1974
(675)/salzburg 1979	(694)/salzburg 1980
793/osaka 1984	(835)/lucerne 1986
(849)/paris 1987	856/berlin 1987

divertimento no 17 in d K334 (8 versions)

307/sankt moritz 1965	(342)/berlin 1967
(385)/salzburg 1969	389/moscow 1969
(694)/salzburg 1980	845/berlin 1987
846/berlin 1987	(855)/lucerne 1987

adagio from divertimento no 17 (1 version)
019/vienna 1946

menuetto 1 from divertimento no 17 (1 version)
(146)/london 1955

serenade no 6 in d K239 "**serenata notturna**"
(2 versions)

375/sankt moritz 1968	771/berlin 1983

serenade no 13 in g K525 "**eine kleine nachtmusik**"
(5 versions)

019/vienna 1946	102/london 1953
210/berlin 1959	307/sankt moritz 1965
712/berlin 1981	

mozart/**adagio and fugue in c minor K546**
(2 versions)
023/vienna 1947   393/sankt moritz 1969

maurerische trauermusik K477 (2 versions)
029/vienna 1947   (724)/salzburg 1981

**german dance no 5 "canary" from deutsche tänze K600
and german dance no 3 "sleighride" from deutsche
tänze K605** (2 versions)
019/vienna 1946   227/berlin 1960

**german dance no 3 "hurdy-gurdy" from deutsche
tänze K602** (1 version)
227/berlin 1960

ave verum corpus K618 (1 version)
147/vienna 1955

mass no 14 in c K317 "coronation mass" (4 versions)
(352)/rome 1967   461/salzburg 1972
560/berlin 1975   812/vatican city 1985

mass no 18 in c minor K427 "great mass" (1 version)
713/berlin 1981

requiem in d minor K626 (7 versions)
221/salzburg 1960   241/berlin 1961
274/vienna 1963   560/berlin 1975
(592)/new york 1976   (691)/salzburg 1980
830/vienna 1986

400

mozart/**cosi fan tutte** (1 version)
117/london 1954

don giovanni (8 versions)

220/salzburg 1960	266/vienna 1963
373/salzburg 1968	392/salzburg 1969
411/salzburg 1970	804/berlin 1985
851/salzburg 1987	(870)/salzburg 1988

don giovanni: crudele? non mi dir (1 version)
030a/vienna 1947

don giovanni: or sai chi l'onore (2 versions)

030a/vienna 1947	(033a)/vienna 1948

don giovanni: batti batti o bel masetto (1 version)
027/vienna 1947

don giovanni: la ci darem la mano (2 versions)

025/vienna 1947	(146)/london 1955

die entführung aus dem serail: martern aller arten
(1 version)
010/vienna 1946

le nozze di figaro (8 versions)

053/vienna 1950	109/milan 1954
(460)/salzburg 1972	489/salzburg 1973
520a/salzburg 1974	(552)/salzburg 1975
605/vienna 1977	644/vienna 1978

mozart/**le nozze di figaro overture** (1 version)
019/vienna 1946

le nozze di figaro: miscellaneous fragments
(1 version)
040/milan 1948-1949

le nozze di figaro: se vuol ballare (1 version)
(025)/vienna 1947

le nozze di figaro: non piu andrai (2 versions)
025/vienna 1947   (146)/london 1955

le nozze di figaro: voi che sapete (1 version)
027/vienna 1947

le nozze di figaro: deh vieni non tardar (1 version)
027/vienna 1947

die zauberflöte (5 versions)
055/vienna 1950   106/rome 1955
254/vienna 1962   520/salzburg 1974
687/berlin 1980

die zauberflöte overture (1 version)
001/berlin 1938

die zauberflöte: bei mannern welche liebe fühlen
(1 version)
025/vienna 1947

MODEST MUSSORGSKY (1839-1881)

boris godunov (3 versions)

306/salzburg 1965   335/salzburg 1966

421/vienna 1970

boris godunov: varlaam's song (1 version)

049/london 1949

khovantschina: entr'acte (3 versions)

118/london 1954   196/london 1959

360/berlin 1967

khovantschina: dance of the persian slaves

(2 versions)

122/london 1954   224/london 1960

pictures from an exhibition (ravel orchestration)

(12 versions)

152/london 1955   155/milan 1955

310/berlin 1965   (665)/salzburg 1979

680/tokyo 1979   827/berlin 1986

(828)/berlin 1986   (842)/salzburg 1987

(854)/salzburg 1987   (860)/cologne 1987

(866)/osaka 1988   868/tokyo 1988

pictures from an exhibition: great gate of kiev

(1 version)

(648)/paris 1978

OTTO NICOLAI (1810-1849)
die lustigen weiber von windsor overture (1 version)
223/berlin 1960

CARL NIELSEN (1865-1931)
symphony no 4 "inextinguishable" (1 version)
713/berlin 1981

JACQUES OFFENBACH (1819-1890)
overtures: barbe-bleue; la belle helene; la grande
duchesse de gerolstein; vert-vert (1 version)
697/berlin 1980

les contes d'hoffmann: barcarolle (4 versions)
118/london 1954   196/london 1959
(648)/paris 1978   697/berlin 1980

orfee aux enfers overture (3 versions)
145/london 1955   224/london 1960
697/berlin 1980

gaite parisienne: ballet suite arranged by rosenthal
(2 versions)
185/london 1958   430/berlin 1971

CARL ORFF (1895-1982)
de temporum fine comoedia (1 version)
488/leverkusen 1973

JOHANN PACHELBEL (1653-1706)
canon and fugue in d, arranged by seiffert (2 versions)
393/sankt moritz 1969   771/berlin 1983

KRZYSZTOF PENDERECKI (born 1933)
polymorphia (1 version)
366/berlin 1968

ILDEBRANDO PIZZETTI (1880-1968)
assassino nelle cattedrale (1 version)
213/vienna 1960

preludio a un altro giorno (1 version)
(078)/rome 1952

AMILCARE PONCHIELLI (1834-1886)
la gioconda: dance of the hours (3 versions)
122/london 1954   224/london 1960
425/berlin 1970-1971

SERGEI PROKOFIEV (1891-1953)
symphony no 1 "classical" (5 versions)
712/berlin 1981   (879)/berlin 1988
(880)/berlin 1988   881/berlin 1988
(886)/salzburg 1989

symphony no 5 in b flat (6 versions)
(133)/torino 1955   (356)/salzburg 1967
377/berlin 1968   (390)/london 1969
(688)/berlin 1980   702/lucerne 1980

peter and the wolf (1 version)
161/london 1956

405

GIACOMO PUCCINI (1858-1924)

la boheme (6 versions)

275/vienna 1963	294/moscow 1964
304/milan 1965	468/berlin 1972
(542)/salzburg 1975	606/vienna 1977

la boheme: si mi chiamano mimi (2 versions)

033a/vienna 1948	(648)/paris 1978

la boheme: donde lieta usci (1 version)

033a/vienna 1948

la boheme: quando m'en vo (1 version)

036/vienna 1948

gianni schicchi o mio babbino caro (1 version)

033a/vienna 1948

madama butterfly (3 versions)

148/milan 1955	509/vienna 1974
530/salzburg 1974	

manon lescaut: intermezzo (8 versions)

(028)/vienna 1947	038/vienna 1948
118/london 1954	196/london 1959
360/berlin 1967	(447)/berlin 1972
705/berlin 1980	824/berlin 1985

puccini/**suor angelica: intermezzo** (2 versions)

360/berlin 1967 705/berlin 1980

tosca (6 versions)

246/vienna 1962 258/vienna 1962

677/berlin 1979 (741)/berlin 1982

(863)/salzburg 1988 (885)/salzburg 1989

turandot (1 version)

718/vienna 1981

turandot: tu che di gel cinta (1 version)

(033a)/vienna 1948

SERGEI RACHMANINOV (1873-1943)

piano concerto no 2 in c minor (3 versions)

467/berlin 1972 (467a)/berlin 1972

495/berlin 1973

MAURICE RAVEL (1875-1937)

alborada del gracioso (1 version)

435/paris 1971

bolero (10 versions)

319/berlin 1966 (544)/salzburg 1975

(557)/lucerne 1975 (581)/salzburg 1976

598/berlin 1977 (669)/salzburg 1979

(734)/tokyo 1981 (816)/salzburg 1985

823/berlin 1985 824/berlin 1985

ravel/**daphnis et chloe: second suite from the ballet**
(7 versions)

281/berlin 1964	(456)/salzburg 1972
640/berlin 1978	(794)/osaka 1984
(797)/tokyo 1984	821/berlin 1985-1986
(822)/berlin 1985	

pavane pour une infante defunte (2 versions)

821/berlin 1985-1986	(828)/berlin 1986

rapsodie espagnole (5 versions)

(032)/torino 1948	092/london 1953
435/paris 1971	(734)/tokyo 1981
839/berlin 1987	

le tombeau de couperin (1 version)
435/paris 1971

la valse (1 version)
435/paris 1971

MAX REGER (1873-1916)
variations on a theme of mozart (1 version)
(182)/berlin 1958

OTTORINO RESPIGHI (1879-1936)
fontane di roma (1 version)
632/berlin 1977

pini di roma (3 versions)
184/london 1958   632/berlin 1977
793/osaka 1984

antiche danze ed arie: third suite (1 version)
393/sankt moritz 1969

EMIL VON REZNICEK (1860-1945)
donna diana overture (2 versions)
024/vienna 1947   (146)/london 1955

NIKOLAI RIMSKY-KORSAKOV (1844-1908)
scheherazade (1 version)
344/berlin 1967

HILDING ROSENBERG (1892-1985)
concerto for strings (1 version)
111/torino 1954

GIOACHINO ROSSINI (1792-1868)
string sonatas nos 1, 2, 3 and 6 (1 version)
375/sankt moritz 1968

overtures: il barbiere di siviglia; la gazza ladra;
l'italiana in algeri; la scala di seta (2 versions)
214/london 1960   426/berlin 1971

rossini/**guillaume tell: overture** (5 versions)

214/london 1960 426/berlin 1971
538/berlin 1975 774/berlin 1983-1984
776/berlin 1983

guillaume tell: passo a tre e coro tirolese (1 version)
185/london 1958

semiramide: overture (5 versions)
(009)/berlin 1942 010/torino 1942
214/london 1960 426/berlin 1971
(447)/berlin 1972

ALBERT ROUSSEL (1869-1937)
symphony no 4 (1 version)
048/london 1949

CAMILLE SAINT-SAENS (1835-1921)
symphony no 3 "organ symphony" (1 version)
727/berlin 1981

FRANZ SCHMIDT (1874-1939)
notre dame: intermezzo (3 versions)
196/london 1959 360/berlin 1967
705/berlin 1980

FLORENT SCHMITT (1870-1958)
psalm 47 (1 version)
(113)/torino 1954

ARNOLD SCHOENBERG (1874-1951)

pelleas und melisande (1 version)
508/berlin 1972-1974

orchestral variations (2 versions)

381/berlin 1969   507/berlin 1972-1974

verklärte nacht (orchestral version) (7 versions)

463/salzburg 1972   503/berlin 1972-1974
(558)/berlin 1975   (590)/new york 1976
(716)/salzburg 1981   (873)/lucerne 1988
875/london 1988

FRANZ SCHUBERT (1797-1828)

symphonies: no 1 in d D82; no 2 in b flat D125;
no 3 in d D200; no 4 in c minor D417 "tragic";
no 6 in c D598 (1 version)
620/berlin 1978

symphony no 5 in b flat D485 (2 versions)

189/berlin 1958   620/berlin 1978

symphony no 8 in b minor D759 "unfinished"
(15 versions)

139/london 1955   (181)/tokyo 1957
209/tokyo 1959   297/berlin 1964
(329)/fukuoka 1966   376/salzburg 1968
534/berlin 1975   679/tokyo 1979
(775)/berlin 1983   (826)/berlin 1986
(843)/salzburg 1987   (844)/salzburg 1987
(853)/salzburg 1987   (861)/frankfurt 1987
(884)/new york 1989

schubert/**symphony no 9 in c D944 "great"** (3 versions)

017/vienna 1946   377/berlin 1968

611/berlin 1978

rosamunde D797: overture, ballet music no 1 and ballet music no 2 (1 version)

620/berlin 1978

ROBERT SCHUMANN (1810-1856)

symphony no 1 in b flat op 38 "spring" (1 version)

428/berlin 1971

symphony no 2 in c op 61 (3 versions)

129/rome 1954   432/berlin 1971

(450)/berlin 1972

symphony no 3 in e flat op 97 "rhenish" (1 version)

428/berlin 1971

symphony no 4 in d minor op 120 (9 versions)

167/berlin 1957   313/vienna 1966

428/berlin 1971   461a/salzburg 1972

(568)/salzburg 1976   (662)/berlin 1979

695/salzburg 1980   847/vienna 1987

871/salzburg 1988

schumann/**piano concerto in a minor op 54**
(6 versions)

031/london 1948	094/london 1953
511/salzburg 1974	729/berlin 1981
(789)/salzburg 1984	(790)/lucerne 1984

overture, scherzo and finale in e op 52 (1 version)
432/berlin 1971

DIMITRI SHOSTAKOVICH (1906-1975)
symphony no 10 in e minor op 93 (6 versions)

340/berlin 1966	(361)/berlin 1967
388/moscow 1969	(580)/salzburg 1976
713/berlin 1981	(750)/salzburg 1982

JEAN SIBELIUS (1865-1957)
symphony no 1 in e minor op 39 (1 version)
711/berlin 1981

symphony no 2 in d op 43 (2 versions)

215/london 1960	705/berlin 1980

symphony no 4 in a minor op 63 (5 versions)

090/london 1953	300/berlin 1965
(305)/helsinki 1965	596/berlin 1976
(638)/berlin 1978	

sibelius/**symphony no 5 in e flat op 82**
(10 versions)

043/stockholm 1949	(065)/london 1951
071/london 1951	170/berlin 1957
224/london 1960	300/berlin 1965
(305)/helsinki 1965	583/berlin 1976
587/berlin 1976	(616)/lucerne 1977

symphony no 6 in d minor op 104 (3 versions)

144/london 1955	350/berlin 1967
705/berlin 1980	

symphony no 7 in c op 105 (2 versions)

144/london 1955	369/berlin 1967

violin concerto in d minor op 47 (2 versions)

297/berlin 1964	441/berlin 1971

en saga op 9 (1 version)
594/berlin 1976

finlandia op op 26 no 7 (8 versions)

071/london 1952	084/torino 1953
196/london 1959	297/berlin 1964
(305)/helsinki 1965	582/berlin 1976
(587)/berlin 1976	780/berlin 1984

karelia suite op 11 (1 version)
705/berlin 1981

sibelius/**pelleas and melisande op 46** (1 version)
740/berlin 1982

the swan of tuonela op 22 no 3 (3 versions)
310/berlin 1965   594/berlin 1976
780/berlin 1984

tapiola op 112 (4 versions)
090/london 1953   297/berlin 1964
594/berlin 1976   780/berlin 1984

valse triste op 44 (7 versions)
185/london 1958   344/berlin 1967
(447)/berlin 1972   (648)/paris 1978
705/berlin 1980   776/berlin 1983
780/berlin 1984

BEDRICH SMETANA (1824-1884)
ma vlast: the moldau (7 versions)
005/berlin 1940   189/berlin 1958
350/berlin 1967   598/berlin 1977
774/berlin 1983-1984   776/berlin 1983
810/vienna 1985

ma vlast: vysherad (1 version)
350/berlin 1967

smetana/**the bartered bride: sweet dream of love**
(1 version)
030/vienna 1947

**the bartered bride: polka, furiant and dance
of the comedians** (1 version)
440/berlin 1971

JOHN PHILIP SOUSA (1854-1932)
marches: stars and stripes forever; el capitan
(1 version)
093/london 1953

JOHANN STRAUSS FATHER (1804-1849)
radetzky march (8 versions)

145/london 1955	188/brussels 1958
225/london 1960	341/berlin 1966
376/salzburg 1968	697/berlin 1980
836/vienna 1987	(884)/new york 1989

beliebte annen polka (1 version)
836/vienna 1987

JOHANN STRAUSS (1825-1899)
accelerationen waltz (1 version)
697/berlin 1980

aegyptischer marsch (1 version)
386/berlin 1969

johann strauss/**an der schönen blauen donau**
(9 versions)

020/vienna 1946	145/london 1955
188/brussels 1958	207/tokyo 1959
341/berlin 1966	376/salzburg 1968
534/berlin 1975	697/berlin 1980
836/vienna 1987	

annen polka (8 versions)

188/brussels 1958	200/vienna 1959
341/berlin 1966	376/salzburg 1968
534/berlin 1975	697/berlin 1980
836/vienna 1987	(884)/new york 1989

auf der jagd polka (4 versions)

188/brussels 1958	200/vienna 1959
386/berlin 1969	697/berlin 1980

elyen a magyar polka (1 version)
697/berlin 1980

die fledermaus (3 versions)

138/london 1955	216/vienna 1960
231/vienna 1960	

johann strauss/**die fledermaus: overture**
(9 versions)

011/berlin 1942	038/vienna 1948
188/brussels 1958	200/vienna 1959
341/berlin 1966	(497)/berlin 1973
534/berlin 1975	697/berlin 1980
836/vienna 1987	

die fledermaus: quadrille (1 version)
697/berlin 1980

frühlingsstimmen waltz (vocal version) (2 versions)

188/brussels 1958	836/vienna 1987

g'schichten aus dem wienerwald (4 versions)

037/vienna 1948	200/vienna 1959
386/berlin 1969	697/berlin 1980

kaiserwalzer (11 versions)

007/berlin 1941	020/vienna 1946
145/london 1955	188/brussels 1958
341/berlin 1966	376/salzburg 1968
(497)/berlin 1973	534/berlin 1975
697/berlin 1980	836/vienna 1987
(884)/new york 1989	

418

johann strauss/**künstlerleben waltz** (5 versions)

005/berlin 1941	020/vienna 1946
142/london 1955	(186)/vienna 1958
697/berlin 1980	

leichtes blut polka (3 versions)

020/vienna 1946	386/berlin 1969
697/berlin 1980	

morgenblätter waltz (1 version)
386/berlin 1969

napoleon-marsch (1 versions)
697/berlin 1980

perpetuum mobile (6 versions)

041/vienna 1949	341/berlin 1966
376/salzburg 1968	697/berlin 1980
836/vienna 1987	(884)/new york 1989

persischer marsch (2 versions)

386/berlin 1969	836/berlin 1980

postillon d'amour polka (1 version)
386/berlin 1969

rosen aus dem süden waltz (1 version)
697/berlin 1980

johann strauss/tritsch-tratsch polka (7 versions)

045/vienna 1949	145/london 1955
225/london 1960	341/berlin 1966
(497)/berlin 1973	534/berlin 1975
697/berlin 1980	

unter donner und blitz polka (7 versions)

045/vienna 1949	145/london 1955
188/brussels 1958	225/london 1960
386/berlin 1969	697/berlin 1980
836/vienna 1987	

vergnügungszug polka (1 version)

836/vienna 1987

wein weib und gesang waltz (2 versions)

045/vienna 1949	697/berlin 1980

wiener blut waltz (3 versions)

044/vienna 1949	386/berlin 1969
697/berlin 1980	

der zigeunerbaron: overture (12 versions)

011/berlin 1942	020/vienna 1946
145/london 1955	200/vienna 1959
341/berlin 1966	376/salzburg 1968
(497)/berlin 1973	534/berlin 1975
697/berlin 1980	776/berlin 1983
836/vienna 1987	(884)/new york 1989

420

johann strauss/**der zigeunerbaron: habet acht!**
(1 version)
035/vienna 1948

JOHANN AND JOSEF STRAUSS
pizzicato polka (6 versions)

020/vienna 1946	139/london 1955
145/london 1955	188/brussels 1958
386/berlin 1969	836/vienna 1987

JOSEF STRAUSS (1827-1870)
delirienwalzer (12 versions)

045/vienna 1949	145/london 1955
200/vienna 1959	(303)/paris 1965
341/berlin 1966	376/salzburg 1968
(447)/berlin 1972	(648)/paris 1978
697/berlin 1980	776/berlin 1983
836/vienna 1987	(884)/new york 1989

ohne sorgen polka (1 version)
836/vienna 1987

tranaktionen waltz (1 version)
045/vienna 1949

josef strauss/**sphärenklänge waltz** (7 versions)

045/vienna 1949	(185)/london 1958
386/berlin 1969	697/berlin 1980
(824)/berlin 1985	836/vienna 1987
(884)/new york 1989	

RICHARD STRAUSS (1864-1949)
ariadne auf naxos (1 version)
115/london 1954

ariadne auf naxos: es gibt ein reich (2 versions)

035/vienna 1948	159/berlin 1956

capriccio: mondscheinmusik and closing scene
(morgen mittag um elf?) (1 version)
819/berlin 1985

elektra (1 version)
291/salzburg 1964

die frau ohne schatten (2 versions)

285/vienna 1964	286/vienna 1964

der rosenkavalier (8 versions)

067/milan 1952	160/london 1956
219/salzburg 1960	222/salzburg 1960
267/salzburg 1963	288/salzburg 1964
760/vienna 1982-1984	787/salzburg 1984

strauss/**der rosenkavalier: orchestral suite**
(1 version)
(185)/london 1958

**der rosenkavalier: kann mich auch an ein mädel
erinnern...quinquin er soll jetzt geh'n** (1 version)
030/vienna 1947

der rosenkavalier: mir ist die ehre widerfahren
(1 version)
026/vienna 1947

salome (2 versions)
604/vienna 1977   613/salzburg 1977

salome: orchestral interlude and closing scene
(1 version)
037/vienna 1948

salome: dance of the seven veils (3 versions)
012/amsterdam 1943   218/vienna 1960
473/berlin 1973

die heiligen drei könige aus mohrenland (1 version)
819/berlin 1985

strauss/**vier letzte lieder** (6 versions)

156/london 1956	289/salzburg 1964
479/berlin 1973	(709)/berlin 1980
743/salzburg 1982	819/berlin 1985

eine alpensinfonie (7 versions)

707/berlin 1980	(738)/berlin 1981
743/salzburg 1982	753/salzburg 1982
771a/berlin 1983	(859)/lucerne 1987
864/salzburg 1988	

also sprach zarathustra (12 versions)

199/vienna 1959	292/salzburg 1964
413/salzburg 1970	478/berlin 1973
(561)/berlin 1975	(569)/salzburg 1976
608/salzburg 1977	(671)/london 1979
675/salzburg 1979	771/berlin 1983
(784)/salzburg 1984	846/berlin 1987

don juan (9 versions)

012/amsterdam 1943	066/london 1951
179/tokyo 1957	211/vienna 1960
(327)/osaka 1966	473/berlin 1972-1973
609/salzburg 1977	762/berlin 1983
793/osaka 1984	

strauss/**don quixote** (12 versions)

292/salzburg 1964	314/berlin 1965
532/berlin 1975	(535)/berlin 1975
(555)/salzburg 1975	(709)/berlin 1980
721/salzburg 1981	825/berlin 1985
(826)/berlin 1986	(841)/salzburg 1987
(843)/salzburg 1987	(844)/salzburg 1987

ein heldenleben (17 versions)

193/new york 1958	197/berlin 1959
202/los angeles 1959	(238a)/edinburgh 1961
289/salzburg 1964	(332)/tokyo 1966
351/florence 1967	389/moscow 1969
434/salzburg 1971	459/london 1972
515/berlin 1975	(528)/new york 1974
(573)/london 1976	(610)/salzburg 1977
806/berlin 1985	(807)/berlin 1985
809/london 1985	

metamorphosen (7 versions)

021/vienna 1947	394/sankt moritz 1969
(561)/berlin 1975	703/berlin 1980
(720)/oxford 1981	(725)/salzburg 1981
799/berlin 1984	

strauss/**sinfonia domestica** (3 versions)

(477)/berlin 1973   487/paris 1973

(511)/salzburg 1974

till eulenspiegels lustige streiche (7 versions)

066/london 1951   137/washington 1955

218/vienna 1960   (296)/berlin 1964

473/berlin 1972-1973   609/salzburg 1977

825/berlin 1986

tod und verklärung (7 versions)

(082)/torino 1953   090/london 1953

(134)/torino 1955   218/vienna 1960

470/berlin 1972-1973   740/berlin 1982

799/berlin 1984

horn concerto no 2 (1 version)

480/berlin 1973

oboe concerto (2 versions)

(289)/salzburg 1964   398/berlin 1969

IGOR STRAVINSKY (1882-1971)

le sacre du printemps (8 versions)

273/berlin 1963-1964   (441)/berlin 1971

458/london 1972   465/lucerne 1972

564/berlin 1975-1977   (618)/berlin 1977

(651)/salzburg 1978   (653)/lucerne 1978

stravinsky/**apollon musagete** (7 versions)

(418)/berlin 1970	(455)/salzburg 1972
462/sankt moritz 1972	676/salzburg 1979
(693)/vienna 1980	(753)/salzburg 1982
(754)/lucerne 1982	

circus polka (1 version)
404/berlin 1970

concerto in d (1 version)
394/sankt moritz 1969

jeu de cartes (1 version)
068/london 1952

oedipus rex (1 version)
079/rome 1952

symphony in c (3 versions)

(238a)/edinburgh 1961	399/berlin 1969
(467a)/berlin 1972	

symphony in three movements (1 version)
134/torino 1955

symphony of psalms (2 versions)

540/berlin 1975	725/salzburg 1981

FRANZ VON SUPPE (1819-1895)
leichte kavallerie: overture (5 versions)

145/london 1955	224/london 1960
398/berlin 1969	(447)/berlin 1972
659/berlin 1978	

**overtures: banditenstreiche; dichter und bauer; ein
morgen ein mittag ein abend in wien; pique dame;
die schöne galathea** (1 version)
398/berlin 1969

HEINRICH SUTERMEISTER (1910-1995)
messa da requiem (1 version)
107/rome 1953

PIOTR TCHAIKOVSKY (1840-1893)
**symphonies no 1 in g minor op 13 "winter dreams"
and no 3 in d op 29 "polish"** (1 version)
633/berlin 1977-1979

symphony no 2 in c minor op 17 "little russian"
(1 version)
661/berlin 1979

tchaikovsky/**symphony no 4 in f minor op 36**
(13 versions)

091/london 1953	126/vienna 1954
212/berlin 1960	339/berlin 1966
358/edinburgh 1967	439/berlin 1971
(501)/tokyo 1973	506/berlin 1973
(577)/salzburg 1976	595/berlin 1976
690/salzburg 1980	791/vienna 1984
(814)/salzburg 1985	

symphony no 5 in e minor op 64 (13 versions)

(071)/london 1952	082/torino 1953
087/london 1953	310/berlin 1965
381/berlin 1969	439/berlin 1971
485/berlin 1973	493/berlin 1973
(510)/salzburg 1974	562/berlin 1975
(575)/salzburg 1976	679/tokyo 1979
782a/vienna 1984	

tchaikovsky/**symphony no 6 in b minor op 74
"pathetique"** (19 versions)

004/berlin 1939	033/vienna 1948
(112)/torino 1954	114/tokyo 1954
140/london 1955	279/berlin 1964
439/berlin 1971	506/berlin 1973
571/berlin 1976	(576)/salzburg 1976
(676)/salzburg 1979	(708)/berlin 1980
710/berlin 1981	(726)/salzburg 1981
(735)/tokyo 1981	777/vienna 1984
(788)/salzburg 1984	(865)/osaka 1988
867/tokyo 1988	

piano concerto no 1 in b flat minor op 23
(8 versions)

257/vienna 1962	349/berlin 1967
402/paris 1970	563/berlin 1975
(575)/salzburg 1976	(662)/berlin 1979
881/berlin 1988	(886)/salzburg 1989

violin concerto in d op 35 (4 versions)

310/berlin 1965	(577)/salzburg 1976
(814)/salzburg 1985	871/salzburg 1988

rococo variations for cello and orchestra op 33
(1 version)
377/berlin 1968

tchaikovsky/**ouverture solennelle "1812" op 49**
(2 versions)
185/london 1958   339/berlin 1966

romeo and juliet, fantasy overture (6 versions)
020/vienna 1946   211/vienna 1960
339/berlin 1966   (576)/salzburg 1976
756/berlin 1982   801/vienna 1984

serenade for strings in c op 48 (2 versions)
339/berlin 1966   703/berlin 1980

capriccio italien op 45 (1 version)
339/berlin 1966

casse noisette: standard ballet suite op 71a
(5 versions)
(071)/london 1952   075/london 1952
239/vienna 1961   339/berlin 1966
756/berlin 1982

evgeny onegin: polonaise and waltz (1 version)
425/berlin 1970-1971

marche slave op 31 (1 version)
339/berlin 1966

tchaikovsky/**sleeping beauty: standard ballet suite op 66a; swan lake: standard ballet suite op 20a** (4 versions)

075/london 1952	196/london 1959
301/vienna 1965	427/berlin 1971

GEORG PHILIPP TELEMANN (1681-1767)
trumpet concerto in d, arranged by grebe (1 version)
514/berlin 1974

WERNER THAERICHEN (1921-2008)
paukenkrieg (1 version)
(618)/berlin 1977

MICHAEL TIPPETT (1905-1998)
a child of our time (1 version)
(081)/torino 1953

GIUSEPPE TORELLI (1658-1709)
concerto op 8 no 6 "christmas concerto" (1 version)
414/sankt moritz 1970

RALPH VAUGHAN WILLIAMS (1872-1958)
fantasia on a theme of thomas tallis (2 versions)

(097)/london 1953	103/london 1953

GIUSEPPE VERDI (1813-1901)

messa da requiem (17 versions)

042/salzburg 1949	127/vienna 1954
191/salzburg 1958	256/salzburg 1962
293/moscow 1964	(309)/epidaurus 1965
343/milan 1967	415/salzburg 1970
449/berlin 1972	554/salzburg 1975
570/salzburg 1976	(593)/new york 1976
(652)/salzburg 1978	682/tokyo 1979
777/vienna 1984	(874)/berlin 1988
(887)/salzburg 1989	

quattro pezzi sacri: te deum (3 versions)

352/rome 1967	401/berlin 1970
(691)/salzburg 1980	

overtures and preludes: aida; alzira; aroldo; attila; un ballo in maschera; la battaglia di legnano; il corsaro; ernani; un giorno di regno; giovanna d'arco; luisa miller; macbeth; i masnadieri; nabucco; oberto; rigoletto; i vespri siciliani (1 version)
560/berlin 1975

aida (6 versions)

056/vienna 1951	205/vienna 1959
(217)/vienna 1960	667/vienna 1979
673/salzburg 1979	(699)/salzburg 1980

verdi/**aida: dance of the priestesses and dance of the moorish slaves** (1 version)
425/berlin 1970-1971

aida: act two ballet music (3 versions)
122/london 1954   224/london 1960
425/berlin 1970-1971

un ballo in maschera (1 version)
882/vienna 1989

don carlo (6 versions)
190/salzburg 1958   553/salzburg 1975
(579)/salzburg 1976   654/berlin 1978
666/vienna 1979   829a/salzburg 1986

don carlo: ella giammai m'amo (1 version)
049/london 1949

falstaff (5 versions)
157/london 1956   174/salzburg 1957
696/vienna 1980   723/salzburg 1981
750a/salzburg 1982

la forza del destino: overture (4 versions)
002/berlin 1939   560/berlin 1975
(648)/paris 1978   659/berlin 1978

verdi/**otello** (4 versions)

236/vienna 1961	412/salzburg 1970
436/salzburg 1971	484/berlin 1973

otello: ballet music (1 version)
425/berlin 1970-1971

la traviata (2 versions)

298/milan 1964	299/milan 1964

la traviata: act one prelude (2 versions)

010/torino 1942	560/berlin 1975

la traviata: act three prelude (4 versions)

010/torino 1942	118/london 1954
196/london 1959	360/berlin 1967

il trovatore (8 versions)

158/milan 1956	255/salzburg 1962
268/salzburg 1963	603/salzburg 1977
603a/vienna 1977	607/vienna 1977
617/berlin 1977	644a/vienna 1978

ANTONIO VIVALDI (1678-1741)

le quattro stagioni: concerti no 1 in e "la primavera" RV269, no 2 in g minor "l'estate" RV315, no 3 in f "l'autunno" RV293 and no 4 in f minor "l'inverno" RV297 (5 versions)

462/sankt moritz 1972   (477)/berlin 1973
786/vienna 1984   (788)/salzburg 1984
858/berlin 1987

trumpet concerto in a flat, arranged by thiede
(1 version)
514/berlin 1974

flute concerto in g minor "la notte" RV439 (1 version)
771/berlin 1983

sinfonia in b minor "al santo sepolcro" RV 169
(2 versions)
414/sankt moritz 1970   (441)/berlin 1971

concerti for strings in g "alla rustica" RV151 and in d minor "madrigalesco" RV219 (1 version)
414/sankt moritz 1970

concerto for two violins in a minor RV523 (1 version)
414/sankt moritz 1970

violin concerti in e "l'amoroso" RV 271 and in d "l'inquietudine" RV 234 (1 version)
414/sankt moritz 1970

RICHARD WAGNER (1813-1883)

der fliegende holländer (3 versions)
737/berlin 1981-1983   (742)/salzburg 1982
(764)/salzburg 1983

der fliegende holländer: overture (3 versions)
223/berlin 1960   523/berlin 1974
(648)/paris 1978

der fliegende hollånder: summ und brumm (1 version)
036/vienna 1948

der fliegende holländer: steuermann lass die wacht!
(1 version)
046/vienna 1949

götterdämmerung (3 versions)
(063)/bayreuth 1951   399/berlin 1969
403/salzburg 1970

lohengrin (3 versions)
565/berlin 1975   (567)/salzburg 1976
783/salzburg 1984

lohengrin: prelude (2 versions)
223/berlin 1960   523/berlin 1974

lohengrin: act three prelude (2 versions)
046/vienna 1949   523/berlin 1974

wagner/**lohengrin: treulich geführt** (2 versions)
(036)/vienna 1948   046/vienna 1949

die meistersinger von nürnberg (4 versions)
058/bayreuth 1951   059/bayreuth 1951
422/dresden 1970   543/salzburg 1975

die meistersinger von nürnberg: overture (8 versions)
002/berlin 1939   006/paris 1941
162/berlin 1957   179/tokyo 1957
202/los angeles 1959   523/berlin 1974
(538)/berlin 1975   (585a)/berlin 1976

die meistersinger von nürnberg: act three prelude
(2 versions)
003/berlin 1939   780/berlin 1984

**die meistersinger von nürnberg: was duftet doch
der flieder; wahnmonolog** (1 version)
(020)/vienna 1946

**die meistersinger von nürnberg: da zu dir der heiland
kam; wach auf!** (1 version)
046/vienna 1949

parsifal (4 versions)
233/vienna 1961   685/berlin 1979-1980
(689)/salzburg 1980   714/salzburg 1981

438

wagner/**parsifal: preludes acts one and three** (1 version)
523/berlin 1974

das rheingold (5 versions)
060/bayreuth 1951   364/berlin 1967
367/salzburg 1968   382/new york 1969
483 and 656/salzburg-munich 1973-1978

siegfried (3 versions)
062/bayreuth 1951   379/berlin 1968
384/salzburg 1969

siegfried idyll (3 versions)
600/berlin 1977   852/salzburg 1987
(862)/berlin 1987

tannhäuser (1 version)
262/vienna 1963

tannhäuser: overture (5 versions)
162/berlin 1957   500/tokyo 1973
538/berlin 1975   852/salzburg 1987
(862)/berlin 1987

tannhäuser: overture and venusberg music
(2 versions)
523/berlin 1974   780/berlin 1984

wagner/**tannhäuser: venusberg music** (2 versions)

122/london 1954 224/london 1960

tannhäuser: freudig begrüssen wir die edle halle
(1 version)
046/vienna 1949

tristan und isolde (5 versions)

070/bayreuth 1952 201/milan 1959

444/berlin 1971-1972 454/salzburg 1972

(482)/salzburg 1973

tristan und isolde: prelude and liebestod (9 versions)

(136)/berlin 1955 162/berlin 1957

365a/berlin 1968 (469)/belgrade 1972

500/tokyo 1973 523/berlin 1974

780/berlin 1984 852/salzburg 1987

(862)/berlin 1987

die walküre (9 versions)

061/bayreuth 1951 164/vienna 1957

187/milan 1958 338/berlin 1966

345/salzburg 1967 348/salzburg 1967

363/new york 1967 378/new york 1968

383/new york 1969

EMIL WALDTEUFEL (1837-1915)
les patineurs waltz (2 versions)

093/london 1953 224/london 1960

440

WILLIAM WALTON (1902-1983)
symphony no 1 (1 version)
104/rome 1953

CARL MARIA VON WEBER (1786-1826)
overtures: abu hassan; beherrscher der geister;
peter schmoll (1 version)
431/berlin 1971

euryanthe: overture (2 versions)
(104)/rome 1953   431/berlin 1971

der freischütz: overture (6 versions)
012/amsterdam 1943   223/berlin 1960
432/berlin 1971   538/berlin 1975
705/berlin 1980   824/berlin 1985

oberon: overture (1 version)
432/berlin 1971

aufforderung zum tanz, arranged by berlioz
(3 versions)
185/london 1958   440/berlin 1971
774/berlin 1983-1984

441

ANTON VON WEBERN (1883-1945)
symphony op 21; passacaglia op 1 (1 version)
507/berlin 1972-1974

five movements op 5 (3 versions)
193/new york 1958   503/berlin 1972-1974
(662)/berlin 1979

six pieces op 6 (2 versions)
(327)/osaka 1966   480/berlin 1972-1974

JAROMIR WEINBERGER (1896-1967)
schwanda the bagpiper: polka (2 versions)
118/london 1954   224/london 1960

GERHARD WIMBERGER (born 1923)
plays for 12 cellos, wind and percussion (2 versions)
(581)/salzburg 1976   (599)/berlin 1977

ERMANNO WOLF-FERRARI (1876-1948)
i gioielli della madonna: intermezzo (1 version)
360/berlin 1967

CHRISTMAS SONGS
**silent night; hark the herald angels; we three kings;
angels we have heard on high; o tannenbaum; god rest
ye merry gentlemen; it came upon the midnight clear;
von himmel hoch; sweet li'l jesus; ave maria (bach);
ave maria (schubert); o holy night; alleluja** (1 version)
237/vienna 1961

NATIONAL ANTHEMS

european anthem arranged by karajan from
beethoven; and the national anthems of the 17
member states of the council of europe: austria,
belgium, cyprus, denmark, west germany,
france, iceland, ireland, italy, luxembourg,
malta, netherlands, norway, sweden,
switzerland, turkey and united kingdom
(1 version)
452/berlin 1972

american national anthem (1 version)
202/los angeles 1959

austrian national anthem (2 versions)
207/tokyo 1959   250/london 1962

british national anthem (1 version)
250/london 1962

german national anthem (2 versions)
320/tokyo 1966   (498)/tokyo 1973

japanese national anthem (3 versions)
207/tokyo 1959   320/tokyo 1966
(498)/tokyo 1973

PRUSSIAN AND AUSTRIAN MARCHES

yorckscher; torgauer; o du mein österreich; unter
dem grillenbanner; des grossen kurfürsten reiter;
pariser einzug; unter dem doppeladler; mir sein
die kaiserjäger; florentiner; finnländische reiterei;
königgrätzer; regimentskinder; wien bleibt wien;
kreuzritter-fanfare; petersburger; fehrbelliner
reiter; pappenheimer; hoch- und deutschmeister;
vindobona; hohenfriedberger; erzherzog albrecht;
tiroler holzhackerbuab'n; preussens gloria;
coburger; kärntnerlieder; die bosniaken kommen;
fridericus-rex-grenadier; alte kameraden;
zigeunerbaron-einzug; nibelungen (1 version)
480/berlin 1973

Books published by Travis & Emery Music Bookshop:

Anon.: Hymnarium Sarisburiense, cum Rubricis et Notis Musicis.
Anon.: Säcularfeier des Geburtstages von Ludwig van Beethoven
Agricola, Johann Friedrich from Tosi: Anleitung zur Singkunst.
Allen, Percy: The Stage Life of Mrs. Stirling: With ... C19th Theatre
Bach, C.P.E.: edited W. Emery: Nekrolog or Obituary Notice of J.S. Bach.
Bateson, Naomi Judith: Alcock of Salisbury
Bathe, William: A Briefe Introduction to the Skill of Song
Berlioz, Hector: Autobiography of Hector Berlioz, (2 vols.)
Buckley, Robert John: Sir Edward Elgar
Burney, Charles: The Present State of Music in France and Italy
Burney, Charles: The Present State of Music in Germany, The Netherlands ...
Burney, Charles: Account of an Infant Musician
Burney, Charles: An Account of the Musical Performances ... Handel
Burney, Karl: Nachricht von Georg Friedrich Handel's Lebensumstanden.
Burns, Robert: The Caledonian Musical Museum .. Best Scotch Songs. (1810)
Cobbett, W.W.: Cobbett's Cyclopedic Survey of Chamber Music. (2 vols.)
Corrette, Michel: Le Maitre de Clavecin
Cox, John Edmund: Musical Recollections of the Last Half Century. (2 vols.)
Crimp, Bryan: Dear Mr. Rosenthal ... Dear Mr. Gaisberg ...
Crimp, Bryan: Solo: The Biography of Solomon
Crotch, William: Substance of Several Courses of Lectures on Music
d'Indy, Vincent: Beethoven: Biographie Critique
d'Indy, Vincent: Beethoven: A Critical Biography
d'Indy, Vincent: Cesar Franck (in English)
d'Indy, Vincent: César Franck (in French)
Dianna, B.A.: Benjamin Britten's Holy Theatre
Dolge, Alfred: Pianos and Their Makers. A Comprehensive History
Fischhof, Joseph: Versuch einer Geschichte des Clavierbaues. (Faksimile 1853).
Fuller-Maitland, J.A.: The Music of Parry and Stanford
Geminiani, Francesco: The Art of Playing the Violin.
Häuser: Musikalisches Lexikon. 2 vols in one.
Hawkins, John: A General History of the Science & Practice of Music (5 vols.)
Holmes, Edward: A Ramble among the Musicians of Germany
Hopkins, Antony: The Concertgoer's Companion - Bach to Haydn.
Hopkins, Antony: The Concertgoer's Companion – Holst to Webern.
Hopkins, Antony: Music All Around Me
Hopkins, Antony: Sounds of Music / Sounds of the Orchestra
Hopkins, Antony: The Nine Symphonies of Beethoven
Hopkins, Antony: Understanding Music

Books published by Travis & Emery Music Bookshop:

Hopkins, Edward & Rimboult, Edward: The Organ. Its History & Construction.
Hunt, John: - see separate list of discographies at the end of these titles
Iliffe, Frederick: The Forty-Eight Preludes and Fugues of John Sebastian Bach
Isaacs, Lewis: Hänsel and Gretel. A Guide to Humperdinck's Opera.
Isaacs, Lewis: Königskinder (Royal Children). Guide to Humperdinck's Opera.
Kastner: Manuel Général de Musique Militaire
Kenney, Charles Lamb: A Memoir of Michael William Balfe
Klein, Hermann: Thirty years of musical Life in London, 1870-1900
Lacassagne, M. l'Abbé Joseph : Traité Général des élémens du Chant
Lascelles (née Catley), Anne: The Life of Miss Anne Catley.
McCormack, John: John McCormack: His Own Life Story.
Mainwaring, John: Memoirs of the Life of the Late George Frederic Handel
Malcolm, Alexander: A Treaty of Music: Speculative, Practical and Historical
Manshardt, Thomas: Aspects of Cortot
Marx, Adolph Bernhard: Die Kunst des Gesanges, Theoretisch-Practisch
May, Florence: The Life of Brahms
May, Florence: The Girlhood Of Clara Schumann: Clara Wieck And Her Time.
Mellers, Wilfrid: Angels of the Night: Popular Female Singers of Our Time
Mellers, Wilfrid: Bach and the Dance of God
Mellers, Wilfrid: Beethoven and the Voice of God
Mellers, Wilfrid: Caliban Reborn - Renewal in Twentieth Century Music
Mellers, Wilfrid: Darker Shade of Pale, A Backdrop to Bob Dylan
Mellers, Wilfrid: François Couperin and the French Classical Tradition
Mellers, Wilfrid: Harmonious Meeting
Mellers, Wilfrid: Le Jardin Retrouvé, The Music of Frederic Mompou
Mellers, Wilfrid: Music and Society, England and the European Tradition
Mellers, Wilfrid: Music in a New Found Land: … … American Music
Mellers, Wilfrid: Romanticism and the Twentieth Century (from 1800)
Mellers, Wilfrid: The Masks of Orpheus: …… the Story of European Music.
Mellers, Wilfrid: The Sonata Principle (from c. 1750)
Mellers, Wilfrid: Vaughan Williams and the Vision of Albion
Newmarch, Rosa: Henry J. Wood
Newmarch, Rosa: Jean Sibelius
Newmarch, Rosa: Mary Wakefield, a Memoir
Newmarch, Rosa: The Concert-Goer's Library
Newmarch, Rosa: The Music of Czechoslovakia
Newmarch, Rosa: The Russian Opera.
Nicholas, Jeremy: Godowsky, the Pianists' Pianist
Niecks, Frederick: The Life oc Chopin. (2 vols.)

Books published by Travis & Emery Music Bookshop:

Panchianio, Cattuffio: Rutzvanscad Il Giovine
Pearce, Charles: Sims Reeves, Fifty Years of Music in England.
Pepusch, John Christopher: A Treatise on Harmony ...
Pettitt, Stephen: Philharmonia Orchestra: A Record of Achievement, 1948-1985
Pettitt, Stephen (ed. Hunt): Philharmonia Orchestra: Discography 1945-1987
Playford, John: An Introduction to the Skill of Musick.
Porte, John: Sir Charles Villiers Stanford.
Quantz, Johann: Versuch einer Anweisung die Flöte traversiere zu spielen.
Rameau, Jean-Philippe: Code de Musique Pratique, ou Methodes.
Rameau, Jean-Philippe: Erreurs sur La Musique dans l'Encyclopédie
Rastall, Richard: The Notation of Western Music.
Rimbault, Edward: The Pianoforte, Its Origins, Progress, and Construction.
Rousseau, Jean Jacques: Dictionnaire de Musique
Rubinstein, Anton : Guide to the proper use of the Pianoforte Pedals.
Sainsbury, John S.: Dictionary of Musicians. (1825). (2 vols.)
Schumann, Clara & Brahms, Johannes: Letters 1853-1896. (2 vols.)
Scott-Sutherland: Arnold Bax
Serré de Rieux, Jean de : Les dons des Enfans de Latone
Simpson, Christopher: A Compendium of Practical Musick in Five Parts
Smyth, Ethel: Impressions That Remained. (2 vols.)
Spohr, Louis: Autobiography
Spohr, Louis: Grand Violin School
Tans'ur, William: A New Musical Grammar; or The Harmonical Spectator
Terry, Charles Sanford: Bach's Chorals – Parts 1, 2 and 3.
Terry, Charles Sanford: John Christian Bach
Terry, Charles Sanford: J.S. Bach's Original Hymn-Tunes - Congregational Use.
Terry, Charles Sanford: Four-Part Chorals of J.S. Bach. (German & English)
Terry, Charles Sanford: Joh. Seb. Bach, Cantata Texts, Sacred and Secular.
Terry, Charles Sanford: The Origins of the Family of Bach Musicians.
Tosi, Pierfrancesco: Opinioni de' Cantori Antichi, e Moderni
Tosi, Pierfrancesco: Observations on the Florid Song.
Tovey, Donald Francis: A Musician Talks, The Integrity of Music
Tovey, Donald Francis: A Musician Talks, Musical Textures
Tovey, Donald Francis: A Companion to "The Art of the Fugue" J.S. Bach
Tovey, Donald Francis: A Companion to Beethoven's Pianoforte Sonatas
Tovey, Donald Francis: Beethoven
Tovey, Donald Francis: Essays in Musical Analysis. (6 vols.).
Tovey, Donald Francis: The integrity of music
Tovey, Donald Francis: Musical Textures

Books published by Travis & Emery Music Bookshop:

Tovey, Donald Francis: Some English Symphonists
Tovey, Donald Francis: The Main Stream of Music.
Van der Straeten, Edmund: History of the Violoncello, The Viol da Gamba …
Van der Straeten, Edmund: History of the Violin, Its Ancestors… (2 vols.)
Walther, J. G. [Waltern]: Musicalisches Lexikon [Musikalisches Lexicon]
Wagner, Richard: Beethoven (Leipzig 1870)
Wagner, Richard: Lebens-Bericht (Leipzig 1884)
Wagner, Richard: The Musaic of the Future (Translated by E. Dannreuther).
Wyndham, Henry Saxe: The Annals of Covent Garden Theatre. (2 vols.)
Zwirn, Gerald: Stranded Stories From The Operas

Music published by Travis & Emery Music Bookshop:

Bach, Johann Sebastian: Sacred Songs for SCTB, arranged by Franz Wullner.
Bax, Arnold: Symphony #5, Arranged for Piano Four Hands by Walter Emery
Beranger, Pierre Jean de: Musique Des Chansons de Beranger: Airs Notes ...
Bizet, Georges: Djamileh. Vocal Score.
Donizetti, Gaetano: Betly. Dramma Giocoso in Due Atti. Vocal Score.
Frescobaldi, Girolamo: D'Arie Musicali per Cantarsi. Primo & Secondo Libro.
Handel, Purcell, Boyce, Greene ... Calliope or English Harmony: Volume First.
Hopkins, Antony: Sonatine
Purcell, Henry et al: Harmonia Sacra … The First Book, (1726)
Purcell, Henry et al: Harmonia Sacra … Book II (1726)
Sullivan, Arthur Seymour: Ivanhoe. Vocal score.
Sullivan, Arthur Seymour: The Rose of Persia. Vocal Score.
Weckerlin, Jean-Baptiste: Chansons Populaires du Pays de France

Other Books, not on Music:

Anon: A Collection of Testimonies Concerning Several Ministers of the Gospel
Amongst People called Quakers, Deceased. [Facsimile of 1760 edn.].
Sandeman-Allen, Arthur: Bee-keeping with Twenty hives.

Available from: Travis & Emery at 17 Cecil Court, London, UK.
(+44) (0) 20 7 240 2129. email on sales@travis-and-emery.com .

Discographies by John Hunt.

3 Italian Conductors and 7 Viennese Sopranos: 10 Discographies: Arturo Toscanini, Guido Cantelli, Carlo Maria Giulini, Elisabeth Schwarzkopf, Irmgard Seefried, Elisabeth Gruemmer, Sena Jurinac, Hilde Gueden, Lisa Della Casa, Rita Streich.

A Gallic Trio: 3 Discographies: Charles Muench, Paul Paray, Pierre Monteux.

A Notable Quartet: 4 Discographies: Gundula Janowitz, Christa Ludwig, Nicolai Gedda, Dietrich Fischer-Dieskau.

American Classics: The Discographies of Leonard Bernstein & Eugene Ormand

Antal Dorati 1906-1988: Discography and Concert Register.

Austro-Hungarian Pianists, Discographies of Lili Kraus, Friedrich Gulda, Ingrid Haebler

Back From The Shadows: 4 Discographies: Willem Mengelberg, Dimitri Mitropoulos, Hermann Abendroth, Eduard Van Beinum.

Carlo Maria Giulini: Discography and Concert Register.

Columbia 33CX Label Discography.

Concert Hall Discography: Concert Hall Society and Concert Hall Record Club

Conductors On The Yellow Label: 8 Discographies: Fritz Lehmann, Ferdinand Leitner, Ferenc Fricsay, Eugen Jochum, Leopold Ludwig, Artur Rother, Franz Konwitschny, Igor Markevitch.

Dirigenten der DDR: Conductors of the German Democratic Republic

From Adam to Webern: the Recordings of von Karajan.

Frosh: Discography of the Richard Strauss Opera Die Frau ohne Schatten

Giants of the Keyboard: 6 Discographies: Wilhelm Kempff, Walter Gieseking, Edwin Fischer, Clara Haskil, Wilhelm Backhaus, Artur Schnabel.

Gramophone Stalwarts: 3 Separate Discographies: Bruno Walter, Erich Leinsdorf, Georg Solti.

Great Violinists: 3 Discographies: David Oistrakh, Wolfgang Schneiderhan, Arthur Grumiaux.

Hans Knappertsbusch: Kna: Concert Register and Discography of Hans Knappertsbusch, 1888-1965. Second Edition.

Her Master's Voice: Concert Register and Discography of Dame Elisabeth Schwarzkopf [Third Edition].

Hungarians in Exile: 3 Discographies: Fritz Reiner, Antal Dorati, George Szell.

Leopold Stokowski (1882-1977): Discography and Concert Register

Leopold Stokowski: Discography and Concert Listing.

Leopold Stokowski: Second Edition of the Discography.

Makers of the Philharmonia: 11 Discographies Alceo Galliera, Walter Susskind, Paul Kletzki, Nicolai Malko, Issay Dobrowen, Lovro Von Matacic, Efrem Kurtz, Otto Ackermann, Anatole Fistoulari, George Weldon, Robert Irving.

Metropolitan Sopranos: 4 Discographies: Rosa Ponselle, Eleanor Steber, Zinka Milanov, Leontyne Price.

Mezzo and Contraltos: 5 Discographies: Janet Baker, Margarete Klose, Kathleen Ferrier, Giulietta Simionato, Elisabeth Hoengen.

Mid-Century Conductors and More Viennese Singers: 10 Discographies: Karl Boehm, Victor De Sabata, Hans Knappertsbusch, Tullio Serafin, Clemens Krauss, Anton Dermota, Leonie Rysanek, Eberhard Waechter, Maria Reining, Erich Kunz.

More 20th Century Conductors: 7 Discographies: Eugen Jochum, Ferenc Fricsay, Carl Schuricht, Felix Weingartner, Josef Krips, Otto Klemperer, Erich Kleiber.

More Giants of the Keyboard: 5 Discographies: Claudio Arrau, Gyorgy Cziffra, Vladimir Horowitz, Dinu Lipatti, Artur Rubinstein.

More Musical Knights: 4 Discographies: Hamilton Harty, Charles Mackerras, Simon Rattle, John Pritchard.

Musical Knights: 6 Discographies: Henry Wood, Thomas Beecham, Adrian Boult, John Barbirolli, Reginald Goodall, Malcolm Sargent.

Philharmonic Autocrat 1: Discography of: Herbert Von Karajan [3rd Edition]

Philharmonic Autocrat 2: Concert Register of Herbert Von Karajan 2nd. Ed.

Philharmonic Autocrat: Discography of Herbert von Karajan (1908-1989). 4th Ed..

Philips Minigroove: Second Extended Version of the European Discography.

Pianists For The Connoisseur: 6 Discographies: Arturo Benedetti Michelangeli, Alfred Cortot, Alexis Weissenberg, Clifford Curzon, Solomon, Elly Ney.

Sächsische Staatskapelle Dresden: Complete Discography.

Singers of the Third Reich: 5 Discographies: Helge Roswaenge, Tiana Lemnitz, Franz Voelker, Maria Mueller, Max Lorenz.

Singers on the Yellow Label: 7 Discographies: Maria Stader, Elfriede Troetschel, Annelies Kupper, Wolfgang Windgassen, Ernst Haefliger, Josef Greindl, Kim Borg

Six Wagnerian Sopranos: 6 Discographies: Frieda Leider, Kirsten Flagstad, Astrid Varnay, Martha Moedl, Birgit Nilsson, Gwyneth Jones.

Staatskapelle Berlin. The shellac era 1916-1962.

Sviatoslav Richter: Pianist of the Century: Discography.

Teachers and Pupils: 7 Discographies: Elisabeth Schwarzkopf, Maria Ivoguen, Maria Cebotari, Meta Seinemeyer, Ljuba Welitsch, Rita Streich, Erna Berger

Tenors in a Lyric Tradition: 3 Discographies: Peter Anders, Walther Ludwig, Fritz Wunderlich.

The Art of the Diva: 3 Discographies: Claudia Muzio, Maria Callas, Magda Olivero.

The Furtwaengler Sound Sixth Edition: Discography and Concert Listing.

The Furtwängler Sound. Discography of Wilhelm Furtwängler. Seventh Edition.

The Great Dictators: 3 Discographies: Evgeny Mravinsky, Artur Rodzinski, Sergiu Celibidache.

The Lyric Baritone: 5 Discographies: Hans Reinmar, Gerhard Huesch, Josef Metternich, Hermann Uhde, Eberhard Waechter.

The Post-War German Tradition: 5 Discographies: Rudolf Kempe, Joseph Keilberth, Wolfgang Sawallisch, Rafael Kubelik, Andre Cluytens.

Wagner Im Festspielhaus: Discography of the Bayreuth Festival.

Wiener Philharmoniker 1 - Vienna Philharmonic and Vienna State Opera Orchestras: Discography Part 1 1905-1954.

Wiener Philharmoniker 2 - Vienna Philharmonic and Vienna State Opera Orchestras: Discography Part 2 1954-1989.

Available from: Travis & Emery at 17 Cecil Court, London, UK.

(+44) (0) 20 7 240 2129. email on sales@travis-and-emery.com .

CPSIA information can be obtained
at www.ICGtesting.com
Printed in the USA
JSHW050511030721
16529JS00001B/5

9 781901 395310